Partners in suspense

MANCHESTER
1824

Manchester University Press

Partners in suspense

Critical essays on Bernard Herrmann and Alfred Hitchcock

Edited by
STEVEN RAWLE
and K. J. DONNELLY

Manchester University Press

Published by Manchester University Press
Altrincham Street, Manchester M1 7JA
www.manchesteruniversitypress.co.uk

British Library Cataloguing-in-Publication Data
A catalogue record for this book is available from the British Library

Library of Congress Cataloging-in-Publication Data applied for

ISBN 978 0 7190 9586 3 hardback

First published 2017

Typeset by Out of House Publishing
Printed in Great Britain
by TJ International Ltd, Padstow

Contents

Contents

Figures and tables

Figures

Tables

Contributors

Richard Allen is Professor of Film and Media Art and Dean of the School of Creative Media, City University, Hong Kong. He is author of *Hitchcock's Romantic Irony* (Columbia University Press, 2007) and numerous scholarly articles about Hitchcock. He is also an editor of the *Hitchcock Annual* and three volumes of Hitchcock essays.

Charles Barr taught for many years at the University of East Anglia, and has since worked in St Louis and in Dublin; he is currently a Research Fellow at St Mary's University, Twickenham. His most recent publication, co-authored with Alain Kerzoncuf, is *Hitchcock Lost and Found: The Forgotten Films* (University of Kentucky Press, 2015).

Royal S. Brown a Professor at Queens College in the City University of New York and at the City University's Graduate Center. He is the author of three books – *Focus on Godard* (Prentice-Hall, 1972), *Overtones and Undertones: Reading Film Music* (University of California Press, 1994), and *Film Musings* (Scarecrow Press, 2006) – as well as numerous scholarly and popular articles and critiques on film and film music. He has also presented papers on these subjects worldwide. He has just completed a book tentatively entitled *The Anti-Orpheus: Jacques Lacan and Narrative Cinema*.

Kevin Clifton is an Associate Professor of Music Theory at Sam Houston State University in Huntsville, Texas. He holds degrees from Austin College and the University of Texas at Austin. He has published articles on the use of music in the films of Hitchcock and Kubrick, and has also examined musical meaning in the music of Poulenc and Bartók.

David Cooper is Professor of Music and Technology and Dean of the Faculty of Performance, Visual Arts and Communications at the University of Leeds. He is a composer and musicologist and has published extensively on the music of Bartók, film music and the traditional music of Ireland. He is author of the Cambridge Handbook on Bartók's *Concerto for Orchestra* (Cambridge University Press, 1996), monographs on Bernard Herrmann's scores for the films *Vertigo* (Greenwood Press, 2001) and *The Ghost and Mrs Muir* (Scarecrow Press, 2005), and the study *The Musical Traditions of Northern Ireland and its Diaspora: Community and Conflict* (Ashgate, 2009). He edited the first modern edition of George Petrie's seminal *The Petrie Collection of the Ancient Music of Ireland* (Cork University Press, 2002, 2005). He is the co-editor with Kevin Dawe of *The Mediterranean in Music: Critical Perspectives, Common Concerns, Cultural Differences* (Scarecrow Press, 2005); with Christopher Fox and Ian Sapiro of *Cinemusic? Constructing the Film Score*

(Cambridge Scholars Publishing, 2008); and, with Rachel Cowgill and Clive Brown, of *Art and Ideology in European Opera: Essays in Honour of Julian Rushton* (Boydell & Brewer, 2010). His recently published major study of Béla Bartók for Yale University Press has received critical acclaim and been described as 'the most impressive musical biography of the decade'.

K. J. Donnelly is Reader in Film at the University of Southampton. He has written *Occult Aesthetics: Synchronization in Sound Cinema* (Oxford University Press, 2014), *British Film Music and Film Musicals* (Palgrave, 2007), *The Spectre of Sound: Film and Television Music* (BFI, 2005), *Pop Music in British Cinema: A Chronicle* (BFI, 2001), and the edited collections *Film Music: Critical Approaches* (Edinburgh University Press and Continuum, 2001), *Music in Science Fiction Television: Tuned to the Future* (co-edited with Philip Hayward, Taylor and Francis, 2012) and *Video Game Music: Studying Play* (co-edited with William Gibbons and Neil Lerner, Taylor and Francis, 2014).

Sidney Gottlieb is Professor of Communication and Media Studies at Sacred Heart University. He has edited two volumes of *Hitchcock on Hitchcock: Selected Writings and Interviews* (Faber and Faber, 1995, repr. 2015) and *Alfred Hitchcock: Interviews* (University of Mississippi Press, 2003), and he co-edits (with Richard Allen) the *Hitchcock Annual* (Columbia University Press), now nearing its twentieth volume. His most recent essays on Hitchcock focus on, among other topics, *Rear Window*, Hitchcock's silent films and the Hitchcock/Truffaut conversations.

Gergely Hubai studied at ELTE, Budapest, and teaches film music history in the Hungarian capital. His main research interests are music in Hitchcock and the James Bond films and rejected film scores. His book on the latter subject, entitled *Torn Music*, was released by Silman-James Press in 2012. He is also the author of 'Murder can be fun: the lost music of *Frenzy*' (*Hitchcock Annual* 17), which marked the first ever analysis of Henry Mancini's rejected score for the director's penultimate film. In addition, he has also authored a few hundred CD booklets for soundtracks.

Pasquale Iannone is a film academic and critic based in Edinburgh. His research interests include European cinema (Italian and French in particular), film aesthetics (sound, music and widescreen), videographic criticism and the representation of childhood on film. He holds a Ph.D. from the University of Edinburgh, where he has taught both undergraduate and postgraduate courses. He is a regular contributor to *Sight and Sound* and his broadcasting work includes film features for BBC Radio 3, BBC Radio 4 and BBC Radio Scotland. He is currently working on a volume on Jean-Pierre Melville's *Army of Shadows* for the BFI/Palgrave.

Murray Pomerance is Professor in the Department of Sociology at Ryerson University. He is author of *The Man Who Knew Too Much* (BFI, 2016), *Moment of Action: Riddles of Cinematic Performance* (Rutgers University Press, 2016), *Marnie* (BFI, 2014), *The Eyes Have It: Cinema and the Reality Effect* (Rutgers University Press, 2013), *Alfred Hitchcock's America* (Polity Press, 2013), among other books, and editor or co-editor of numerous volumes including *Thinking in the Dark: Cinema, Theory, Practice* (with R. Barton Palmer, Rutgers University Press, 2015). He is editor of the 'Horizons of Cinema' series at SUNY Press and the 'Techniques of the Moving Image' series at Rutgers University Press, as well as co-editor of 'Screen Decades' and 'Star Decades' at Rutgers.

Steven Rawle is an Associate Professor in Film and Media at York St John University. He is the author of *Performance in the Cinema of Hal Hartley* (Cambria, 2011) and co-author of *Basics Filmmaking: The Language of Film* (2nd ed., Bloomsbury, 2015). His writing has appeared in *Film Criticism, Scope, Asian Cinema* and the *Journal of Japanese and Korean Cinema*, in addition to numerous book chapters on topics relating to independent American and Japanese cinema.

William H. Rosar is a Research Associate in the Center for Brain and Cognition at the University of California, San Diego, where he studies how film music is perceived and related brain processes. He is also founder of the Film Music Society in Los Angeles and editor of the *Journal of Film Music*.

Jack Sullivan is Professor of English and Director of American Studies at Rider University and Westminster Choir College. His books include *Elegant Nightmares: the English Ghost Story from LeFanu to Blackwood* (Ohio University Press, 1980), *Words on Music, New World Symphonies: How American Culture Changed European Music* (Yale University Press, 1999) and *Hitchcock's Music* (Yale University Press, 2006). He has written for the *Hitchcock Annual, Opera*, the *New York Times, Washington Post, Wall Street Journal, American Record Guide* and *Carnegie Hall Stagebill*. He is currently writing a book on New Orleans jazz.

Tomas Williams is an independent researcher and education adviser at Exeter College. He completed his Ph.D. at the University of Exeter, exploring the life and work of émigré cinematographer Eugen Schüfftan. He is currently working in a project exploring the collaboration between Hitchcock and the British cinematographer Jack Cox.

Acknowledgements

Partners in suspense began life as a conference, staged in York in March 2011. Consequently, there are many people to thank who contributed to the successful running of the conference and therefore to the volume you now hold in your hands. Thanks should firstly go to Robert Edgar for initially conceiving the project for the conference. Many people helped make the event a resounding success, at York St John University and beyond: Gary Peters, Head of Research, and Steven Purcell, then Dean of the Faculty of Arts, were unwavering in their support of the event; Vanessa Simmons, Hilary Hunt, the Faculty's events team, and the team at the Royal York Hotel helped everything run smoothly; Mat Lazenby at LazenbyBrown, who designed the striking promotional images for the conference, and Paul Richardson who turned them into moving images; and also to Neil Sinyard for his unwavering support. Thanks should also go to The Tippet Quartet, whose performance of composer, and York St John music lecturer, David Lancaster's 'Vertigo' illuminated the conference. Mark Herman's discussion of collaboration with composers was also greatly appreciated. One of the highlights of the event was York St John's Head of Music Production Ben Burrows' new score for *The Lodger*, performed by The Tippet Quartet at York's City Screen, which capped a short season of Hitchcock films that coincided with the conference: thanks go to Ben, and also to Dave Taylor at City Screen and the programmers at Picturehouse Cinemas for working with us to set up the season. Finally, thanks go to everyone who contributed to the event, echoes of which are felt throughout the collection: colleagues and students in Film and TV Production at York St John, Film Studies students at York College, and all of our academic contributors, sadly not all of whom we have been able to include in the collection. Thanks also to everyone at Manchester University Press, particularly Matthew Frost, and their readers, for their support.

Steven would especially like to thank Lorna for all her reassurance and encouragement, then and now.

Richard Allen's chapter, 'The Sound of *The Birds*', has previously been published in *October* 146, Fall 2013, pp. 95–118. Reprinted with permission.

Introduction

K. J. Donnelly and Steven Rawle

For a decade from 1955, Alfred Hitchcock worked almost exclusively with one composer: Bernard Herrmann. From *The Trouble with Harry* (1955) to the bitter spat surrounding *Torn Curtain* (1966), the partnership gave us some of cinema's most memorable musical moments, taught us to stay out of the shower, away from heights and never to spend time in corn fields. Consequently, fascination with their work and relationship endures fifty years later. This book brings together new work and new perspectives on the relationship between Hitchcock and Herrmann. Featuring chapters by leading scholars of Hitchcock's work, the volume examines the working relationship between the two and the contribution that Herrmann's work brings to Hitchcock's idiom, as well as expanding our understanding of how music fits into that body of work. The goal of these analyses is to explore approaches to sound, music, collaborative authorship and the distinctive contribution that Herrmann brought to Hitchcock's films. Consequently, the book examines these key works, with particular focus on what Elisabeth Weis (1982: 136) called 'the extrasubjective films' – *Vertigo* (1958), *Psycho* (1960), *The Birds* (1963) – and explores Herrmann's palpable role in shaping the sonic and musical landscape of Hitchcock's work, which, the volume argues, has a considerable transformative effect on how we understand Hitchcock's authorship.

The collection examines the significance, meanings, histories and enduring legacies of one of film history's most important partnerships. By engaging with the collaborative work of Hitchcock and Herrmann, the chapters in the collection examine the ways in which film directors and composers collaborate, and how this collaboration is experienced in the films themselves. In addition, the collection addresses the continued hierarchisation of vision over sound in the conceptualisation of cinema and readdresses this balance through the exploration of the work of these two significant figures and their work together during the 1950s and 1960s.

'From his first sound films', Weis remarked, 'Hitchcock has treated sound as a new dimension to cinematic expression' (1982: 14). Music is often fundamental to how we consider Hitchcock's authorship, and he forged a number of partnerships with composers over his career, including Miklós Rózsa, Dimitri Tiomkin, but most notably Herrmann. Jack Sullivan suggests:

A supremely calculating technician often accused of coldness, Hitchcock needed music more than most movie-makers. Music tapped into the Romanticism beneath his classical exterior. Certainly his most dreamlike moments – the ones we never forget – are profoundly connected to music. (2006: 322)

As Donald Spoto argues, Hitchcock and Herrmann united in their romanticism: the pair 'shared a dark, tragic sense of life, a brooding view of human relationships, and a compulsion to explore aesthetically the private world of the romantic fantasy' (Spoto, 1999: 355). A romantic 'in every sense of the word', according to Royal S. Brown (1982: 16), Herrmann's contribution to Hitchcock's oeuvre is ultimately defining. Brown identified in Herrmann's scores what he called 'The Hitchcock chord'. A 'minor major-seventh in which there are two major thirds and one minor' (20), 'the Hitchcock chord' evokes for Brown a Wagnerian motif that he also sees prefigured in Herrmann's score for Orson Welles's *Citizen Kane* (1941), as well as in films produced during the Hitchcock collaboration, such as 'the much less subtle' *The 7th Voyage of Sinbad* (Nathan H. Juran, 1958) (1982: 21), although its most clear appearance is in Hitchcock's canonical films.

Hitchcock's works have a universalism that marks them out as different from most other films. Almost everyone will be familiar with at least one of his films, which were, and are, as gratifying to popular audiences as to those interested in cinema as an art form. He is quite probably the only film director to have achieved this distinction. Not only did Alfred Hitchcock make much of his visual image, making cameo appearances in his films, but he also had his own, instantly recognisable musical theme, Charles Gounod's 'Funeral March of a Marionette', which was used as his musical signature in the *Alfred Hitchcock Presents* television series. During his introduction to one of these episodes, Hitchcock informs the audience that the music is written first, then the images and story are found to fit it. Although a joke, this suggests something of the truth: that Hitchcock prized the possibilities offered to him by film music.

While it is widely accepted that Hitchcock produced perhaps the most outstanding body of films in Anglo-American cinema, the importance he ceded to music has rarely been registered. Hitchcock's interest in film technique and the vocabulary of cinema led directly to a fascination in his films with the expressive, aesthetic and narrative possibilities of both diegetic and non-diegetic music. Indeed, it was far from fortuitous that Hitchcock's most enduring and highly acclaimed films, made between the mid-1950s and the early 1960s, involved the convergence of his career with that of Bernard Herrmann, who arguably remains the single most outstanding composer of music for films.

Hitchcock and Herrmann's first collaboration was on *The Trouble with Harry* (1955). As a comic score, it is a rarity in Herrmann's oeuvre, yet its most prominent moments are either sinister or pastoral. Herrmann reconstituted his score into a concert suite called 'A Portrait of Hitch', evidencing film music's common dual function (working both in and outside film) as well as personifying the film's music precisely *as* its larger-than-life director.

Alfred Hitchcock was famed for his cameo appearances in his own films, yet in the remake of *The Man Who Knew Too Much* (1956) Hitchcock also encouraged

Herrmann to make a cameo appearance. His appearance at the Albert Hall, conducting the London Symphony Orchestra, marked a rare moment when Hitchcock allowed a collaborator to 'do as he did' – almost an admittance of equal status, one might speculate. However, Hitchcock did not allow Herrmann to write a new cantata for the sequence, reusing Arthur Benjamin's 'Storm Clouds' cantata from the 1930s original.

Hitchcock's films include probably the most famous use of music in a film, the stabbing violins used in the shower scene of *Psycho* (1960), and one of the most celebrated romantic scores in the cinema for the stately paced *Vertigo*. In both cases Herrmann was absolutely defining in the final Hitchcock product. A focus on music in films allows us to realise that another strong personality is 'in the text', rather than simply focus on the omnipotent director, writer or producer. It may not be visible – like Hitchcock in his cameos – but in certain cases it is highly identifiable.

Hitchcock was persistent in his interest in music: eight of the central protagonists in his films were supposedly musicians. In the 1930s, Hitchcock had published an article on his views about the use of music in films, and it detailed what he thought should be the primary uses of film music: first, to create 'atmosphere', to create excitement and tension; and second, for 'psychological' effect, to express the unspoken and to work as a counterpoint to the visuals (Hitchcock, 1933–34). Interestingly, his description of musical functions delineates a fertile zone for experimentation, largely through avoiding the more mundane functions of film music, such as providing coherence and continuity, and establishing space and place. Indeed, Hitchcock's interest in style and form arguably led to an indirect interest in the language of film music as an integral element of film. This meant that he allowed and encouraged a degree of experimentation by composers, predominantly within the production context of the dominance of the classical Hollywood style.

With respect to serious writing about film, a significant proportion of it discusses Alfred Hitchcock's films and life. Interestingly, although there is far less published about film music, a significant amount of it pertains to Bernard Herrmann (including Cooper, 2001, 2005; Rosar, 2001; Schneller, 2012; Blim, 2013; Brown, 1994; Larsen, 2005; Wierzbicki, 2008). The dominant status of these two is testified to by the regular publication of the *Hitchcock Annual*, the 'Herrmann Studies' special issue of the *Journal of Film Music*, and the issue of *Popular Music History* on Herrmann's music.[1] Indeed, the history of cinema arguably has not had such a notable pairing of two great authorial figures. While Hitchcock clearly took the lead, Herrmann's input is without doubt imperative, with music expressing what cannot be achieved pictorially (Manvell and Huntley, 1975: 80). Herrmann claimed that 'Hitchcock himself was not a musically sensitive man, but according to Herrmann, he had "the great sensitivity to leave me alone when I am composing"' (Moral, 2002: 136). Indeed, Herrmann claimed that he 'finished the picture 40%' (quoted in Brown, 1994: 14).[2] Hitchcock surely would not have approved such a statement, particularly as he was extremely proprietorial about his films and even downplayed the contributions of others. Spoto (1999: 495) notes that the Truffaut interviews 'hurt and disappointed just about everybody who had ever worked with Alfred Hitchcock, for the interviews reduced the writers, the designers, the photographers, the composers, and the actors to little else than elves in the master carpenter's workshop'. However, as befits great collaborators, Hitch and Benny Herrmann were great friends during their halcyon period. Norma Shepherd, the third Mrs Herrmann, recalled Herrmann's stories of regular dinners at the Hitchcocks' in the late 1950s:

> Benny used to wash dishes with Hitch, and they'd talk about what they'd do if they weren't in the film business. Benny wanted to run an English pub, until someone told him you actually had to open and close at certain hours. Hitchcock then turned to Benny, his apron folded on his head, and said solemnly, 'a hanging judge'. (Smith, 1991: 193)

Something in the psyches of the two men resonated and the films upon which they collaborated remain over half a century later among the cream of cinematic history.

Hitchcock's partnership with Herrmann ended in acrimony during the scoring (literally) for *Torn Curtain*. As a number of the contributors to this collection attest, Hitchcock's request for a more contemporary-sounding score for the film led to the very public break-up of the collaboration. Elmer Bernstein's rediscovery and subsequent recording of the unused score, just prior to Herrmann's death in 1975 (as Hubai's chapter discusses), ensured it was introduced to the public domain, while the subsequent inclusion of the unused portions of the score on Universal's DVD and Blu-ray releases of the film has reminded viewers of the contribution that Herrmann made to Hitchcock's oeuvre, even though John Addison's more conventional score is retained throughout the film itself (this is discussed in Rawle's chapter about the ways in which the Herrmann–Hitchcock partnership has been reimagined in the digital domain). The partnership cast a long shadow over the two men until the end of their careers. As Steven C. Smith noted, Henry Mancini's score for *Frenzy* (1972) was rejected for being too Herrmannesque – 'If I want Herrmann, I'd *ask* Herrmann' (quoted in Smith, 1991: 293). Mancini later confessed that he didn't understand the comparison and that the score sounded nothing like Herrmann's music.

Herrmann subsequently went on to work with other notable directors, his reputation built on the collaboration with Hitchcock. Following the end of his relationship with Hitchcock, he worked with François Truffaut (*Fahrenheit 451*, 1966),[3] and Martin Scorsese (*Taxi Driver*, 1976), but perhaps most notably with Brian De Palma, for whom Herrmann scored two films, *Sisters* (1973) and *Obsession* (1976). Following Herrmann's death, De Palma drew on the influence of Hitchcock and Herrmann, with what Royal S. Brown (1994: 237) describes as two 'post-Bernard-Herrmann-cum-Italian-bel-canto scores done by Pino Donaggio', *Carrie* (1976) and *Dressed to Kill* (1980). The *Carrie* score liberally interpolates the *Psycho* strings as a motif whenever Carrie's psychokinesis strikes. Prior to the beginning of their partnership, however, De Palma had never considered Herrmann to score his Hitchcock-inspired thrillers: he simply assumed Herrmann was dead, having not seen a Herrmann-scored film since *The Birds* in 1963. Smith (1991: 320–2) recounts a story about De Palma's first meeting with Herrmann, who he described as 'a short stout man, with silver gray hair plastered down [on] his head, thick glasses [who] carried an ominous-looking walking stick'. De Palma and his editor Paul Hirsch had used the love theme from *Marnie* (1964) as temp music in *Sisters*. With 'unbelievable horror', Herrmann thumped his cane on the ground and demanded they stop the film. 'I don't want to hear *Marnie* when I'm looking at your movie. How can I think about anything new with that playing?' Herrmann asked. De Palma explained that he and Herrmann talked about how the director wanted no title music, something with which the composer disagreed ('they'll walk out', he explained). He explained why De Palma couldn't get away with using Hitchcockian devices:

'You are not Hitchcock! He can make his movies as slow as he wants in the beginning! And do you know why?'
   [De Palma] shook his head.
   'Because he is Hitchcock and they will wait! They know something terrible is going to happen and they'll wait until it does. They'll watch your movie for ten minutes and then they'll go home to their televisions.'

Herrmann told De Palma he'd write a title cue and had an idea for two Moogs. While Smith argues that the opening sequence is the film's 'most effective', he also criticises the score for being 'Herrmann's most self-derivative … tediously repetitive and overscaled for the low-budget film it accompanies' (1991: 332). The Hitchcock connection was difficult to leave behind, much more so in *Obsession*, a 'free paraphrase of *Vertigo*'s Tristan and Isolde story', in Smith's terms, with a score he describes as 'Herrmann's cinema requiem, a summation of his film skills' (341). William Wrobel (2003) has well documented Herrmann's 'self-borrowings' across his work in film, television, radio and his opera. Herrmann's attachment to the Hitchcockian oeuvre goes beyond self-borrowing or the echoes of his work following his death, such as in Elmer Bernstein's recreation of Herrmann's *Cape Fear* (1962) score in Martin Scorsese's 1992 remake, such is the enduring fascination with this decade-long tempestuous creative collaboration and its products.

The book takes a roughly chronological approach to the work of the partnership, examining first the working processes and the relationship between Hitchcock's earlier authorship and his work with Herrmann. Later chapters explore the musicological significance of Herrmann's contribution to Hitchcock's films, although some chapters examine music in the overall context of Hitchcock's body of work. Jack Sullivan's opening chapter sets the context for the working collaboration, utilising the Conradian metaphor of the 'secret sharer' to argue that Herrmann was 'Hitchcock's secret sharer, a catalyst for energies darker and riskier than Hitchcock's cool sensibility normally permitted'. Sullivan, like a number of the contributors, contextualises Hitchcock's fascination with music, and its significance in his overall style. The 'secret sharer' dynamic was, Sullivan argues, what led fatefully to the bitter end of the partnership over *Torn Curtain*. Charles Barr's chapter takes musicality as a fundamental metaphor for Hitchcock's work, in particular his approach to editing. Looking across Hitchcock's oeuvre, from his silents (and the influence of Griffith) through the Herrmann partnership to his final John-Williams-scored *Family Plot* (1976), Barr sees the construction of Hitchcock's suspense sequences as musical in the precision and patterning of shots, shot lengths and their pacing.

Kevin Clifton's chapter stretches back into Hitchcock's work prior to the Herrmann partnership to explore the similarities between the score for *Rope* (1948), Hitchcock's first colour film, an attempt to give the illusion of being shot in a single take. Clifton argues that we can hear echoes of *Rope*'s score, based largely on Francis Poulenc's *Mouvement Perpétuel* (1918), in Herrmann's score for *Vertigo*. The 'musical ambivalences' of both scores provide counterpoints for the two film's narrative complexities. Likewise, Sidney Gottlieb begins with *Vertigo* as a means of tackling the significance of music in Hitchcock's oeuvre. Gottlieb's chapter argues that recovery and rehabilitation are at the core of Hitchcock's thinking about music, with its therapeutic possibilities. Looking predominantly at *Rear Window* (1954) and *Waltzes from Vienna* (1934), an underexplored Hitchcock work also considered by Sullivan's chapter, as well as Hitchcock's Herrmann-scored remake of *The Man Who Knew Too Much* (1956), Gottlieb sees the therapeutic power of music as a defining feature of Hitchcock's thematic use of music, in the Herrmann era but also prior to that.

As the title of his chapter testifies, Royal S. Brown takes a Lacanian approach to Herrmann's work with Hitchcock. Drawing on Kristeva's Lacanian pre-Symbolic notion of 'the specular', Brown finds Herrmann's music, not just his film work with Hitchcock, but also his concert and radio music, to demonstrate the full specular potential of the cinema. Drawing on Laura Mulvey's theories, Brown shows how Herrmann's deployment of the Hitchcock chord (as referenced above) in *Vertigo* and *Psycho* in particular, removes film's Symbolic discursive attachments, in a manner similar to atonal or experimental music, and returns it to its specular potential.

Murray Pomerance's chapter on the 'neglected' (by scholars and cinephiles) remake of *The Man Who Knew Too Much* looks at the different role played by Herrmann in orchestrating and organising the film's music, as well as his appearance in the finale of the film as the orchestra's conductor in the Albert Hall. Pomerance examines the historical circumstances of the film's scoring, Herrmann's cues, as well as his orchestration of Arthur Benjamin's 'Storm Clouds' cantata and the two Jay Livingston/Ray Evans songs, 'Que Sera, Sera' and 'We'll Love Again'. Continuing in an analytical vein, Pasquale Iannone turns towards *Vertigo* and *Psycho* to explore how the two films share in Herrmann's music 'a depiction of troubled, unstable subjectivity'. Looking specifically at an underexplored aspect of Hitchcock's films, the car journey, Iannone considers two car journeys taken by the protagonists of *Vertigo* and *Psycho*, Scottie and Marion respectively. Arguing that it would be easy to consider these scenes as having little significant value in terms of narrative action, Iannone asserts that the use of Herrmann's music and internalised sounds adds inestimable value in the ways that it contributes to our understanding of the characters' anxieties and subjectivities. David Cooper also analyses *Vertigo*'s score, albeit for its resonances with theatre and dance, with traces of the waltz, tango and habanera, as well as strong Wagnerian overtones, from his *Tristan und Isolde* opera (1859). Cooper's starting point, however, is Herrmann's later *Echoes* for string quartet and the ways in which it resonates with much of his film music. Additionally, the chapter argues that much of Herrmann's musical contributions can be contextualised in relation to his contemporaries, including Lyn Murray, the composer who suggested Herrmann to Hitchcock following his score for *To Catch a Thief* (1955) and the subsequent influence this had on the Hitchcock–Herrmann partnership.

Richard Allen's chapter on *The Birds* examines its electronic soundtrack. An unconventional mixture of sounds and electronic effects, the Herrmann-supervised soundtrack highlights Hitchcock's embrace of new and innovative technologies. Allen also considers the role of the Mixtur-Trautonium, the electronic instrument devised and played by Oskar Sala. Like Iannone's chapter, Allen's examines the ways in which the soundtrack produces anxiety and expresses internality. Returning to the orchestral, K. J. Donnelly argues that *Marnie*'s score seems retrogressive in its conventionality in comparison with *The Birds*. While Hitchcock considered Herrmann's score to be 'self-plagiarised', Donnelly considers Herrmann's use of conventional film scoring techniques to be novel in Herrmann's scores. A romantic score for an unromantic film, Donnelly argues, is a misdirection, but also a score that later became 'uncoupled' from the film's images on CD and in Herrmann's concert music.

The three chapters that follow all turn toward *Torn Curtain*, the film that brought Herrmann's partnership with Hitchcock to an abrupt end. First, Tomas Williams examines the variations in the different extant scores for the scene in which the East German security officer Gromek is protractedly murdered by Paul Newman's hero. Three different versions exist: Hitchcock's final version, with no music and only diegetic sound (as Hitchcock had also wanted the murder in the shower in *Psycho*); and the two rejected cues by Herrmann and Addison. Williams critiques the three versions, only to side with Hitchcock on which version is most successful. Gergely Hubai then goes on to look at the history of Herrmann's rejected score and later recordings, and their place in a discography. Hubai considers the role of Elmer Bernstein in bringing the score into existence – the first rejected score ever to be recorded and released – and how portions of that music found its way into other films, such as Bernstein's score for Scorsese's *Cape Fear*. William Rosar's 'post-mortem' of the Herrmann–Hitchcock relationship focuses on what occurred between the two men during the fateful sessions in which Hitchcock fired Herrmann when he was dissatisfied with what the composer was developing for *Torn Curtain*. Rosar, however, searches more broadly for reasons why the partnership broke down, including Hitchcock's philosophies about film scoring and exploring the history of the working relationship between the two men, looking in particular at the process of spotting and scoring *Psycho* that caused such friction and created a precedent for what happened on *Torn Curtain*, albeit with a very different outcome.

Steven Rawle is more concerned with the contemporary framing of the legacy of the partnership in the digital realm. Thinking about how authorship is framed and textualised on the DVD and Blu-ray and in artefacts accompanying CD releases, Rawle argues that, perhaps understandably, mainstream film cultures have difficulty conceiving of authorship as multiple or collective. The paratexts and deep texts of the digital home video releases of *Vertigo*, *North by Northwest* (1959), *Psycho* and *Torn Curtain* offer evidence of the ways in which the Herrmann–Hitchcock partnership is memorialised by the film studios that release Hitchcock's work – Hitchcock remains a palpable draw for viewers, but, as the DVD threatens to recede into history, this also comes at the cost of making the Hitchcockian-Herrmannian (echoing Bazin) unthinkable, as well as threatening to reduce film (again echoing Bazin's worry) to less than the sum of its parts.

Just as Weis and Sullivan argued, music and sound are fundamental to understanding Hitchcock's cinema, while the partnership with Herrmann provided it with many of its most famous and culturally significant moments. The chapters in the collection all contribute to our understanding of this distinctive oeuvre and how it fits more broadly into Hitchcock's overall body of work.

Notes

1　The *Hitchcock Annual* (which has been published every year since 1992); *Journal of Film Music* 1: 2/3, Fall/Winter 2003 (edited by James Wierzbicki); *Popular Music History* 5: 1, 2010 (edited by Edward Green).
2　In different sources the percentage quoted varies, but Brown is a reliable source.
3　Although the film was released subsequent to the fallout between Hitchcock and Herrmann, Truffaut had met with Herrmann to discuss scoring *Fahrenheit 451* prior to his dismissal from *Torn Curtain*. In a letter to Hitchcock from November 1965, Truffaut explains, 'In London I met Bernard Herrmann who will be writing the score for *Fahrenheit 451*. We had a long talk together about you and I feel that, in him, you have a great and genuine friend' (Truffaut, 1988: 290).

References

Blim, Dan (2013), 'Musical and Dramatic Design in Bernard Herrmann's Prelude to "Vertigo" (1958)', *Music and the Moving Image* 6: 21–31.

Brown, Royal S. (1982), 'Herrmann, Hitchcock, and the Music of the Irrational', *Cinema Journal* 21:2: 14–49.

Brown, Royal S. (1994), *Overtones and Undertones: Reading Film Music*. Berkeley and London: University of California Press.

Cooper, David (2001), *Bernard Herrmann's Vertigo: A Film Score Handbook*. Westport, CT: Greenwood Press.

Cooper, David (2005), *Bernard Herrmann's 'The Ghost and Mrs Muir': A Film Score Guide*. Lanham, MD: Scarecrow Press.

Hitchcock, Alfred (1933–34), 'Alfred Hitchcock on Music in Films', *Cinema Quarterly* 2:2: 80–3.

Larsen, Peter (2005), *Film Music*. London: Reaktion.

Manvell, Roger and John Huntley (1975), *The Technique of Film Music*. London: Focal Press.

Moral, Tony Lee (2002), *Hitchcock and the Making of Marnie*. Manchester: Manchester University Press.

Rosar, William H. (2001), 'The Dies Irae in *Citizen Kane*: Musical Hermeneutics Applied to Film Music', in K. J. Donnelly (ed.), *Film Music: Critical Approaches*. Edinburgh: Edinburgh University Press, pp. 103–16.

Schneller, Tom (2012), 'Easy to Cut: Modular Form in the Film Scores of Bernard Herrmann', *Journal of Film Music* 5: 1/2: 127–51.

Smith, Steven C. (1991), *A Heart at Fire's Center: The Life and Music of Bernard Herrmann*. Berkeley: University of California Press.

Spoto, Donald (1999), *The Dark Side of Genius: The Life of Alfred Hitchcock*. London: Da Capo.

Sullivan, Jack (2006), *Hitchcock's Music*. New Haven and London: Yale University Press.

Truffaut, François (1988), *Correspondence, 1945–1984*, ed. Gilles Jacob and Claude de Givray, trans. Gilbert Adair. New York: Cooper Square Press.

Weis, Elisabeth (1982), *The Silent Scream: Alfred Hitchcock's Sound Track*. East Brunswick, NJ and London: Associated University Press.

Wierzbicki, James (2008), *Film Music: A History*. New York: Routledge.

Wrobel, William (2003), 'Self Borrowing in the Music of Bernard Herrmann', *Journal of Film Music* 1: 2/3: 249–71.

1

Bernard Herrmann: Hitchcock's secret sharer

Jack Sullivan

Partners in Suspense celebrates a great director–composer collaboration that fascinates even people who normally don't think about film music. This chapter addresses that partnership both as a very special professional connection between a director and composer and also as an intense Conradian relationship that was as volatile as it was productive. Because he was so meticulously involved with the musical process, Hitchcock often had a close working relationship with his composers, but here the connection was stronger and deeper: Herrmann was a risky alter-ego, a 'secret sharer' who took his cinema into darker places than it had gone before, tying the two artists together in ways that enhanced their careers even as it threatened their sense of identity.

Before examining this collaboration, it is necessary to evaluate precisely how Bernard Herrmann fits into Alfred Hitchcock's overall musical achievement. We tend to forget just how rich and varied that achievement was and how deeply Hitchcock had experimented with music long before he met Herrmann. When we consider Hitchcock's music at all, we tend to think about *Vertigo* (1958) or *Psycho* (1960), but how often do we think about the music in *Rebecca* (1940) or *Spellbound* (1945) or *Rear Window* (1954), even though these changed the way film music was received and marketed? And how often do we think about the incredibly diverse genres Hitchcock explored, more than any director in history, not only dense symphonic scores, but popular songs, Strauss waltzes, jazz, cabaret, rock tracks, Cageian noise effects, and electronic experiments?

Herrmann is the gold standard for Hitchcock's symphonic sound, but his predecessors are significant too, and the pop songs that were the occasion of Hitchcock–Herrmann imploding were already part of Hitchcock's musical experimentation for some thirty years. Herrmann was openly resistant to producing popular songs, but there is evidence that Hitchcock was grumpy as well, precisely because he had already worked with dozens of vernacular tunes both successfully and unsuccessfully and had been fighting with studios over the issue of how to use them since *Spellbound*. As I wrote in *Hitchcock's Music* (2006), even the quarrel over Herrmann's alleged repeating of his own themes in *Marnie* wasn't new, but a revisiting of the same controversy with Miklós Rózsa in *Spellbound*.

For Hitchcock, the very act of making movies was musical. He compared himself to conductor, composer, and orchestrator, making analogies between scoring and movie-making, storyboards and musical notation. Close-ups, he said, were like trumpet solos, long shots 'an entire orchestra performing a muted accompaniment' (Truffaut, 1983: 335). Twice he said that his relationship with his audience was that of an organist playing his instrument.

From the start of his career, Hitchcock depicts singers and songs, conspiracies and codes, musicians and ensembles, stages and dressing rooms. Often the quality of the singing or playing is as important as the music: the nervous performances of Marlene Dietrich and Farley Granger bring on guilt and catastrophe; the confident singing of Doris Day saves her son's life.

Music could be traumatic and overpowering, like the poisoning scene in Roy Webb's underrated score for *Notorious* (1946) or surpassingly delicate like the distant vocalise in *I Confess* (1953). It could be life-saving or death-dealing, sometimes both, as in *The Lady Vanishes* (1939). Either way, it is a vital force in the flawed humanity of Hitchcock's characters. Miss Lonelyhearts could be speaking for Hitchcock when she tells the composer at the end of *Rear Window*, 'You have no idea what this music means to me.'

Hitchcock's music comprises the low-budget British films, full of popular ditties, marching bands, theatre orchestras, street singers, and other diegetic sounds; the great symphonic period from *Rebecca* to *Marnie* (1964), where Hollywood Golden Age money and composers allowed him to experiment with elaborate scores; and the final years of decline, where musical excellence was harder to achieve. These categories are not mutually exclusive: *Waltzes from Vienna* (1934, originally released in the USA as *Strauss' Great Waltz*) and the original *The Man Who Knew Too Much* (1934) both feature a brilliant symphonic scene, though it is diegetic; Hitchcock's Hollywood films sometimes eschew symphonic music altogether, notably *Rope* (1948), which has only seven cues, and *The Birds* (1963), which relies on electronic effects and haunted silence. The entirely diegetic *Rear Window*, Hitchcock's most imaginative fantasia on popular song, is actually an American riff on British Hitchcock, an extension of the method in *Waltzes from Vienna*, *The Lady Vanishes*, and others where serenades and waltzes drift into the protagonist's window, full of charm but also menace.

In a unique category is *The Man Who Knew Too Much* remake (1956), not only a radical expansion of the original British version but a culmination of Hitchcockian methods with both popular and classical. After *Rear Window* and *The Man Who Knew Too Much*, Hitchcock really had nowhere else to go with popular song and kicked out singers from *The Wrong Man* (1956), *Vertigo* and *Topaz* (1969), even though the studio put him under pressure to do the opposite and even though singers were already scheduled in these films (USC and Margaret Herrick archives).

Hitchcock forged a musical style very early. As with many of his themes and cinematic designs, he sounded important signatures at the beginning, then spent the rest of his career playing endlessly fascinating variations. *The Pleasure Garden* (1925), *The Ring* (1927) and *Downhill* (1927, released in the USA as *When Boys*

Leave Home) depict dancers, cabarets, and stages as exuberant counterpoint to disaster. When sound became available in 1929, he quickly immersed himself in the new medium. In *Blackmail* (1929), Cyril Ritchard sings 'Miss Up to Date' to Anny Ondra in a seductive aria that ends with the singer stabbed to death by the heroine, linking music to a disturbingly ambiguous psychodrama. 'Miss Up to Date' moves with astonishing subtlety from source music to symphonic underscore, unveiling a music of the subconscious that establishes an interior point of view and blurs the distinction between diegetic and non-diegetic long before those terms were codified. *Blackmail* even experiments with noise music in the breakfast knife montage and with elaborate aural transferences. All this in 1929, and several score details – spectral harp and organ, barren timpani solos, abrupt silence following huge crescendos, spinning arpeggios linked to circular designs – became signatures as well.

The most important musical experiment from Hitchcock's early period was *Waltzes from Vienna*, a behind-the-scenes look at the musical and sexual conquests of the Strauss family. This unique combination of musical and Oedipal drama depicts Johann Strauss Jr's overthrow of his father as the Waltz King through the inspiration, composition and premiere of the 'Blue Danube' waltz, his muse energised by both his younger and older lovers. In its depiction of an onstage orchestra from multiple points of view and its revelation of how dramatically music can change lives, this Hitchcockian operetta anticipates numerous orchestral scenes in his later films. The young Strauss's premiere of his new waltz is a personal triumph and a landmark in Viennese culture, but a betrayal of his father and younger lover. In a memorable scene depicting the premiere of the new waltz, Hitchcock takes out all non-musical sound, dialogue and street noise, as he does in Herrmann's maestro cameo in *The Man Who Knew Too Much*, so the music becomes a force of its own; the dancers are moved as if by a magical power, much as Miss Lonelyhearts is transported in *Rear Window*.

Waltzes from Vienna is a striking predecessor of later Hitchcock films in its poetic depiction of music floating in windows and up staircases. Like *Rear Window*, it shows the composition of a song from conception through noodlings and rehearsals to full performance. In a poignant coda, the defeated father wanders among empty chairs in the bandstand following his son's triumph. When a girl requests his autograph, he calls her back, and wistfully adds 'senior' under his name, proud of his son in spite of himself. As the lights go down on the bandstand, his silhouette moves off-camera on a bittersweet 'Blue Danube' cadence, ending the film with the exquisite ambiguity that Hitchcock strived for in music.

Hitchcock was as sour about *Waltzes from Vienna* as the critics, but it was a valuable musical laboratory, as revealed by an astonishing interview he did for *Cinema Quarterly* in 1933 when editing the film. He spoke about music as a new tempo in editing, as counterpoint rather than imitation, and as an 'underlying idea' that illuminates a film's psychology, all principles he enacted through his career. Anticipating Erich Wolfgang Korngold, whose sumptuous orchestrations he used in *Waltzes from Vienna*, he tied cinema to opera, something he had hinted at in the Wagnerian shaving scene in *Murder!* (1930) (Hitchcock, 1933–34: 244).

Singers are everywhere in Hitchcock, momentarily turning films like *The Lady Vanishes*, *The Man Who Knew Too Much* and *Stage Fright* (1949) into musicals. Even non-singers have a way of suddenly bursting into song, as in 1*Train* (1950) or playing a significant motif on the piano, as in *The Paradine Case* (1947) and *Stage Fright*. In the latter, *Blackmail,* and *The Man Who Knew Too Much*, he hired popular singers for leading roles, mimicking the position of opera director.

One of Hitchcock's favourite forms was the waltz, a staid form he invested with near-mystical properties. Again, *Waltzes from Vienna* is the template. The film's coda brought the curtain down on the era of Johann Strauss senior, whose Radetzky March opens the film, and ushers in the new Viennese waltz. By the 1930s, however, the latter signified an old order nostalgia for an old order lost in the onslaught of modernism; Hitchcock used waltzes to embody crumbling worlds and treacherous charm in a number of films, including *Rebecca, Suspicion* (1941), *Shadow of a Doubt* (1942) and *Strangers on a Train* (1951).

Ballet was also a central design in Hitchcock, including the kinetic chases in *The 39 Steps* (1935), *Foreign Correspondent* (1940) and *North by Northwest* (1959); Miss Torso dances under Jeff's gleefully voyeuristic gaze in *Rear Window*; Paul Newman and Julie Andrews escape from the Soviets during a ballet of Tchaikovsky's *Francesca Da Rimini*, an extravagant music-suspense sequence that brings this wooden film to sudden life. Hitchcock also experimented with jazz, layering it with double meanings, a suave surface masking dread in *Rich and Strange* (1931, originally released in the US as *East of Shanghai*), *Saboteur* (1942) and *The Wrong Man*.

Hitchcock's use of vernacular music was always strong and original, but his symphonic scores are even more celebrated. Often, the basic design of a film – crisscross in *Strangers on a Train*, obsessive spirals in *Vertigo*, slashing lines in *Psycho* – is established immediately by the music well before the story begins, and remains in our heads long afterward.

Hitchcock's work with big symphonic scores began in 1939 with *Rebecca*. Spooked by a pair of novachords, Franz Waxman's sensuous score envelops the film from beginning to end. Several long scenes, notably the mesmerizing tracking shot as Joan Fontaine approaches Manderley's west wing, delete all dialogue and non-musical sounds, creating a huge space for Waxman's haunted pedal point.

Working closely with Hitchcock through a meticulous set of music notes, Waxman wrote a triumphantly successful score (Selznick archive). It made such a powerful impression that the *Standard Symphony Hour* asked Waxman to compose a symphonic suite immediately after the premiere, transforming movie music into classical. Sensing a new way of promoting a movie over a long period, David Selznick, who had angrily denounced the music, suddenly became very happy about it, and renewed Standard's request two years later (Selznick archive).

Miklós Rózsa's score for *Spellbound* went a step further. It was programmed as a concert suite by Leopold Stokowski and broadcast on the radio before the film's release, helping to sell the movie in advance. Like *Rebecca*, *Spellbound* became a popular Hitchcock concert piece, a 'Spellbound Concerto', unveiling another shivery electronic instrument, the theremin, which quickly became a Hollywood marker for spooks and breakdowns.

Spellbound is an example of what Hitchcock called the 'psychological use' of music, a revelation of the subconscious rather than just a mood setter or character marker. Ambivalence is built into the music's structure: the love theme and the 'paranoia' theme are variants of each other, revealing the thin line between love and terror, one of Hitchcock's favourite themes. In the lengthy, hypnotic razor-blade scene, Hitchcock moves music forcefully to the foreground, making it equal with his camera.

It was during his Selznick period that Hitchcock first tried to get Bernard Herrmann. Selznick remarked during the search for *Spellbound*'s composer that he could not 'see anyone to compare with Herrmann', but the latter was unavailable (Selznick archive). When Hitchcock finally landed him a decade later, the timing was ideal. By the mid-1950s, the lush, melodic style of Raksin, Steiner and Korngold had peaked, making Herrmann's menacing chord patterns and incisive motifs all the more refreshing. (On Broadway, a similar pattern was unfolding, as Oscar Hammerstein was displaced by his most brilliant student, Stephen Sondheim, whose *Sweeney Todd: The Demon Barber of Fleet Street* (1979) is an homage to Hitchcock–Herrmann.)

Herrmann's brooding intensity and harmonic asperity are indelibly linked with Hitchcock's mature work. Their personalities were dramatically opposite – Hitchcock regal and controlling, Herrmann notoriously moody and prone to ranting outbursts. Yet the two were deeply simpatico: both had an uncompromising professionalism, a contempt for mediocrity, a dark sense of irony, an exuberant enthusiasm for eating and drinking, and a loathing for the Hollywood establishment matched by a longing for its approval. One huge difference, which became increasingly significant as Herrmann offended studio heads, was Hitchcock's canny ability to work with superiors he despised versus Herrmann's endless capacity for self-destructive blowups.

Herrmann was Hitchcock's secret sharer, a catalyst for energies darker and riskier than Hitchcock's cool sensibility normally permitted. His outcast status and emotional impulsivity constituted a Conradian alter-ego that moved Hitchcock's cinema into a new, darker dimension. Franz Waxman's sweeping lyricism, Dimitri Tiomkin's boisterous theatricality and Lyn Murray's glamorous fizziness were innovative but hardly risky; indeed, they guaranteed a certain commercial cachet. Herrmann, however, pushed Hitchcock's cinema deeper than ever into a world of dread and obsession. It's hard to imagine daring films like *The Wrong Man* and *Vertigo* existing at all without the interior narration of Herrmann's music; even the delightful *North by Northwest* has unexpected moments of yearning and trauma.

There is a witty, sardonic side as well. In Conrad's words, the secret sharer is 'one of those creatures that are just simmering all the time with a silly sort of wickedness', a description that could easily fit Herrmann – or Hitchcock as well (Conrad, 1910: 27). Indeed, their first collaboration was *The Trouble with Harry* (1955), which simmers with mischief and irony. Delivering Hitchcock's signature counterpoint, Herrmann flooded this absurdist comedy with some of his most pastoral music. This is Herrmann's most Elgarian score. Herrmann revered Elgar as 'one of the very greatest of the masters'. In an article for the Elgar centenary in 1957, he analysed what he saw as an inspired doubleness in Elgar, an 'intellectual cynicism' coupled with a 'deep sense of the country scene and pastoral tranquillity' (Herrmann, 1957: 3). This sounds very much like the score for *The Trouble with Harry*.

Herrmann's love for British music and culture was one more reason he got on so well with Hitchcock. Besides their strong artistic connection, the two had luck on their side. Lyn Murray got them together for lunch following his work for *To Catch a Thief* (1955); they immediately hit it off, as he thought they would, and Hitchcock had the power to bring Herrmann aboard. As Donald Spoto reminded me, Herrmann became available precisely when Hitchcock became his own producer:

> Remember that Hitchcock had no choice of composer until he also produced his films – and even then he had to use mostly studio personnel. His clout enabled him to have Herrmann, who was not attached to a studio in any case. (Spoto, personal communication)

During their early collaborations, Hitchcock and his secret sharer had, as Conrad would call it, 'a mysterious communication' that allowed each to tap into the other. Each reflected the other in 'an immense mirror' of sensibility and 'pure intuition' (Conrad, 1910: 26–7). They got along splendidly as both friends and colleagues. The closeness of their partnership is reflected in Hitchcock's notes for their next project, *The Man Who Knew Too Much*. To make his intentions clear, Hitchcock supplied his composer with his own music notes. These became increasingly detailed and imaginative as he worked with composers through four decades. Just how precisely he imagined sounds is revealed by his manipulation of the fateful cymbal crash at the end of Herrmann's imperious main title in *The Man Who Knew Too Much*, a sound montage that subconsciously prepares the audience for what is to come: 'At the very outset, the ring of the cymbals should carry over into the whine of the tires on the roadway' (Herrick archive).

As counterpoint to Arthur Benjamin's choral-orchestral extravaganza, Herrmann wrote malevolently spare chords as Hitchcock's camera tracks James Stewart and Doris Day through empty streets and alleyways. This was a new sound, sparse and lonely, a perfect realisation of the anxiety and emptiness gripping a couple who have lost their child. Because Herrmann had Hitchcock's trust, the director's notes have a relaxed, witty tone, illustrated by his directive in the hilarious final scene, where the frustrated partiers have collapsed into a stupor

following endless Buñuelian interruptions: 'After Jimmy Stewart's line about picking up Hank, Mr Herrmann will take over ... a few ladylike snores might be
permitted' (Herrick archive).

In Conrad's tale, the captain achieves self-mastery by tuning in to his dark side.
Their next project, *The Wrong Man*, was darker than ever. Herrmann's 'Wrong
Man Prelude' is a Latin jazz number with a corrosive undertone – champagne
poured over acid. Misunderstood by critics, who claimed it was too dour for a
proper jazz number, it perfectly embodies Manny's ostensibly upbeat, but dangerously vulnerable existence as a working musician struggling to support his family.

Much of the score grows from Manny's walking bass motif; it stalks like an
anxious ghost through the film, spinning out of control as the camera frantically
circles Manny's terrified face as he is thrown into a cell (one without a bathroom,
apparently; according to the files, the censor made Hitchcock remove the toilet
from the cell). Hitchcock imagined music as a preternatural force, abstract yet
strangely alive, a concept implied in the music notes for *The Wrong Man*, where
Herrmann's music should 'sneak in' Manny Balestrero's cell like a 'very soft'
invader, and where the notes specify the music should evoke Vera Miles' 'vacant
look' before her imprisonment in an asylum. We often think of movie music as filling an emptiness on the screen, but under Hitchcock's direction Herrmann could
evoke emptiness as a palpable energy: absence as 'the highest form of presence', in
James Joyce's phrase.

Hitchcock's clout in keeping Herrmann aboard is demonstrated in their most
important collaboration, *Vertigo*. An early studio memo states that the music was
to be furnished by Paramount staff, but Hitchcock hired Herrmann, kicking out
several pop cues in the process (Herrick archive; Smith, 1991: 222). The two continued to enjoy an easy give and take that transcended each man's implacable independence. Hitchcock invited Herrmann on to the set before scenes were shot to
discuss ideas, timing and spotting, an aural storyboarding paralleling the visual.

In some instances, Herrmann coaxed Hitchcock into more music. There is evidence he allowed Herrmann to call the shots in a way he never had with his previous composers. The notes for the restaurant scene state a preference for a 'moment
of silence, when Scottie feels the proximity of Madeleine'. Hitchcock wanted to
banish music and also 'take all the sounds of the restaurant away', leaving us
with 'Scottie's sole impression of her'. But he left the final decision to Herrmann,
who wrote 'Madeleine's Theme' for the scene, a piece of melancholy sensuality
that haunts the remainder of the movie. The removal of all sound other than the
score, a Hitchcock signature since *Waltzes from Vienna*, allows the music to have
an overwhelming presence and eroticism. There is a shivery moment of silence
before the music floats in, and we can imagine why Hitchcock wanted to extend
it. But he allowed Herrmann to make the call, and the music transforms the scene
from hushed expectancy to deep romantic yearning.

In other instances, it was Hitchcock who called for more music, asking
Herrmann to supply a longing he knew was beyond the power of his camera. For the famous dressing scene, he again took out all other sounds because

'Mr Herrmann may have something to say here', finally telling him, 'We'll just have the camera and you' (Herrick archive; Smith, 1991: 222). He allowed Herrmann ten minutes of Wagnerian sensuality unlike anything in cinema.

By *Vertigo*, Hitchcock's cinema was indelibly tied to his composer. We can't think of these films without thinking of the music. From the moment Herrmann's three-note motif begins spiralling in *Vertigo's* main title, plunging the listener into the cinema's most elegant nightmare, Scottie Ferguson's obsession becomes ours. In the words of John Williams, Hitchcock's final composer, *Vertigo's* music 'spins along this relentless path that gives a sense of timelessness … of the unstoppability of a destiny' (AFI DVD, 2011). This is the closest music comes to hypnosis, repealing forever the cliché that a movie score should stay discreetly in the background.

Herrmann was originally meant to share the stage with Norman O'Neill, in a re-enactment of a Hitchcock musical obsession from nearly twenty years in the past. During *Rebecca*, Hitchcock had tried to find O'Neill's wordless chorus, 'Prelude and Call', from J. M. Barrie's 1920 ghost play *Mary Rose*, so he could use it in the film, and he tried again with *Vertigo*. Both are projects involving voices from the dead, and Hitchcock was apparently convinced this cue would be perfect each time. The search proved fruitless in both instances and has been a subject of endless speculation, but a letter I received from Katherine Jessel, O'Neill's granddaughter, reveals that 'The Call' (like Poe's purloined letter) was right under Hitchcock's nose. Hitchcock's production people 'were not very enterprising in their search', says Ms Jessel in a bewildered letter from 2009. 'Not only had *Mary Rose* been produced on Broadway in 1920, but the music was published that year – the famous "Prelude and Call" being available for Orchestra as well as piano version. One would have thought Selznick could have obtained this music from the publisher' (Jessel, personal communication). It is just as well the searches failed, for it is hard to imagine any music more ghostly than Herrmann's evocations of Madeleine, or, for that matter, Franz Waxman's of Rebecca.

Vertigo was not exactly a box office triumph. No one in 1958 wanted to see Jimmy Stewart break down and land in an asylum, and no one wanted to see Kim Novak, the love of his life, plummet to her death – twice! It was all too dark for the 1950s, and Hitchcock yanked the movie out of circulation.

It was Herrmann's music that kept *Vertigo* alive when it vanished from sight until the 1980s. The score survived on a stunning Mercury Living Presence LP, its 'unstoppability' keeping the movie in people's imaginations. I remember seeing *Vertigo* when it opened in 1958 and being blown out of my chair by Herrmann's score, even though I was far too young to really grasp the convoluted story; *North by Northwest* and *Psycho* followed in the next two years, and I was hooked on Hitchcock–Herrmann forever.

Vertigo's stock is now breathtakingly high: in a *New York Times* review Alex Ross (1997) rates it as the cinema's finest score; another former *Times* critic, Joseph Horowitz, told me he believes *Vertigo* is greater than any American symphony. (These generalisations seem like ridiculous hyperbole until one tries to think of exceptions.)

Herrmann reprised themes from *Vertigo* in cliff-hanger and romance scenes for his next Hitchcock comedy, *North by Northwest*, but his most distinctive contribution was a spectacular fandango and a pulsing chord pattern that forecast what we now call minimalism. Hitchcock and Herrmann were at the top of their game and still perfectly in sync, revelling in the sheer joy of movie- and music-making. It was the last time their relationship would be so easy.

With *Psycho*, their partnership was plunged into unsettled waters. 'The Murder' is probably the most widely referenced of all film cues, yet Hitchcock's music notes reveal that he originally wanted the shower scene to not be scored, and for the picture as a whole to have scant music. This was not really new, since Hitchcock had used silence to powerful effect in the knife killings in *Blackmail* and *Sabotage* (1936). But, halfway through production, he worried that *Psycho* was looking like a dud. He told Herrmann that he was contemplating cutting *Psycho* up for television on *The Alfred Hitchcock Hour* (Smith, 1991: 237). Herrmann, who believed passionately in the project, was appalled by this possibility. He became a secret sharer in the most literal sense, writing the shower cue on the sly against Hitchcock's explicit directive.

The immediate effect was to right a ship that was about to go down. Herrmann was convinced the film only needed his music. Legend has it that he asked Hitchcock to chill, to go on his Christmas vacation and forget the whole thing, then come back and they could discuss it. On the way out the door, Hitchcock said, 'remember, no music in the shower scene!' When Hitchcock returned, Herrmann sat him down and played the shower scene with and without his secretly written cue. Hitchcock immediately reversed himself, stated it was better with the music (a rare admission of error), and became energised about the film.

Yet the struggle over *Psycho's* music appears more complicated than that. As late as 21 January, the music sheet, a scant one for Hitchcock, still calls for no music during the shower scene. Screenwriter Joseph Stefano told me that Hitchcock actually didn't come back after a Christmas vacation because he didn't go away in the first place; he and his family went over to the Stefanos' house for Christmas. It is true that Herrmann talked Hitchcock into numerous cues before late January, including the much-quoted 'Madhouse' motif, but the shower cue apparently came late in the game, understandably so, since giving in to it was a dramatic relinquishment of Hitchcock's authority. By the end, he had relinquished quite a bit. Beginning with the least music, *Psycho* ended up with more than in any Hitchcock film except *Vertigo*. In Stefano's words, 'Bernie took the picture and turned it into an opera' (interview with the author).

The terrifying modernity of *Psycho* was something new, another landmark in Herrmann–Hitchcock. This is not just true of the shower cue, which I think we make too much of, but the entire score, a symphony of dread unlike anything in cinema. Stefano, who was treated to the score in a private screening by Hitchcock, told me Hitchcock knew the music would knock his socks off, and it did: 'Hitchcock said the music raised *Psycho's* impact 33 percent. It raised it for me by another thirty.' Stefano was particularly awed by the 'geyser of sound' which he imagined Herrmann lying on the floor and sending up as the lovers rise from the bed in the opening hotel scene. 'You should go watch that!' he told me (interview with the author).

By now, Herrmann worried that Hitchcock resented his pivotal role in these films' successes. Herrmann too was in a dependent position, his career tied to his partnership with Hitchcock so closely the two were becoming synonymous. As Conrad describes it, each partner in the secret sharer dynamic becomes 'as dependent on' the other as on his 'own personality … it was very much like being mad, only it was worse because one was aware of it' (Conrad, 1910: 37).

In *The Birds*, Herrmann was no longer the music star but one part of an intricate sound team; because this was an electronic soundtrack, Hitchcock himself was able to exercise an unusual amount of control. This time he was captain of the ship, and he was resolute about having no music – at least, not the kind normally supplied by Herrmann. Hitchcock 'scored' *The Birds* in his lengthiest, most meticulous notes, delineating an astonishing variety of bird sounds, from those that 'assail the ears of the audience to perhaps an almost unbearable degree' to 'the equivalent of a brooding silence' (Herrick archive).

Herrmann boasted to colleagues that he co-directed *The Birds*, a statement that cannot have sat well with Hitchcock, especially since he was now under active pressure from Lew Wasserman and MCA to terminate the 'lazy' and 'derivative' Herrmann and get somebody more modern (Spoto, 1983: 491). Herrmann was a throwback to an age of symphonic film music that would soon disappear and be more profitably replaced with pop hits. At least, that was the prevailing Hollywood myth.

The failure of *Marnie* made matters worse, plunging Hitchcock into an angry, vulnerable mood. According to Truffaut, *Marnie* 'cost him a considerable amount of his self-confidence', and he was 'never the same again' (Truffaut, 1983: 327). During *Torn Curtain*, long-standing issues involving authorship and envy came to a boil. In November 1965, Hitchcock sent Herrmann a testy telegram commissioning *Torn Curtain*, but also warning him that if he didn't change his tune, and make it a pop one, he risked becoming a has-been and dragging Hitchcock down with him. Like Conrad's captain, Hitchcock dreaded risking his career to a sharer who was already banished by the corporation.

When Herrmann responded that he appreciated Hitchcock's 'suggestions', a Hitchcock surrogate fired back that these were no such thing, but 'requirements'. This was a verbal escalation on Hitchcock's part: the music notes for *Psycho* are called 'Mr Hitchcock's Suggestions', so Herrmann was simply repeating a term Hitchcock himself normally used. Clearly the era of suggestions was over.

Incorrigibly independent as ever, and perhaps eager to save a film that looked like another disaster, Herrmann ignored all the warnings, writing a dense, brassy, brutal score with no pop elements – exactly what Hitchcock forbade; he also, as in *Psycho*, created an electrifying cue for the central murder scene even though Hitchcock specified no music. Upon hearing the Prelude at Goldwyn Studio,

Hitchcock angrily rejected Herrmann's score in front of the orchestra, a bruising public humiliation, then drove to Universal and apologised for hiring Herrmann in the first place. The greatest director–composer team in Hollywood history was suddenly over. Herrmann regarded his friendship with Hitchcock as one of the high points of his life, and that was over as well (Smith, 1991: 273).

Many blame Hitchcock for this debacle, but the firing involved ambivalent, complicated emotions on both sides. Hitchcock stuck his neck out to defend Herrmann to his corporate superiors and felt deeply betrayed when Herrmann defied his instructions. Still, did he really believe that Herrmann – who not only regularly defied authority but was implacably loyal to the symphonic tradition – would write a series of pop tunes to order? Herrmann certainly did defy Hitchcock, but he probably believed his score could bring to life a cold, inexpressive film.

In the Conrad analogy, the captain in crisis can regain mastery only if he learns to control his combustible alter-ego, but Hitchcock believed Herrmann had become uncontrollable. Joseph Stefano told me that Hitchcock simply 'didn't like the score'. That was the issue, and there was no turning back. Hitchcock's relationship with his composer had always been a subtle barometer of his independence and confidence, both of which were at an all-time low. Even if he had felt more confident and given Herrmann an opportunity for revision, it's by no means clear Herrmann could have given Wasserman and company what they wanted – or thought they wanted.

After Hitchcock let him go, Herrmann presented himself in interviews very much like the liberated secret sharer in Conrad's final lines, 'a free man, a proud swimmer striking out for a new destiny', away from Hitchcock, who had sold out to corporate pop tune mediocrity (Conrad, 1910: 61). But, as Donald Spoto and Steven C. Smith document, Herrmann and Hitchcock were both deeply affected by the break-up: Herrmann fell into a profound depression, and Hitchcock was so mortified that he hid behind a door when Herrmann came to his office for a reconciliation (Smith, 1991: 273; Spoto, 1983: 491). I asked John Williams what he believes is behind the firing. He remembers Peggy Robertson saying Hitchcock thought 'Benny was repeating himself and quoting himself', but he believes the break-up was about deeply personal issues that

> had nothing to do with music or film. Hitchcock may have felt that his style was too dependent on Herrmann's music, and that may have wounded his pride. They ended up being two matadors opposing one another. (Williams, interview with the author)

The irony, of course, is that Truffaut, De Palma and Scorsese snatched Herrmann up after Hitchcock cast him into the water. Contrary to what the corporation believed, the new wave 1960s generation idolised Herrmann; he was totally in tune with the times, as far as we were concerned. It was corporate Hollywood that was out of touch.

Hitchcock–Herrmann left behind a celebrated legacy, but precisely what it constitutes is hard to pin down. I've asked several prominent critics what they make of it. The sceptic is Steven C. Smith, Herrmann's biographer:

It didn't really change anything in Hollywood; not until the '70s did makers of thrillers like De Palma begin to have Herrmann-esque scores, and it wasn't until the '80s that major Herrmann plagiarism really kicked in on movie soundtracks. I think it's fair to say that in recent years, those BH–AH scores have been recognized by non-film music buffs as memorable in their own right, and they're certainly masterpieces; but outside of composers studying (or stealing) the way those scores work, I don't think they were game-changers – just exceptional examples of a composer-director partnership. (Smith, personal communication)

Alex Ross (1997) believes the partnership showed us what music could accomplish in a Hollywood movie. Occasionally a film like *There Will Be Blood* features a score that creates its own powerful space, but Ross believes this is rare in contemporary film scoring.

On the other hand, *Musical America*'s editor, Sedgwick Clark, believes the legacy continues strongly in the team of Steven Spielberg–John Williams, Hollywood's premiere director and composer. The two have been together since *Jaws* (1975), already much longer than Hitchcock–Herrmann. Herrmann and Williams have a very different style, Clark admits, but the point is:

John Williams has a style, an unmistakable, instantly recognizable sound. You can't say that about many composers nowadays. As Spielberg has gravitated from brash action-adventure and magical fantasy films to the deeply humanistic themes of *Schindler's List* and *Lincoln*, Williams has been inspired to compose music of rare subtlety amid today's anonymous electronic scores. (Clark, personal communication)

A great deal can be said for Clark's view. Williams' rocket to fame took off just as Herrmann's was coming down and is widely regarded as saving large-scale symphonic film music. Williams and Herrmann are similar in their loyalty to symphonic tradition, their insistence on orchestrating everything themselves, and their low regard for those who don't. For these composers, sound is substance.

Herrmann was an important mentor to Williams, and the Herrmann–Hitchcock collaborations formed some of his earliest, most indelible impressions. He rarely goes to movies, but he did see *Vertigo* and never got over the music. He actually called Herrmann to ask his permission to do *Family Plot* (1976). Very much like a passing of the torch.

Hitchcock was attracted to Williams because of his sensational music for *Jaws*, which Spielberg credits with saving the film, much as Herrmann rescued *Psycho*. Williams sees important similarities in Hitchcock and Spielberg, for both have:

great trust in music … both are interested in intimate details like tempo and spotting. Much of their filmmaking style has to do with their use of music –music that has an idiosyncratic stamp. Steven is a different personality, sunnier, more optimistic, less sceptical – a very different view of life. But where music is concerned and its function, they are very similar. (Williams, interview with the author)

There are other parallels as well. Hitchcock regarded music as an actual presence in his films, 'a character in the métier', says Williams. Spielberg uses the same metaphor in regard to Williams, stating that his scores 'are like characters' and that, in *Close Encounters of the Third Kind* (1979), he became 'the major character' (New York Philharmonic archive).

Hitchcock never abandoned symphonic sound, as his hiring of Williams illustrates. Williams' *Family Plot* provided Hitchcock with a charming swansong, reprising musical signatures developed over his career: pulsing chase rhythms, sinister harp sounds, sudden silences after false crescendos, and fusions of orchestral and 'real' sounds, especially bells. Hitchcock even got an ethereal chorus, something he had wanted since his first fruitless search for Norman O'Neill's music in *Mary Rose*. Lonely timpani solos, a longtime Hitchcock trademark, are played by Williams' father, who performed under Herrmann during the Hitchcock era.

Herrmann, who was very ill and had less than a year to live, gave Williams 'his blessing' to do this score, without his customary diatribes. Perhaps, after a decade, the same length of time he had been with Hitchcock, he had made his peace. It's important to remember the deep trust the two men built during most of their relationship. As Williams puts it, 'Herrmann's contribution was very striking and very strong, but Hitchcock was a director who placed his faith in that. Most directors would be afraid of music that operatic.' Given their strong personalities, their perfectionist sensibilities, their dramatically different temperaments and the work-for-hire nature of the business, it's remarkable the partnership of Alfred Hitchcock and his secret sharer lasted so long and yielded so much glorious music.

References

All quotations are from the following film archives unless otherwise indicated.

British Film Institute (BFI), Library and Information Services, London, UK
David Selznick Collection, Harry Ransom Humanities Research Center, University of Texas, Austin, Texas
Margaret Herrick Library, The Alfred Hitchcock Collection, Academy of Motion Picture Arts and Sciences, Beverly Hills, California
Museum of Modern Art, Film Study Center, New York, New York
New York Philharmonic archive, Lincoln Center, New York, April 2006
RKO Studio Collection, Arts Library Special Collections, Young Research Library, University of California, Los Angeles, California
Syracuse University Library, Department of Special Collections, Syracuse, New York
Warner Brothers Archive, School of Cinema-Television, University of Southern California, Los Angeles, California

Texts
Conrad, Joseph (1910), *The Secret Sharer*. New York: Signet.
Herrmann, Bernard (1957), 'Elgar, A Constant Source of Joy', in H. A. Chambers (ed.), *Edward Elgar Centenary Sketches*. London: Novello & Co.
Hitchcock, Alfred (1933–34; 1995), 'Alfred Hitchcock on Music in Films', *Cinema Quarterly* 2:2: 80–3. Reprinted in Sidney Gottlieb (ed.), *Hitchcock on Hitchcock: Selected Writings and Interviews*. London: Faber and Faber, pp. 241–5.

Ross, Alex (1997), 'Casting the Spells of "Vertigo"', *New York Times*, 6 October, p. H17.

Smith, Steven C. (1991), *A Heart at Fire's Center: The Life and Music of Bernard Herrmann*. Berkeley: University of California Press.

Spoto, Donald (1983), *The Dark Side of Genius: The Life of Alfred Hitchcock*. Boston: Little, Brown.

Sullivan, Jack (2006), *Hitchcock's Music*. New Haven: Yale University Press.

Truffaut, François (1983), *Hitchcock/Truffaut*. New York: Simon & Schuster.

Correspondences with the author

Sedgwick Clark, 28 May 2014
Katherine Jessel, 14 October 2009
Steven Smith, 11 August 2009
Donald Spoto, 4 January 2005

Interviews with the author

Maurice Jarre, 8 June 2005
Joseph Stefano, series of interviews, 1999–2005
John Waxman, series of interviews, 1999–2005
John Williams, 29 January 2003

DVD

American Film Institute, *The Art of Collaboration: Steven Spielberg, John Williams*. 30 December 2011.

Hitchcock, music and the mathematics of editing

Charles Barr

'Construction to me, it's like music.'

(Hitchcock, 1995: 298)

'Every piece of film that you put in the picture should have a purpose. It's like notes of music. They must make their point.'

(Hitchcock, 1995: 290)

I am no kind of music expert, and am not equipped to write about music as such, in the manner of other contributors to this volume such as Jack Sullivan, author of a definitive chapter on 'Hitchcock and Music' in the recent collection *A Companion to Alfred Hitchcock* (2011). Instead, I want to offer some sort of tentative exploration of what Hitchcock may have meant by the analogies that he often articulated between film construction and music. This means going right back to his formative years, and specifically the work of D. W. Griffith.

My own chapter in that same *Companion* dealt with the topic of 'Hitchcock and Early Film-Makers': his relation to some of his predecessors and contemporaries in silent cinema, and what he drew from them. A special inspiration, for Hitchcock as for many others, was Griffith's 1916 epic *Intolerance*, subtitled 'Love's Struggle Throughout the Ages'. The film tells in parallel four stories of persecution and resistance from different historical periods. This is what Griffith wrote in the publicity for the film:

> The stories begin like four currents looked at from a hilltop. At first the four currents flow apart, slowly and quietly. But as they flow, they grow nearer and nearer together, and faster and faster, until in the end, in the last act, they mingle in one mighty river of expressed emotion. (Griffith, quoted in Hansen, 1991: 330)

This works, I argued, as a metaphor for Hitchcock's own cinematic formation. Four main currents of influence come together. Griffith and American cinema; the cinema of Germany, where Hitchcock worked extensively in the mid-1920s; and the new Soviet cinema, which he was exposed to a little later – he always enthused to interviewers about the impact of all three. And, of course, his roots in (and his collaborators from) British culture and cinema, even though he was not always so quick to acknowledge these. The four currents come together to form the 'one mighty river' of his cinema. It is precisely his openness to this wide range of models and of influences, and his skill in drawing on them and blending them together into a purposeful cosmopolitan form of cinematic narrative, that has helped to make him such a central figure in film history.

From another angle, Hitchcock's cinema can be seen as, likewise, representing an especially artful blending, and integration, of a range of antecedent artistic forms or media. Again there seem to be four main currents feeding in to the 'mighty river' of the newly evolving twentieth-century medium of cinema, as he theorised it in articles and interviews, and as he practised it. To put it very schematically: cinema has strong affinities with *literature* for narrative, with *theatre* for performance and with *painting* for visual composition. And, also, if less obviously, with *music* – for the ways in which its compositional work is laid out in temporal sequence. My initial quotations are only two among many, found in articles and interviews of widely differing dates.

'Construction to me, it's like music … Every piece of film that you put in the picture should have a purpose. It's like notes of music. They must make their point'. So what analogies can be made between the note and the 'piece of film', the shot? I would suggest there are three. First, length: how long the note is held, how long the shot is held. Second, 'volume', the loudness of a note in some way corresponding to the scale of the shot, the emphasis of the close-up being stronger than that of the long shot – Hitchcock sometimes articulated that analogy himself (Truffaut, 1969: 346).[1] But the fundamental and indispensable element is *repeatability*, based on fixed position. A note has a fixed position within a scale, and a fixed camera position can be seen as, in its way, a cinematic equivalent of this, involving repeatability of the set-up, and repeatability – with variations – of the shot.

The British writer Paul Rotha, in his enormously ambitious and influential 1930 volume *The Film Till Now*, expressed strong views on this subject of repeatability:

> The elementary principles of editing are as follows. First, it should be the aim of the director never to use a shot on the screen more than once if it has been taken from the same angle of vision, unless he should desire to emphasise a particular viewpoint. The screen will thus be kept constantly fresh and interesting to the audience. To show a thing more than once from the same angle is to invite monotony …

'… unless he should desire to emphasise a particular viewpoint' (Rotha, 1930: 291):[2] such repetition is evidently a rare special case, an unusual exception that proves the rule: that is, it supports, by its specialness, the validity of the general principle. Here Rotha demonstrates a profound lack of understanding of – or maybe just a profound lack of sympathy with – one of the fundamental principles, or building blocks, of cinematic narrative, as it had been developed and systematised in the early years, when Hitchcock was growing up and beginning his fascinated study of the medium. The key figure here is Griffith, whom Hitchcock in a journal article in 1931 would call 'the Columbus of the screen', the man who mapped out new territories (Hitchcock, 2005).

His main pioneer contribution was not the so-called invention of the close-up, or of cross-cutting within a scene, but the practice that he refined long before he started using close-ups or 'scene dissection' at all, namely doing what Rotha said you should not do: showing things more than once from the same angle; repetition of camera positions, and cutting back and forth between those positions to create quite complex structures and narratives. Again, Griffith did not invent the principle, but he used it with a new kind of intensity and eloquence.

One could use in illustration virtually any of the 450-odd short narratives that he made for the Biograph company between 1908 and 1913, based on consistent and rigorous structural principles. Typical – but especially neat and (still) powerful – among the 1910 films is *The Unchanging Sea*, based on a poetic narrative by Charles Kingsley about members of a fishing community. The opening shot shows a young fisherman and a girl outside her home. Soon they are married, and soon after that he is called out to sea; his boat fails to return. We, unlike his wife, discover that he has been washed up elsewhere, but has lost his memory. By the time he regains it and is reunited with his wife, their daughter (played by Mary Pickford) is fully grown. At regular points in this story, we return to the exterior of the home, which is invariably shown from the same fixed position as in the initial shot. In all, there are nine of these shots of the home, intercut with a small number of other locations, themselves handled in the same repetitive way. Analysis shows that the film is made up of twenty-nine shots in all, divided between only five camera set-ups. Two of the three initial ones – the home (A), and a view looking out to sea (B) – are illustrated in Figure 2.1; the C shots, only three in all, look inland to another area of the beach. The other two set-ups (D and E) show the island on which the man is cast away. The shot-by-shot structure of the narrative can be set out in a tabular chart (two consecutive numbers in the same column, for instance 4-5, indicate that a title has intervened) (Table 2.1a).

The nine shots of the home exterior, column A, show a succession of moments separated in time. 1: courtship. 4: they enter the home as a married couple. 5 (after an intertitle): he is called out to sea, and she goes to see him off – they exit frame left. 7: she goes to look for his return, again exiting left. 13: she holds their baby. 16: mother and child, now older. 19: mother and child, now grown up. 21: a young man calls to court the daughter. 25: now married, they say

Figure 2.1 *The Unchanging Sea* (1910, Dir: D.W. Griffith). (L to R) A (shot 1): the home; B (6): farewell; A (13) fatherless baby (Biograph Company/American Mutoscope & Biograph).

Table 2.1a Distribution of set-ups across a scene in *The Unchanging Sea* (Griffith, 1910)

A	B	C	D	E
1				
	2			
		3		
4				
5				
	6			
7				
	8			
	9			
			10	
			11	
				12
13				
	14			
				15
16				
	17			
				18
19				
		20		
21				
	22			
				23
			24	
25				
	26			
	27			
		28		
	29			

goodbye, exiting frame left and leaving the mother bereft. The happy ending, reuniting the parental couple, takes place on the beach, so there is no final return to the home.

It is clear that all of these nine shots will have been taken successively, following a precise script and storyboard: the camera remains fixed until all the A shots have been completed, everyone then moves on to one of the beach locations, and they run through that set of shots, and so on to the end, leaving the editors to do the mechanical work of breaking down the footage and assembling the shots in the correct scripted order. This is obvious enough from looking at the film, and it is confirmed by an unusual surviving version of another of the Biograph shorts (less economical and less powerful than *The Unchanging Sea*), *The Transformation of Mike* (1912), held by the British Film Institute (BFI). In the old (pre-DVD) Distribution Library Catalogue, the 16mm print was described thus: 'This version of the D. W. Griffith film gives first of all the entire footage in the order in which it was shot, followed by the finally edited film. Useful in discussion of the film making practices of the time' (Petley, 1978: 226). The first part, the unedited footage, corresponds exactly to what we can infer of the way *The Unchanging Sea* was planned and realised: a series of bits of action all taken from the same set-up, then a series from another set-up, making no kind of narrative sense, simply waiting to be edited into the scripted order, as supplied in the second part of the print.

This two-part item illuminates not simply 'the film making practices of the time', but principles of cinema that extend far beyond those early silent years: the ability to shoot out of continuity, and to construct narrative jigsaw-style in the editing. In the short films for Biograph, Griffith went beyond his contemporaries in the forceful economy with which he applied the system, providing a demonstration of the medium's potential as telling in its way as the celebrated editing experiments set out years later by the Russians. The extreme economy of the strategy explains the remarkable speed with which the films were turned out – no fewer than 141 of them in 1910 alone, the year of *The Unchanging Sea*[3] – and at the same time it establishes a strong and eloquent 'musical' principle that will be built into the development of the mature medium, even though neither Griffith himself in his longer films, nor others, will generally use it in quite such a simple way. I've never forgotten the response of an undergraduate class on early cinema when I first tried out a version of this kind of chart. One of them remarked that, if you turned it on its side, the chart would look like a musical score. Table 2.1b gives an idea of what the student meant.

As Jack Sullivan emphasises at the start of his chapter in *A Companion to Alfred Hitchcock* (2011), 'Hitchcock envisioned movie-making musically, comparing himself to composer, maestro, and orchestrator, making numerous analogies between scoring and moviemaking. Storyboards, he said, were like musical notation' (219). It was surely Griffith, the 'Columbus of the screen' whom he had admired from his early teenage years onwards, who first drew him in this direction, demonstrating so clearly the attractive economy and expressivity of this form of storyboarding, or 'scoring'. I will now work through four characteristic Hitchcock sequences which operate on the same kind of compositional principle. One from his first silent film as director, *The Pleasure Garden* (1925); one from his last film, *Family Plot*, made fifty-one years later; and, in between, one from a British sound film, *The Skin Game* (1931), and another from a Hollywood film, *The Birds* (1963). It is tempting to use more famous set pieces, like the scene of James Stewart trailing Madeleine in the early stages of *Vertigo* (1958), or of Cary Grant waiting at the prairie bus stop in *North by Northwest* (1959), but those are familiar enough already. None of my four scenes has any musical score, but I suggest that, like those more celebrated scenes, they embody the structural principles which Hitchcock plausibly regarded as musical, and which he applied consistently throughout his directing career.

Table 2.1b Distribution of shots across a sequence in *The Unchanging Sea* (Griffith, 1910)

Table 2.2 Distribution of shots across a sequence in *The Pleasure Garden* (Hitchcock, 1925)

boat									9			12		
boat							7							
boat		2				6								
shore				4									13	
shore			3					8			11			14
shore	1				5					10				

Figure 2.2 *The Pleasure Garden* (1925, Dir: Alfred Hitchcock). (L to R) Shore: the wife; Boat: the husband (Bavaria Film/Gainsborough Pictures/Münchner Lichtspielkunst AG).

A key sequence in *The Pleasure Garden* echoes, as it happens, that Griffith short film from 1910, *The Unchanging Sea*: a wife waves goodbye from the shore to her husband. There is a binary opposition between him on the ship and her on the shore, the two never being seen in the same shot (Figure 2.2): the sequence thus follows the Griffith-derived principles articulated by the Soviet theorist Lev Kuleshov, years before Hitchcock would have had a chance to read these Soviet formulations.[4] There are three camera set-ups on each side, each trio offering simple variations on the presentation of man and woman respectively (Table 2.2).

Now consider a scene from an early sound film *The Skin Game*, based on a play by John Galsworthy. Some critics have dismissed it as a dull film in which Hitchcock took little interest: he had to be loyal to the high-prestige play text, and the cumbersome quality of early sound cinema apparatus resulted in a lot of long static takes. In the margins of the dialogue scenes, however, he was continuing to engage in bold formal experimentation. Like the musical film he made not long after it, *Waltzes from Vienna* (1934), *The Skin Game* deserves to be redeemed from obscurity, not least for scenes like the central one of the auction. The story is based on a conflict between two families, the Hillcrists, representing old money, and the Hornblowers, representing new. At the auction, they bid against each other for a house of great personal and symbolic importance: at the climax of the bidding we

Figure 2.3 *The Skin Game* (1931, Dir: Alfred Hitchcock). (L to R) Shot 1: Auctioneer; shot 2: Hornblower; shot 3: Hillcrist (British International Pictures).

get a rapid montage of eighteen shots in thirty-six seconds, cutting between the rival bidders and the auctioneer (Figure 2.3):

Auctioneer
     Hornblower
          Hillcrist
     Hornblower
          Hillcrist
Auctioneer
     Hornblower
          Hillcrist
     Hornblower
          Hillcrist
     Hornblower
          Hillcrist
Auctioneer
     Hornblower
          Hillcrist
     Hornblower
          Hillcrist
Auctioneer

A precisely timed and rather beautiful symmetrical construction is in evidence here: shots of the auctioneer, always from the same set-up, are intercut with quick alternating shots of the bidders, in blocks of four, then six, then four (see Table 2.3). To do a full structural or 'musical' analysis of this scene, as of the previous one, one would need to do more than put in a lot of crude blobs or 'notes' – taking into account also the precise length of each shot, and also the 'scale' of shot, the loudness of the close-up against the quieter long shots. For fully accurate notation, a film print rather than a DVD would be necessary, in order to measure the number of frames, which would mean working from a 35mm archival film print. This is exactly what David Bordwell and Kristin Thompson do, in recent editions of their now-classic textbook on *Film Art*, using 35mm prints to produce stills and analyse key scenes – one of them a suspense scene from *The Birds*, in which Melanie ('Tippi' Hedren) and others try, unsuccessfully, to warn a motorist about

Table 2.3 Distribution of shots across a sequence in *The Skin Game* (Hitchcock, 1931)

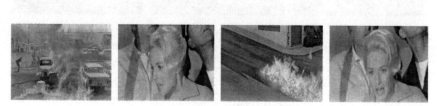

Figure 2.4 *The Birds* (1963, Dir: Alfred Hitchcock). Cross-cutting between Melanie and the growing fire (Universal Pictures).

the danger of dropping a match on to a petrol-soaked forecourt (2013: 224–5). Access to the film print means that they can count the precise number of frames within a quick sequence built on alternation between Melanie and the fire that blazes up (Figure 2.4). The shots are measured in frames, starting with the four shots illustrated.

Fire	73 frames [3 seconds + one frame]
Melanie	20 frames
Fire	18
Melanie	16
Fire	14
Melanie	12
Fire	10
Melanie	8
Fire, wider	34
Melanie	33

The arithmetical pattern created by Hitchcock and his editor George Tomasini, with seven successive shots reduced by two frames each time, can surely not be accidental. In all, the sequence of ten shots runs for 233 frames, slightly under ten seconds; the next shot in contrast is a high-angle one showing the town and the fire below, revealed as a literal bird's-eye view when birds enter the foreground, and this runs for twenty-five seconds. The contrast offers rich scope, for someone with the will and the competence, for further exploration of the musical analogy, going beyond basic patterns of repetition of shots/notes into issues of tempo, scale and 'volume'.

To return to *The Skin Game*: a scene later in the film offers a comparable arithmetical structure that is easier to measure because its shots are much longer. Two romances are frustrated by the hostilities that exist between the two families. In two successive scenes, the respective romantic couples talk, and part unhappily; at the end of each scene, the man goes out. The first scene, between Charles Hornblower and his wife Chloe, is played out in a long take of two minutes and twenty-two seconds: after Charles's exit, a five-second reaction shot of Chloe registers the pain that she feels. The following scene, between Jill Hillcrist and Rolf Hornblower, is played out in a long take of two minutes and twenty-two seconds: after Rolf's exit, a five-second reaction shot of Jill registers the pain that she feels. The formal repetition helps to enforce a striking dramatic parallel, and the precise equation between the duration of the two scenes suggests that Hitchcock was keen to exploit it to the full, and in doing so to have some mathematical fun. It reminds me of a dictum that can be traced back to a contemporary of his in the British Film Industry, one of my favourite of all film quotations: 'The movies aren't drama, they aren't literature, they are pure mathematics.' It is spoken by a film editor in Christopher Isherwood's *roman-à-clef* about the British cinema of the 1930s, based on his own involvement as a young writer on *The Little Friend* (1934, directed by Berthold Viertel), whose editor was Ian Dalrymple. One feels that Hitchcock would have endorsed the editor's dictum, with some emendation. Movies for him were rooted both in literature and in drama, but *also* in the 'music' of mathematics, or, if you like, the mathematics of music: the perception of the profound connections between the two goes back at least as far as Pythagoras. Dan Auiler's book *Hitchcock's Notebooks* provides some neat confirmation of the way he sketched out, or 'scored', key sequences, using forms of chart that are comparable to those that I have set out above. In a later suspense sequence in *The Birds*, children leave the school and are violently attacked by crows. Auiler reproduces nine successive notebook pages written in Hitchcock's own hand, in which he lays out the whole sequence shot by shot, specifying the length of shot not in time but in physical measurement; a typical section of fourteen shots, measured in feet, is designed to run 2-1-1-1-half-half-2-1-2-1-1-2-1-3. Three feet of 35mm film = two seconds, so this is another piece of rapid rhythmic editing, as duly realised in the film (Auiler, 1999: 507). Another handwritten chart sketches out the suspenseful cross-cutting at the climax of *Strangers on a Train* (1951), cutting back and forth between Guy's tennis match and Bruno's return to the fairground to plant incriminating evidence: the alternating structure, accelerating in tempo, is laid out in clear tabular form. In Auiler's words, 'Hitchcock divided the page in two columns – Bruno and Guy – and then began to bounce the film back and forth between them' (1999: 485).

Hitchcock's final film, *Family Plot*, functions as a summation of this aspect of his formal concerns and practices. It was widely recognised as a low-pressure film compared with his finest work, playful rather than intense, a 'pure cinema' exercise in neat plotting and in shot-by-shot construction. The review in *Sight and Sound* at the time of its release, by the American critic Jonathan Rosenbaum, picked out a sequence that illustrates this quality to perfection:

> Best of all is a hair-raising sequence with Blanche and George in a car without brakes barrelling down a steep mountain road. An ultimate expression of Hitchcock's

Figure 2.5 *Family Plot* (1976, Dir: Alfred Hitchcock). (L to R) shot A;
shot B; shot C (Universal Pictures).

storyboard technique – clearly devised at a desk rather than during shooting or at an
editing table – its suspense derives from algebraic essentials, where the purest kinds
of 'musical' variations can be played on the threats of passing cars, culminating in a
wonderfully timed procession of motorcyclists. (Rosenbaum, 1976: 188–9)

So the familiar reference points are still here after fifty years, and longer if one
goes back to Hitchcock's early mentor, Griffith: storyboard, mathematics, music.
As is confirmed by documents and interviews, Hitchcock did indeed storyboard,
or 'score', the sequence from his desk, disdaining the idea of going with the camera
crew to shoot the location footage of the downhill ride, happy instead to direct the
shots of Blanche and George in a studio mock-up of the car. The car – as we know,
but they don't – has been sabotaged by an enemy, so that brake fluid is leaking out
rapidly as they begin their descent. The sequence is built up out of an extremely
simple set of elements (Figure 2.5).

A: frontal shots of the couple inside the car, with back projection
B: subjective shots, their viewpoint through the windscreen
C: exterior details, e.g. of the brake fluid leaking
D: interior details, e.g. of George's foot on the brake pedal
E: occasional wider shots of the car

A and B are dominant, and the camera position for both of them remains the
same: so the fifty-seven-shot sequence really does sustain the same economical,
'musical' compositional principles that were already operating in that Griffith
short film of 1910, which was likewise based on fixed camera and on no more than
five elements (Table 2.4).

This is Hitchcock's last major set piece of cinematic action, based on suspense,
virtually wordless, an almost literal enactment of his often-stated belief that cinema should give its audience the experience of a rollercoaster ride. It seems fitting
that it should so clearly hark back to his formative experiences of silent cinema,
first as student and then as practitioner, and that it should so clearly employ the
storyboarding strategies which he saw as analogous to scoring, and to which
Rosenbaum plausibly applies the two adjectives 'algebraic' and 'musical'.

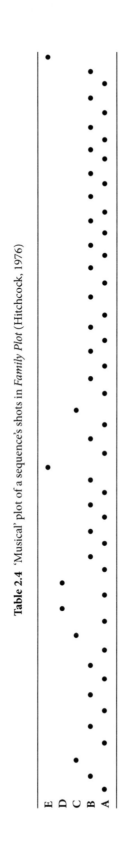

Table 2.4 'Musical' plot of a sequence's shots in *Family Plot* (Hitchcock, 1976)

Notes

1 'It was like music, you see, the high shot with the violins, and suddenly the big head with the brass instruments clashing.' From discussion of the scene of the death of Arbogast in *Psycho* (Truffaut, 1969: 346). The interview book was first published in French in 1966; different editions have different pagination.
2 The passage stayed unaltered in successive updated versions of the book, the last being the fourth edition (London: Spring Books, 1967).
3 For details of the short films made by Griffith for Biograph, see Bowser (1973).
4 In 1925, when he shot *The Pleasure Garden*, Hitchcock could not have been familiar with the new Soviet films or the related theoretical writings, themselves strongly influenced by Griffith. Pudovkin's *Film Technique and Film Acting* was not published until 1929.

References

Auiler, Dan (1999), *Hitchcock's Secret Notebooks*. London: Bloomsbury.

Bordwell, David and Kristin Thompson (2013), *Film Art: an Introduction*, 10th ed. New York: McGraw-Hill.

Bowser, Eileen (1973), *Biograph Bulletins, 1908–1912*. New York: Octagon Press.

Hansen, Miriam (1991), *Babel and Babylon: Spectatorship in American Silent Film*. Cambridge: Harvard University Press.

Hitchcock, Alfred (1995), 'On Style', interview in *Cinema* magazine, 5:1, August-September 1963. Reprinted in Sidney Gottlieb (ed.), *Hitchcock on Hitchcock: Selected Writings and Interviews*. London: Faber and Faber, pp. 285–302.

Hitchcock, Alfred (2005), 'A Columbus of the Screen', *Film Weekly*, 21 February 1931. Reprinted in *Hitchcock Annual* 14: 46–9.

Petley, Julian (1978), *BFI Distribution Library Catalogue*. London: BFI.

Rosenbaum, Jonathan (1976), '*Family Plot*', *Sight and Sound* 45:3: 188–9.

Rotha, Paul (1930), *The Film Till Now: A Survey of the Cinema*. London: Jonathan Cape.

Sullivan, Jack (2011), 'Hitchcock and Music', in Thomas Leitch and Leland Poague (eds), *A Companion to Alfred Hitchcock*. Chichester: John Wiley, pp. 219–36.

Truffaut, François (1969), *Hitchcock*. London: Panther Books.

The anatomy of aural suspense in *Rope* and *Vertigo*

Kevin Clifton

I vividly remember seeing Hitchcock's *Vertigo* (1958) for the first time as a gradu-ate student in Austin, Texas, in the 1990s. I was hypnotised in the darkened theatre as I listened to Bernard Herrmann's swirling arpeggios and watched Saul Bass's spiralling visuals during the opening credits. Something – or *someone* – took a hold of me that afternoon. Since that day, Herrmann's music, especially the opening Prelude, has been something akin to a musical *dark passenger*[1] in my life, lurking just underneath the veil of my own musical reality. I often find myself humming its haunting tune – if you can even call it a tune – out of the blue and for no apparent reason. And, like many of the characters in the film, I too have been bewitched, and in my case by *Vertigo*'s strange music.

It is well known that early reviews of the film were not positive. John McCarten wrote in the *New Yorker*: 'Alfred Hitchcock … has never before indulged in such farfetched nonsense' (McCarten, 1958: 65). Initial reviews typically ran the gamut from the film being too long and too complicated, to being too slow. The pendu-lum has since swung the other way, of course, and *Vertigo* is now acclaimed as one of Hitchcock's best films, ranking near the top of many 'Best Of' film polls. General audiences and film scholars alike agree that the film elicits powerful emotions in the filmic viewer, which certainly resonates with my own initial reaction. Germane for this book, film-music scholars, such as Jack Sullivan (2008), Graham Bruce (1985: 139–81), David Cooper (2001), Antony John (2001: 516–44) and Dan Blim (2013: 21–31), among others, have written extensively on the effective use of music in *Vertigo*, with Cooper's film-score guide being the most comprehensive study.

This chapter moves beyond current film music scholarship on *Vertigo* by offer-ing an investigation on how its music can be heard in relation to *Rope* (1948), Hitchcock's first colour film, released ten years prior. The basic plotline for both films is strikingly similar: a murder occurs relatively early in each film, after which a main character psychologically spirals downwards fuelled by an obsessive-compulsive behaviour. With respect to their accompanying soundtracks, in *Rope* Hitchcock mainly employed pre-existing music, specifically the *Mouvement Perpétuel* (1918) by the French composer Francis Poulenc. The opening and end-ing credits for *Rope*, as well as its promotional movie trailer, feature an orches-trated version of Poulenc's piano music, and in a pivotal scene in the film one of the deranged killers plays the *Mouvement Perpétuel* at the piano while being cross-examined by a rather inquisitive party guest. Thus, Poulenc's music saturates *Rope*'s soundtrack and is elevated to an enigmatic character in its own right in the filmic narrative, much like Herrmann's iconic music scored specifically for *Vertigo*. Elsewhere I have argued that the music in *Rope* can be interpreted on different analytical levels: discrete levels of purely musical forces as well as possible extra-musical meanings.[2] Working outwards from this interpretive framework, it is possible for the listener to hear reverberations – or musical echoes – from *Rope*'s modernist soundtrack in Herrmann's musical backdrop for *Vertigo*. The music used in both films, both pre-existing as well as newly composed, features dramatic moments of aural suspense in which the music actively yearns for closure – hence, working *against* the trope of psychological obsession – yet concomitantly resists this closure at the same time, perpetuating dramatic suspense on a purely sonic level. As we will see and hear, these moments of musical ambivalences – or suspenseful *open endings* – brilliantly counterpoint the narrative complexities of both films.

Unraveling *Rope*'s soundtrack

In 1947, Hitchcock, along with his then – business associate Sidney Bernstein, formed a short-lived production company called Transatlantic Pictures Corporation. This company allowed Hitchcock to promote *Rope* as he saw fit, thus asserting his creative independence away from the standard marketing procedures of the time (see Clifton, 2013a). The movie trailer for *Rope*, which Hitchcock himself directed, is unique in that he used 'special shoot footage' not seen in the feature film. In fact, the movie trailer provides a compelling backstory for the film akin to a filmic prequel in that we are introduced to David and Janet as a couple in New York City's iconic Central Park – in the feature film, David is murdered in the very first scene. The movie trailer's opening pastoral scene shows couples strolling by arm-in-arm, and David even proposes marriage to Janet, which she playfully resists. Undeterred by her unwillingness to accept his proposal, David tells her that she can say 'yes' later that night at Brandon and Philip's dinner party. In a surprising turn of events, the feature film is not about whether or not Janet will accept David's proposal of marriage, but whether or not David's own body will be discovered in the trunk at the dinner party.

The background music featured in the movie trailer is David Buttolph's orchestral transcription of Poulenc's *Mouvement Perpétuel*. The piano music has been strategically altered to fit into a Hitchcockian world of dramatic suspense, where things are not always what they appear to be. Buttolph took Poulenc's original music and altered it to fit within the ecological space of the urban park setting. The opening is reminiscent of Debussy's erotic *Prelude to the Afternoon of a Faun* (1894), appropriate for a lazy day at the park with contemporary drones of the bagpipe as well as pastoral wind instruments to evoke the playful shepherd's pipe. Within the first section of the movie trailer, aural suspense can be detected in the

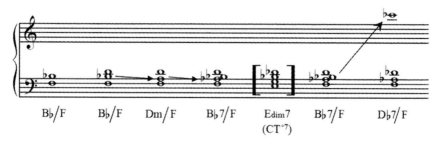

Figure 3.1 Colouristic chord successions and bass drone in the first section of *Rope*'s movie trailer (Chester Music).

use of the bass drone and the colouristic chord successions, sonorities that do not follow a functional harmonic syntax. The shifting sonorities above the drone result instead from smooth voice leading, mostly by descending half-steps that have long been associated with *musical grief*.[3] This extra-musical association can help guide an interpretation of the colouristic chords that accompany the image track during David and Janet's courtship in Central Park.

As shown in Figure 3.1, the first two B-flat sonorities represent the possibility of David and Janet's coupling, affirmed by the accompanying *Love Theme* – this theme is presented when David and Janet are introduced sitting on the park bench.[4] The next chord, a D-minor sonority, serves as a voice-leading chord to B-flat 7. It contains the pitch A-natural, scale degree 7, also known as the *leading tone* because of its half-step relationship to B-flat, the most important pitch in the diatonic collection. Heard within this tonal context, the pitch A-natural has been stripped of its natural voice-leading tendency to resolve upwards to the B-flat, and instead trudges downwards to the pitch A-flat, the tonal centre of the *Exotic Theme*.[5] The pitch A-flat is a symbolic point of *otherness* within the musical texture, both in terms of its chromaticism as well as being linked with the killers themselves later in the movie trailer.[6] B-flat 7 thus embodies tension, but not in a traditional musical way, where the major–minor seventh chord behaves like a functional dominant-seventh sonority. Notice that B-flat 7 does not resolve to E-flat as would be expected in a traditional applied-dominant resolution.

There is a nod to traditional voice leading in that the pitch A-flat, the seventh of the B-flat 7 sonority (e.g. B-flat–D–F–A-flat), moves down – or *resolves* – by step to the expected pitch, G. This traditional voice-leading motion, however, resonates more convincingly within the broader interpretive context of the grief motif (e.g. B-flat down to A; A down to A-flat; and now, A-flat down to G). Further, the pitch G is harmonised not by an E-flat sonority, but instead by a harsh-sounding common-tone diminished-seventh chord, as the pitch B-flat – the embodiment of David and Janet's tonal anchor – is held over and *all* of the remaining voices join forces and move down the motivic half-step. E dim 7 is next followed by another statement of B-flat 7 as the voices reverse their direction while the pitch B-flat remains steadfastly anchored into place. The tonal pillar of B-flat 7 can be interpreted as a dramatic musical metaphor where two pitches – namely, B-flat and A-flat – struggle for polarity or supremacy over the other. Up until this point, B-flat seems to be in control. As the first section of the movie trailer comes to a close, however, it is the A-flat – and, by filmic association, Brandon and Philip – that gains the upper hand, since this pitch is a member of the culminating D-flat 7 sonority: indeed, the pitch B-flat, and its extra-musical association with David and Janet's love, has been eerily silenced. The ascending melodic motion to the climactic C-flat signifies a new emotional state, one of rising anxiety.

In the feature film, Philip's diegetic performance at the piano echoes many of the musical procedures heard previously in the movie trailer. As I have argued elsewhere (see Clifton, 2013b: 66–70), at the very moment in the music where Philip could have found closure, he gets stuck playing the last bar, obsessively trying to figure out a way to end the music in a tonally convincing manner. This can be viewed as a musical manifestation of his desire to get away with murder. The music itself is structured in such a way that it ends open-ended and this is not possible. Throughout the piece, the right hand unfolds a background pattern in B-flat major from scale degree 5 down to scale degree 2, while the left hand is firmly anchored throughout the piece on scale degree 1. At the precise moment in the last bar where the right hand could have found closure down to scale degree 1, it reverses its direction – much like the culminating gesture at the end of the first section of the movie trailer – and ends instead on an A-natural, the leading tone. This musical moment dramatically encapsulates Philip's profound ambivalence over what he has done. His hands at the keyboard, the very hands used to kill his friend earlier in the film, are combative agents and are at odds with each other.

We can further dissect the musical material of the left hand in order to investigate how each discrete bar of the *perpetual mobile* provides kinetic momentum in terms of both rhythm and pitch. These elements are part and parcel of Philip's obsessive nature and can provide a glimpse into his conflicted psyche sublimated in the music, as it were. Elsewhere I have argued that the minimalist music fits well within the mise-en-scène that Hitchcock creates for *Rope* (see Clifton, 2013b: 68–9). Once the left hand starts, it does not stop its hypnotic groove until the very last bar, where the music simply fades away rather than coming to a definitive ending. The unyielding rhythm of the left hand consists of a steady stream of quavers, an example par excellence of musical obsession.

Figure 3.2 illustrates that the texture of the *Mouvement Perpétuel* can be divided into four distinct textural strands, with Strand 1 (hereafter S1) and S2 located in the left hand, and S3 and S4 in the right hand. Each textural strand has its own particular pitch content. S1 consists of an alternation of scale degrees 1 and 5, the tonic and the dominant in B-flat major. If we dissect each bar in the left hand from the score as a discrete interpretive unit, S1 always culminates with scale degree 5, the root of the dominant triad – this interpretation in bar 1 is strengthened by S3's E-flat and S4's C, both members of the dominant-seventh sonority. In addition, S2's culminating pitch, G, can be interpreted as a major ninth above the root. Heard within this context, each one-bar unit, which always culminates with the

Assez modéré ♩ = 144

Figure 3.2 Textural strands in Poulenc's *Mouvement Perpétuel* (bars 1–2)
(Chester Music).

pitches F and G in the left hand – the outer frame of a dominant-ninth sonority (e.g. F–A–C–E-flat–G) – can be interpreted as *mini-half cadences* where the
harmonic motion to the dominant potentially comes to a brief pause before starting anew again on the tonic in the next bar. I use the term 'mini-half cadences'
analogous to *subphrases*, since tonal elements are set in place for potential harmonic repose, but other factors, such as rhythm, undermine these moments as
true arrival points. This heightened awareness of potential ebb and flow in the left
hand circulates just underneath the surface of the unyielding rhythmic impulse.
This is another example of how music both yearns for closure – in this case, in the
form of potential harmonic repose – yet actively resists it at the same time through
the unyielding kinetic motion.

In sum, the use of music in *Rope* helps tell a story of Philip's conflicted psyche
on a purely sonic level. The rhythmic ostinatos provide a glimpse into his highly
obsessive nature, one that is terrified of being caught. Throughout the film, Philip
is portrayed as weaker than Brandon, his partner in crime, even though it was
Philip who actually murdered David. His conflicted feelings over what he has done
are effectively portrayed in his musicalised guilt at the piano, demonstrated, in
part, by his failed attempts to achieve musical closure. Tonality, as we have seen,
was not on his side. In the end, there was no musical closure for Philip, nor was
there an escape from his predicament with Brandon. Rupert, the inquisitive party
guest played by James Stewart, successfully catches Brandon and Philip in their
web of deception and discovers David's body in the trunk.

The film ends with Rupert firing three gunshots out of their apartment window,
while Philip sits defeated at the piano and Brandon mixes himself a drink, ever
defiant. And in the far-off distance, the police sirens indicate that balance will soon
be restored. As the sirens become louder and more pronounced in the soundtrack
mix, Philip plays a sad-sounding version of the *Love Theme* with his right hand, a
last musical testament for his dead friend. The ending credits bring back Buttolph's

orchestral transcription of the *Mouvement Perpétuel*. The last musical theme heard in *Rope* is none other than a heroic transformation of the *Love Theme*, now scored triumphantly for brass instruments. This theme culminates with a final drawn-out perfect authentic cadence (V → I), with the leading tone finally allowed to resolve upwards by half-step to scale degree 1. At the arrival of the final tonic triad, a sense of prevailed justice for David is masterfully encoded in the music: indeed, Poulenc's music gets the last authoritative word in the film. Throughout the movie trailer and the feature film, the leading tone – and, by association, the dominant harmony – has been rendered powerless time and time again. The music at *Rope*'s end effectively ties together the musical forces at play throughout the movie trailer and the feature film. The aural stage is thus set to next investigate how *Vertigo*'s music can be interpreted as musical reverberations from *Rope*, where Herrmann's use of non-diegetic music underscores filmic themes of intense psychological obsession as well as doomed lovers. Before we think about his music, however, a contextual overview of the plot will be provided.

Hearing musical doubles on *Vertigo*'s soundtrack

The plot for *Vertigo*, which is based on the 1954 French crime novel *D'entre les Morts* (*The Living and the Dead*) by Boileau and Narcejac, focuses on an ex-policeman, John 'Scottie' Ferguson (played, once again, by James Stewart), and his unhealthy obsession with Madeleine, the wife of one of his college friends, Gavin Elster. Elster hires Scottie to watch over Madeleine (played by Kim Novak) to see where she goes during the day. We later find out that this is all an elaborate ruse put on by Elster so that he can murder his real wife. In their initial meeting, Elster plants the seed in Scottie's mind that Carlotta Valdes, Madeleine's great-grandmother who committed suicide, possibly possesses her from beyond the grave. Elster confesses to Scottie that he fears for Madeleine's life because she has been acting strange. The first section of the film ends with Madeleine, who is actually played by Judy Barton, an imposter unbeknownst to Scottie, leading him up a bell tower at Mission San Juan Bautista, just outside of San Francisco. Unable to follow Madeleine/Judy to the top of the tower because he suffers from a debilitating case of vertigo, Elster hurls his real wife off the tower, killing her instead: his modus operandi all along. Elster knew ahead of time that Scottie suffered from vertigo, and he took a calculated risk that Scottie would not be able to climb the stairs in pursuit; the real Madeleine's death was later declared a suicide. What he did not know, however, is the depth to which Scottie would fall in love with Madeleine's doppelganger.

The second section of the film begins with an exploration of Scottie's depression after he thinks the woman he fell in love with is dead. After his eventual release from a sanatorium, he mindlessly retraces all of the places in San Francisco where he previously saw Madeleine. When he meets Judy – whom he initially sees as a vulgar imitation of Madeleine – he eventually convinces her to change her appearance so that she can look like Madeleine in every possible way. He manipulates Judy's body as a site to resurrect the past – to resurrect Madeleine from the dead – and because of her love for him, Judy plays along with his twisted fantasy. His fantasy comes crashing down, however, when he discovers that Judy is really Madeleine (or a copy of Madeleine) when she absentmindedly wears Carlotta's necklace from the first section of the film. He puts two and two together and realises that he has been duped. In the last scene of the film, he forces Judy to re-enact the earlier bell-tower scene that led to his madness. While she begs for his forgiveness, he is still unable to let go of the past. And, just like the real Madeleine, she too falls to her death, leaving Scottie all alone once again, but now cured of his acrophobia.

The movie trailer for *Vertigo* provides background information for the filmic audience. Like his dual roles with *Rope*, Hitchcock served as both movie director and film producer for *Vertigo*. The trailer begins with an orchestral musical passage from Herrmann's Prelude, what many film-music scholars have called the *Love Theme*, a passage of music that features the melodic shadow of the 'Madeleine' cue accompanied by swirling arpeggios (see Blim (2013) for a comparative study of the two musical cues). Against this musical backdrop, an image of a dictionary fills the screen and the music doubles back in on itself to repeat the same passage at a much softer level in the audio mix, perhaps a musical foreshadowing of a *ghostly double*. Meanwhile, the camera zooms forward and focuses in on the definition of 'vertigo', which is then read aloud by a faceless male narrator: 'Vertigo, a feeling of dizziness … a swimming in the head … figuratively a state in which all things seem to be engulfed in a whirlpool of terror'. At the precise moment that 'terror' is read aloud, the background music synchronises a stinger chord for dramatic effect. The image of the dictionary starts to spin akin to a whirlpool and next morphs into Saul Bass's artful spiral design. Bass's intricate circular image, which contains a hollow oval in its centre evocative of a human eye, continues to rotate, and the camera tracks forward with the *Vertigo* title following suit. The remainder of the trailer features key scenes from the film, accompanied by Herrmann's music composed especially for *Vertigo*. The narrator provides a continuous thread of voice-overs throughout the remainder of the trailer that makes sense of the filmic montage (e.g. 'The story of a love so powerful it broke down all barriers between past and present … between life and death'). The trailer also shows the heartbreaking scene when Judy agrees to be made over to look like Madeleine. The audience is even made aware of Novak's dual performances by large marketing slogans that brand the novelty of the film: 'KIM NOVAK … [PLAYS] *TWO* AMAZING ROLES'. To help facilitate my musical reading of *Vertigo*, we will think about how Herrmann's iconic Prelude sets the stage for the upcoming filmic narrative, one that deals with conflicting *dualities* around every corner.

Figure 3.3 provides a piano reduction of the first eight bars of the Prelude. Flutes and Violin 1 play the upper arpeggios, while clarinets and Violin 2 play the lower arpeggios. The topsy-turvy figures, which mechanically repeat every bar, are suggestive of a mirror-like reflection of each other. As one arpeggio descends (or comes closer into view), the other ascends (or goes farther from view), and vice versa (see Blim [2013] for a detailed discussion of musical spirals and musical

Figure 3.3 Herrmann's Prelude from *Vertigo* (bars 1–8) (Sony/ATV Music Publishing/ Famous Music LLC).

mirrors in the Prelude). The differences in instrumental timbre and register make it rather easy for the filmic viewer to aurally identify the two distinct textural strands. Further, the two strands could signify different musical agents within the texture, an evocation, as it were, of the many *double identities* featured in *Vertigo*, from Madeleine's supposed possession by her great-grandmother, to Madeleine being played by Judy in Elster's diabolical scheme, to Judy's uncanny makeover to resurrect the dead Madeleine in Scottie's twisted fantasy. On the surface, the unyielding triplet rhythms and mirror-like patterns perpetuate a constant parade of *arpeggio doubles*. However, an investigation into the pitch content of each corresponding arpeggio reveals that the doubles are not truly inversionally equivalent as one might expect from an exact mirror inversion (e.g. in bar 1, beat 1, the upper arpeggio begins with a descending G-flat augmented triad, while the lower arpeggio begins with an ascending E-flat minor triad). The intervals between the first two notes of each arpeggio are simply not the same, nor are they enharmonically equivalent: D-natural down to B-flat is a major 3rd, and E-flat up to G-flat is a minor 3rd. The next two eight notes in both arpeggios are mirror inversions: B-flat down to G-flat || G-flat up to B-flat. Herrmann saturates the score with this inversional dyad by means of a contrapuntal technique called a *voice exchange*, a procedure that interchanges two tones between two musical agents (in this case, arpeggios). The term *voice exchange* is a perfect metonym for the film, and the Prelude effectively sets the stage for the upcoming plot of 'mixed-up' identities. In addition, notice that the two harmonic dyads just before each voice exchange are E-flat/D-natural (on beat 1) and C-natural/D-natural (on beat 2).

These pitches are the very source material for the ominous tune played by the low brass instruments starting in bar 3. The stripped-down melody, which only consists of four notes, can be divided into a periodic design in compound triple metre. The antecedent phrase consists of the D-natural descending down a step to the C-natural on each hypothetical downbeat – an expanded presentation of the *grief motif* – and the consequent phrase consists of the E-flat down to D-natural. With these last two pitches, balance is restored as the melody comes to rest back on its original starting pitch, D-natural, but not without a certain sacrifice. The initial grief motif has been compressed from a major second to a minor second, perhaps a musical warning – from bad to worse – of future events to come. The use of polymetre in the first eight bars – compound duple in the two upper strands versus compound triple in the low brass melody – separates musical agents into different time zones, a possible metrical opposition for the various conflicting identities in the upcoming filmic narrative. As the music progresses, the low brass take longer and longer to resolve down a step, as if time is no longer quantifiably measurable, while the two upper strands mechanically keep a constant duple pulse.

The *Love Theme*, shown in Figure 3.4, is stated in compound duple with no hint of a conflicting metrical double. Notice too that throughout the passage there is only a single arpeggio strand in a submerged lower register. At least for the time being, musical doubles have been purged from the soundtrack. The melody begins with an initial statement of the *grief motif* transferred into the treble clef; the first two pitches – D-natural down to C-natural – recall the first two notes of the ominous low brass melody from bars 3–4. Now, the pitches are reminiscent of a *musical sigh*, as the D-natural (a non-harmonic tone) can be interpreted as a lingering *appoggiatura* to the C-natural, harmonised by an A-flat major triad. The melody next descends a step to B-natural, depicting another intensification of *grief* as the initial major-second interval compresses to a minor second. The pitch B-natural is harmonised by a bold new sound, an A-minor triad marked at a louder dynamic level of *forte*. The harmonic concept of shifting sonorities up a half-step – from A-flat major to A minor – is accomplished by retaining the third of the A-flat major triad – the pitch C-natural – and raising its root and fifth up a semitone. The melody ends with a sweeping gesture down a perfect fifth to the pitch E-natural. This relatively large leap is effective because leaps of fifths are seldom heard in Herrmann's melodic palette for *Vertigo*, preferring instead to use restrictive steps or smaller leaps. The next section in the passage (bars 93–6) features the same lovesick melody: indeed, another type of *musical double*. This time Herrmann reverses the modality from C minor to C major by retaining the root and fifth and shifting the 3rd up a semitone. From start to finish, the two statements of the *melodic double* are tonally progressive, from A-flat major → A minor || C minor → C major, thus bookended by a large-scale chromatic-mediant relationship: A-flat major → C major, both major keys. In bar 97 there is a tonal pulling or a snapping back to the A-flat tonal centre, but this time around the modality is a grief-stricken A-flat minor. The *Love Theme* ends with a climactic arrival point in bar 99, marked *ff* in the score, on a B-flat augmented triad (e.g. B-flat–D–F-sharp – notice

Figure 3.4 Herrmann's Prelude from *Vertigo* (bars 89–101): *Love Theme* (Sony/ATV
Music Publishing/Famous Music LLC).

the *enharmonic doubling* of B-flat as A-sharp in the treble clef). This climactic
chord can be interpreted as a *harmonic double* in the passage: first as a functioning
altered dominant with a raised fifth in the key of E-flat (e.g. B-flat–D–F-sharp),
and second as an *enharmonic double* for the upcoming swirling arpeggios in the
last section of the Prelude. This type of doubling is reserved solely for the musicians reading the score, since the filmic viewer would not be able to tell the aural
difference between these two enharmonic sonorities.

   Shown in Figure 3.5, the last section of the Prelude brings back many of the
musical elements from the first eight bars shown in Figure 3.3. First, the *arpeggio
doubles* return to the two upper strands. The lower strand now moves twice as fast
as its upper counterpart, depicting intensification of the whirlpool motif – and,

Figure 3.5 Herrmann's Prelude from *Vertigo* (bars 101–6) (Sony/ATV Music Publishing/ Famous Music LLC).

by extension, the word 'terror' – from the movie trailer. The compressed E-flat/ D-natural *grief motif* also returns in full force, stated as harmonic clashes on beats 1 and 2 throughout the passage. An investigation of the pitch content of the low brass sonority in bar 102 reveals that the dyadic pair D-natural/C-natural also makes one last appearance. This time the *grief motif* is accompanied by A-flat from the *Love Theme* – this pitch is given tonal salience by being placed at the bottom of the three-note sonority. There is potential for hearing large-scale tonal transcendence at this moment in that C-natural shifts the modality of A-flat back to major. In other words, by mixing pitches from A-flat major and A-flat minor throughout the Prelude, which can be interpreted as an example of mode mixture or *modal doubling*, Herrmann's music suggests that love may find a way to conquer all.

The Prelude ends with a final outburst on the pitch D-natural – a recollection of the first note of the ominous theme from bar 3 – stated by the low brass underneath a solitary arpeggio figure (e.g. D–G-flat–B-flat). Throughout the Prelude, D-natural has been associatively linked with the pitch C-natural, either as stepwise melodic events or as harmonic dyads, depictions of *musical grief*. The Prelude ends with a final declamatory statement of just the D-natural, with C-natural nowhere to be seen or heard. Like the dead, it has vanished from the musical texture. Because the filmic viewer has heard this particular dyadic pair so often throughout the Prelude, it is not difficult to provide a mental resolution to the *ghostly* pitch C-natural. To put it another way, the audience has been conditioned to hear something that does not actually make a sound. By actively engaging with the music and the filmic viewer's cognitive abilities in such an imaginative way, Herrmann nudges the listener to let go of reality and to expect the unexpected. He asks the filmic viewer to consider the very real possibility of hearing *musical ghosts*.

In light of my earlier reading of *Rope*, it is possible to hear musical reverberations of murder, obsession and doomed lovers in both films. *Vertigo*'s opening
Prelude, saturated with a preponderance of *musical doubles*, as we have seen, can
also shed a glimpse into Scottie's tormented psyche. Like Philip's strange behaviour
in *Rope*, the obsessive rhythmic drive in the Prelude – the unyielding triplet patterns – paints a musical portrait of Scottie as a grief-stricken madman obsessed
with a singular vision: to remake the past. The only other time in *Vertigo* when
the *arpeggio doubles* return to the soundtrack is during Judy's transformational
makeover at the beauty salon, providing a clear interpretive pathway between sight
and sound in the filmic narrative. The triplet patterns represent in musical terms,
as it were, the physical and metaphysical embodiment of the Scottie/Madeleine/
Judy love triangle that serves as the heart and soul of *Vertigo*. As we have seen, the
arpeggio doubles feature mirror inversions of the G-flat/B-flat dyad, symbolic of
the dualism between Madeleine and Judy. At the Prelude's end, the other pitch in
the arpeggio, D-natural, can be understood – all along – as a stand-in for Scottie
himself, a pitch that yearns for closure yet can only find it in his imagination – into
the past – with an entity that is no longer there.

Notes

1 The notion of a *dark passenger* was recently expressed in the Showtime television series
   Dexter, which aired from 2006 to 2013. Dexter – the main character, who is a blood spat-
   ter pattern analyst as well as a serial killer – learns to control the dark side of his persona
   after witnessing the brutal killing of his mother.
2 See Clifton (2013a: 63–74). The author provides a detailed study of the use of music in the
   film by considering three analytical levels: (1) 'Pure' musical codes, (2) 'Cultural' musical
   codes and (3) 'Cinematic' musical codes.
3 An excellent example of the descending half-step as a musical signifier for *grief* is the
   chromatic ground bass from Henry Purcell's 'Dido's Lament' from his opera *Dido and
   Aeneas* (1689). The bassline (e.g. G–F-sharp, F–E, E-flat–D …) serves as a unifying element in the *passacaglia* and underscores the dramatic intensity of Dido's despondency in
   the aftermath of losing Aeneas just before her suicide. These descending half-steps can
   also be heard as *musical sigh* figures.
4 I label the *Love Theme* as the tuneful B-flat major melody from Poulenc's original
   (bars 1–2).
5 I label the *Exotic Theme* as the highly chromatic melody from Poulenc's original (bars
   14–17). The melody begins on A-flat and ends on E-flat, which can be interpreted as a
   traditional tonic–dominant tonal relationship.
6 When Brandon and Philip are singled out in the second section of the movie trailer as
   'the two who were responsible for everything', the accompanying background music is
   the A-flat *Exotic Theme*.

References

Blim, Dan (2013), 'Design in Bernard Herrmann's Prelude to *Vertigo*', *Music and the Moving Image* 6:2: 21–31.

Bruce, Graham (1985), *Bernard Herrmann: Film Music and Narrative*. Michigan: UMI Research Press.

Clifton, Kevin (2013a), 'Sound and Semiotics in Hitchcock's Coming Attraction: Locating and Unraveling Meaning in *Rope*'s Movie Trailer', published proceedings for 12th International Congress on Musical Signification, Université catholique de Louvain, Louvain-la-Neuve.

Clifton, Kevin (2013b), 'Unravelling Music in Hitchcock's *Rope*', *Horror Studies* 4:1: 63–74.

Cooper, David (2001), *Bernard Herrmann's 'Vertigo': A Film Score Handbook*. Westport, CT: Greenwood Press.

John, Antony (2001), ' "The Moment That I Dreaded and Hoped For": Ambivalence and Order in Bernard Herrmann's Score for *Vertigo*', *Musical Quarterly* 85:3: 516–44.

McCarten, John (1958), '*Vertigo*', *New Yorker* 34: 65.

Sullivan, Jack (2008), *Hitchcock's Music*. New Haven, CT: Yale University Press.

4

The therapeutic power of music in Hitchcock's films

Sidney Gottlieb

Vertigo (1958) contains not only some of the most memorable music in a Hitchcock film but one of his most grim pronouncements about the limited power of music. After the apparent death of Madeleine before his eyes, Scottie is institutionalised, comatose, beyond hope and help. Midge's rueful comment perfectly sums up his desperate condition – which is indeed aesthetic as well as psychological and metaphysical – as, to coin a phrase, *Amadeus absconditus*. Mozart isn't going to be nearly enough to pull Scottie back from among the dead, she tells his doctor, and after voicing this dark wisdom Midge herself disappears. There is much powerful music throughout the film, but it is, as Royal Brown aptly names it, the music of the irrational, arguably both preserver and destroyer, but unequally so, making the notion of music therapy – and perhaps any kind of therapy – untenable (Brown, 1982). Mozart, the symbol of our dreams of reparation and recovery, never sounded so tinny.

Music is central, and problematic, throughout Hitchcock's films: not only from the beginning but even before the beginning. *The Blackguard* (1925), credited to Graham Cutts, but 'authored' by Hitchcock in several ways (he wrote the script, assisted on the artistic design and evidently shot several sequences), revolves fundamentally around music, musicians and the perils of art in a tumultuous world that pulls one towards chaos rather than harmony. And music continues to be prominent in the silent films he directed, not heard (at least via synch sound) but visualised and thematised, embodied in scenes of musical performance and dancing that are spectacles and dramas. Dance is a sadly neglected correlate and complement of Hitchcock's music throughout his silent films especially, and it would be well worth closely examining these paired motifs in such films as *The Pleasure Garden* (1925), which even in its title sequence features an exuberant but also frenzied dance that typifies not only the main characters' vocation but also their mentality; *Downhill* (1927), where one of the lowest stages in Roddy's decline is his role as a dancing gigolo; and *Champagne* (1928), where dancing is an image of the vitality and the threat of Jazz Age 'liberation' for women.

But my focus is more specifically on music of reparation and recovery throughout Hitchcock's films, evident in numerous sequences, some undeveloped and momentary, others more fully orchestrated, as it were, where the composition and performance of music are specifically linked to the resolution of serious personal and interpersonal challenges and dilemmas, and not only change and shape but save a relationship and even a life. I won't catalogue these exhaustively, but it is worth calling attention to at least several examples, some of the best of which are in his films of the 1930s, watersheds of experiments with sound and music. Music is associated with introspection and problem solving (counterpointing its association with problem-causing aspects of theatricality, self-dramatisation and the carnivalesque) in *Murder!* (1930). Bob Lawrence and his associate Clive use a witty adaptation of churchsong to communicate counter-subversively in the temple of the assassins in *The Man Who Knew Too Much* (1934). Richard Hannay's compulsive whistling of Mr Memory's theme song as he subconsciously processes and finally solves the mystery of *The 39 Steps* (1935) is part of a subtext in the film of music that saves (hymns that helped me, the joke goes, after a printed collection of them protects him from a bullet) and soothes ('play something' is the plea and command at the end, in the hope that the orchestra can restore harmony after chaos has erupted). And in *The Lady Vanishes* (1938) the old chestnut of the song containing the coded message is only part of an evocation of music that can not only save civilisation but save us from civilisation: Gilbert, an amateur (in the best sense of the word, animated by love) musicologist, draws on folk traditions of song and dance to offer an alternative to fascists like Dr Hartz and fops like Iris's fiancé. Skipping ahead several decades for my last example, while we normally associate Bernard Herrmann with music of murder, the uncanny and the mysteries of death, the remake of *The Man Who Knew Too Much* (1956) repeatedly links music with reparation and recovery, especially as it asserts a very powerful (and positive) emotional intimacy between mother and child. Hitchcock often spoke about the formative power of elders telling children scary stories at bedtime, schooling them in suspense, horror and what he called the 'enjoyment of fear', but here we see a different kind of formative primal scene, the mother singing a pop lullaby to her child – a song that rescues him later on and to some extent rescues her as well, insofar as it is an assertion, not only of her role as a mother but also an independent and resourceful woman and artist.

  The Man Who Knew Too Much lends itself to and deserves full analysis for its presentation of the therapeutic function of music, but my focus will be on two other films – one very well-known, the other hardly known at all. *Rear Window* (1954) comes first to mind as Hitchcock's most fully articulated affirmation of what Jack Sullivan (2006: 169–82) calls 'The Redemptive Power of Popular Music', and I'll try to add a bit to his fine discussion, particularly by identifying what I think are some key models for Hitchcock of films dramatizing characters saved by song. I'll then concentrate on a much earlier film, *Waltzes from Vienna* (1934), which rarely comes to anyone's mind as an example of anything good about Hitchcock, but is a fascinating exploration of the composition and performance of a song, key parts of the process by which a man works out and overcomes complex parental and romantic problems, in effect saving himself by becoming himself, capable of independence and love.

Rear Window is often taken to be one of Hitchcock's most insightful portrayals and analyses of visual spectacle, highlighting the dangers and pleasures of the look (see Gottlieb, 2017). But it is also a detailed examination of the counterpart to this, auditory spectacle. Walter Ong, one of the great theorists of sound, may well be as relevant to our understanding of this film as Laura Mulvey, one of the great theorists of cinematic sight (see Ong, 2002; Mulvey, 1975). *Rear Window* is a case study of people as audieurs as well as voyeurs, and, as Jack Sullivan and Elisabeth Weis remind us, we must be alert to the soundscape as well as the landscape of the film, a soundscape filled with music (see Weis, 1982: 107–24; Weis and Thom, 2007).

There are multiple reference points to consider in analysing Hitchcock's presentation of the positive aspects of music in *Rear Window* (which are not, by the way, completely detached from their more problematic aspects: the fact that I do not focus on the latter does not mean that I am unaware of their prominence and significance). First, the composer is of course a key figure. In a neighbourhood subtly identified as a community of artists – if not artist freaks, akin to the group of circus performers on the railroad car in *Saboteur* (1942), who turn out to be admirably fair and compassionate, compared to 'normal' and especially upper-class people – he is the most dedicated, and, even though he works in a pop genre (like Hitchcock himself, as some have suggested), he seems far more serious and committed to his art than the idiosyncratic sculptor (ironically, one reason why her sculpture is so bizarre may be that she doesn't hear well, in an environment where sound is a medium of connection with and knowledge about other people); the professional whistler (termed the Siffleuse in the screenplay); the singer practising scales heard occasionally in the background; Miss Torso, for whom the term 'ballet dancer' is primarily a euphemism; and even Jefferies, the photographer who no longer uses a camera primarily for taking pictures. In one of the most extensive of the dispersed but connected narratives woven into the film – particularly prominent because we not only see but hear him constantly, which is not the case with the other ancillary characters – the composer uses determined creativity to overcome nagging thoughts of personal inadequacy, frustration, incipient despair, loneliness, artistic blockage and the ravages of time: an ad on the radio about impending listless middle age as well as Hitchcock's cameo next to a clock, reinforced by the sight and sound of other timepieces in the film, evoke the formidable challenge – *tempus fugit*.[1]

The composer's song emerges in bits and pieces out of some inscrutable process of sustained effort (a process dramatised and analysed in great detail in *Waltzes from Vienna*, as we'll see later), consolidating his identity and organising the world around him, like Wallace Stevens's jar placed upon a hill in Tennessee and Robert Frost's momentary stay against confusion. His music interconnects him with the outside world. Ong reminds us of the socialising force of sound (and, I would add, music in particular), contrasted with the privatising and personalising bias of sight, and indeed throughout *Rear Window* sound is centripetal and sight is centrifugal. Song knits; sight separates – and shreds. The composer's music draws a lively crowd of musicians into his room who share in the creation of the song and it generates an audience who contribute to the creative circuit by listening appreciatively. Miss Lonelyhearts is the most notable of this audience, rescued from suicide by the melody and not only rescued from loneliness but returning the favour as she ends up in the composer's room at the end, presumably a couple in the making. (In the screenplay, he ends up with Miss Torso, but the change to Miss Lonelyhearts reinforces the depth of the romantic power of music and averts any kind of joking trivialisation of his art: he doesn't write music simply to pay the bills, as Jefferies cynically suggests, nor as a means of picking up attractive women.) Lisa is also part of the audience, mesmerised and energised by the song. These two individual focal points of the effects of music capture most of our attention, and I'll talk briefly about them before moving on to the often unnoticed effects on a somewhat broader audience.

The embedded story of Miss Lonelyhearts is a rather straightforward dramatisation of the power of music to save a person from a desperate act and from intolerable isolation. Unable to sustain herself with imaginary relationships – her mimed performance of a date is one of the most poignant moments in the film – and justifiably repulsed by the aggressiveness of her real gentleman caller, she is ready to pull down the curtains on her life and take enough sleeping pills to knock out all of New Jersey, as Stella notes. Hearing the song, though, makes her change her mind, put down the pills and open the curtains. The rest of her story is told elliptically, but the later vignettes are revealing: she is briefly seen rushing to look out to the courtyard, concerned by Jefferies' cry for help, a sign that she is now more socially engaged; and then she graduates from the immaterial connection with the music to a material connection with the composer, standing alongside him at the end. The fact that the song was not intended for her and enters her life somewhat serendipitously in no way undermines or ironises its power and lasting effect, and in some ways magnifies it. The sense of the uncanny in Hitchcock's films is often linked to the proposition that 'chaos happens' (a somewhat more elegant way of rephrasing a common epithet of our day). It is all the more magical and refreshing, then, to experience an uncanny Hitchcock moment linked to an affirmation that sometimes 'music happens'.

Lisa's relationship to the composer's song is more complex. She is a particularly avid listener, comments appreciatively on how 'beautiful' and 'enchanting' it is, speculates thoughtfully on its origin – 'Where does a man get inspiration to write a song like that?'– and is alert to its significance, that it seems 'written especially for us' (her and Jefferies, that is). She laments that she is not 'creative' like a songwriter, but in resonating deeply and personally to the song – at one point she hums the tune (a contrast with *Shadow of a Doubt* (1943), where a song jumping from head to head is more eerily worrisome) – she participates in the process, a kind of creative contagion, and her receptivity is a sure sign that she is not what Jefferies tries to caricature her as, a self-involved domestic philistine (which ironically is a more accurate description of Jefferies). There is an intimation that Lisa is endangered by the music: at exactly the same moment that Miss Lonelyhearts is enchanted away from killing herself, Lisa, shown in a stunningly effective long-shot split screen that parallels her and Miss Lonelyhearts, is so captivated by the song that she fails to notice Thorwald's return to the apartment. But even at this moment of vulnerability and danger, music is one of Lisa's great resources: it may not be evident as we watch this sequence, but, as Steven DeRosa notes, in the pre-script material outlining the story, John Michael Hayes, the screenwriter, specifies that 'Lisa reveals that the song inspired her to fight for her life' when Thorwald assaults her (DeRosa, 2001: 29).

Lisa is connected to the song in another way, revealed to us only at the very end of the film, when we hear that it specifically mentions and is presumably titled and about 'Lisa', but in a complex and not directly mimetic way. That art has unexpected and unintended consequences is yet another part of its great value: just as playing the song was not intended to save Miss Lonelyhearts, writing it was not intended to shape, woo or flatter Lisa. The composition of the song, 'Lisa', calls attention to, parallels and supports the construction of the woman, Lisa. All these processes are complex and difficult, but ultimately successful here, and Hitchcock shrewdly avoids two major traps. He does not explain the song as the result of the composer being inspired by an idealised woman whom he loves from afar, even across the courtyard. Lisa Fremont is not Petrarch's Laura, and this is a laudable instance of Hitchcock avoiding a cliché (even a cliché that has produced great art).[2] And he avoids a potentially even more dangerous trap of having the song directly construct a woman in a self-serving and manipulative way. Lisa is not Galatea, and one of the notable achievements of this film is that Hitchcock shows that he is capable of, as it were, taking the pig out of Pygmalion, of showing the process of the artistic construction of a woman as something other than the result of compensatory and problematic male control. *Rear Window* is not *Vertigo*, a tale of abusive re-creation; nor is it, more pertinent to my specific subject today, *Blackmail* (1929). When in that film the artist sings a song at the piano, it is part of his coercive strategy to mould Alice into 'Miss Up To Date', that is, 'Miss Ready for an Evening of Sex at My Command', and although he concludes by asserting 'And that's a song about you, Alice', we recognise that it is in fact a song about him, a projection of his desire and bad intentions. Hitchcock has come a long way in *Rear Window*, where the composer's song is a higher form of art, not rhetoric, engaged but disinterested; where its composition and performance is a complement, a commentary and occasionally an intervention without an intrusion; and where its simple final statement – most of the lyrics are, I think, purposefully obscured except the final word, the last in the film, which acknowledges that it is a song about Lisa – is a celebration, an enunciation and annunciation far beyond the reach of the usual Pygmalions.

The final reference point for my examination of the positive effects of music here is not individual but collective, and involves not the audience in the film but the audience of the film, to whom the music is equally – and perhaps primarily – directed. Sullivan calls *Rear Window* 'the most musically allusive of Hitchcock's films' (176), and although, as is often noted, the music is almost exclusively diegetic, it is mostly for the attention and benefit of the film's audience. *Rear Window* is a cautionary tale about perception and interpretation, and it begins with a remarkable illustration of how the film audience is drawn into Jefferies' predicament: as the camera pans across his room, we see carefully placed clues that fill us in on the details of his backstory and personality – what his profession is, how he got hurt, how his life is split between positive and negative images of women, and so on. What happens in the beginning sequence? Nothing in terms of the actions of the characters. But it establishes voyeurism as one of the key themes, links us with Jefferies' habits and indicates that what happens in the film happens not only onscreen but in the minds of the audience. The point of this sequence is not only to introduce us to Jefferies visually – pure cinema *par excellence* – but to implicate us in what turn out to be his characteristic actions and missteps, which involve incessant perceptions and, inevitably, misperceptions. For us as for Jefferies, as we soon find out, perception prompts speculation and interpretation and a kind of epistemic arrogance that we need to be shaken from. In the first sequence of the film we congratulate ourselves on our grasp of the world within our field of vision. Nearly everything that happens from this point on serves to show how shaky this grasp is.

The hunger for perception and interpretation evident in this first sequence persists throughout the film, and not only visually but aurally, primarily in the form of the many songs we listen to, not as sonic wallpaper, which they are primarily for the people within the film, but as clues and comments about the characters and the action. How is this a positive effect of music in the film? Music helps make *Rear Window* a parable of careful listening as well as careful watching. In Hitchcock's most extended comments on the use of music in films, his interview with Stephen Watts at the time he was working on *Waltzes from Vienna*, he emphasises the palpable but subliminal place of music: 'I might argue that I do not want the audience to listen consciously to the music at all. It might be achieving its desired effect without the audience being aware of how that effect was being achieved' (Hitchcock, 1995: 243). In *Rear Window*, he more than occasionally works in the opposite way, inviting the audience to consciously attend to and interpret the meaning even more than the mood of the songs. For example, the song 'That's Amore' in the background of one sequence contributes to our awareness that the entire film is an examination of love, with all its joys, difficulties, dramas and dangers. At a particularly significant moment, Lisa calls attention to one of the key challenges and 'issues' of the film: 'Tell me what you see, and what you think it means.' The constant presence of music that we listen to and puzzle through underscores that *Rear Window* revolves around the parallel injunction Hitchcock presents to us: 'Tell me what you hear, and what you think it means.' The film never presumes that we can stop being voyeurs and audieurs or ever escape the unreliability of perception, but we can become more aware of these as facts of life and become less subject to their associated perversions and vulnerabilities. Music can be therapeutic not only by saving and healing but also by instructing and educating, making us more thoughtful and aware.

In asserting the therapeutic function of music, Hitchcock may be drawing from and echoing a large store of conventional wisdom about how music soothes the savage breast, is a litmus test of character (as in Shakespeare, people who have music wherever they go are better and perhaps more fortunate than those who have none, and are thereby fit for 'treasons, stratagems, and spoils'; *Merchant of Venice* 5.1.85) and is often associated with romance and reconciliation. But he may very well have a specific cinematic model in mind when it comes to crafting fables of the therapeutic function of music: D. W. Griffith, one of the few filmmakers Hitchcock praised unreservedly and acknowledged as an influence, and certainly a filmmaker he borrowed from repeatedly in his theories of pure cinema, his notion of the auteur and also in key techniques and particular moments.[3] In a subtle homage to Griffith, Hitchcock embeds his own version of a Biograph film in *Rear Window*. I am thinking particularly of *Pippa Passes* (1909), which Griffith often referred to as one of his favourites, and was the first film reviewed by the *New York Times*, a watershed moment in the acceptance of film as a serious art form. It is also, according to Scott Simmon, a particularly important work in Griffith's struggle to establish film as a progressive medium, artistically and especially morally, proposing that serious filmmakers could be a beacon at a time when politicians, religious leaders and captains of industry were hypocrites, fundamentally bankrupt, clueless and unreliable (Simmon, 1993: 150–1). Briefly, Griffith bases his film on Browning's well-known poem, removing the problematic and tragic elements from the original to create a consistently positive drama of the saving power of song. The young girl Pippa awakens to the sun streaming in her room, grabs her guitar and passes through the world playing and singing a song with the message 'God's in his heaven, and all's right with the world'. The film is filled with operatic gestures, tilted heads and rapt facial expressions, non-naturalistic elements but effective indicators of the real power of music. Pippa's song inspires a wayward drunk to return to his wife and child, a hoodwinked husband to forgive the less than virtuous women he has married, and a woman to resist the temptation to have her unexciting husband murdered by a potential lover. Hitchcock does not retain Griffith's simplistic moralising and crude piety and Victorianism (which perhaps I should add were rejected by many Victorians as well, including Browning), but I do think that he was quite taken by Griffith's cinematic spectacle of the saving power of song.

Griffith, a master of narratives of rescue, recovery and redemption, repeated the scenario of *Pippa Passes* in another short film, *The Wanderer* (1913), substituting a flute-playing man for a guitar-playing young woman, and then developed the theme more fully in a feature-length film, *Home, Sweet Home* (1914), which may also have left its mark on Hitchcock. Griffith's film is framed as a biography of John Howard Payne. It begins by showing him living a life away from home and the woman he loves, undergoing experiences of loss and sadness that hasten his premature death but also prompt the composition of what came to be an enormously popular song, a touchstone for domesticity – and in fact played briefly, not without a tinge of irony, as Hitchcock's wanderers return home at the end of

Rich and Strange (1932). Griffith's film ends with the visionary redemption of Payne, ascending to heaven and a reunion with an angelic form of his lost love. But the middle section of the film is a dramatisation of the power of his song, played by a variety of musicians and saving a variety of souls. In the first episode, a young man hears the song and is saved from his new-found citified ways, and in a variation of the patented Griffith ride-to-the-rescue, he hastens to return to Apple Pie Mary and secure a life with a home and a family. In the second episode, the song is not enough to prevent two brothers from killing each other in an argument over money, but it does stop their grief-stricken mother from killing herself. And, in the third episode, a woman discouraged by her indifferent and preoccupied husband contemplates an adulterous affair, but hears the song through the (rear?) window played by a violinist in a room 'across the way' and, reminded of her vows, associated with an earlier playing of the song, spurns her tempter and reconciles with her husband. Even summarised this briefly, these Griffith films, in their general import and even some of their specific details, are plausible influences on, and models for, Hitchcock's dramatisation of the life-changing effects of music.

The example of Griffith looms large not only in *Rear Window*, an acknowledged masterpiece, but also in *Waltzes from Vienna*, an acknowledged failure that may seem somewhat more interesting and successful if we pay particular attention to it as a complex story about the therapeutic power of music. It does not literally picture a song saving someone from death, but it is a film in which music, as process and product, is linked with the rejection of entrapping domesticity, lifeless repetition, regimented work and backward-looking conventionality, and, more positively, with creativity, freedom, eros, the future and, not only individuality and independence, but the ability to interact, to form vital romantic, familial and communal bonds. Not all music in this film has such a utopian aura and effect: Hitchcock opposes the musical and the non-musical, but he also carefully distinguishes between the music of convention, power, age, stasis and vanity, and the music of youth, growth, movement and creative expression. When the elder Strauss announces that 'In Germany, they worship titles; here in Vienna, artists are superior', he presumably speaks for the one large union of creative spirits opposed to the world of realpolitik, but upon closer examination he represents a kind of music that itself needs therapy and renovation. His statement is not so much the credo of a fiery revolutionary as that of the head of an entrenched institution, defensive, jealous of and dependent on the power and patronage of the ruling class. And, while the elder Strauss is portrayed as a formidable figure, he is noticeably nervous and beleaguered. Ironically, he is even more vulnerable to the 'anxiety of influence' than his son. Much of the film of course focuses on Schani's ultimately successful struggle to escape from his father's shadow, but there are repeated vignettes showing that the elder Strauss is not so fortunate or resourceful, unable to improve upon his own masterpiece, the Lorelei waltz, once a sign of his creativity, now a sign of his ossification. My focus will be on the more positive, therapeutic aspects of music in the film, but not without this brief   acknowledgement of some characteristic Hitchcockian complexity and ambiguity in his treatment of this subject.

Schani's problems are multiple and interrelated – Oedipal, artistic, interpersonal and sociocultural – and are all addressed and resolved by music. Oedipally, he needs to find a way to assert himself as an independent person, as something other than his father's son. At the beginning of the film, he literally plays second fiddle in his father's orchestra (again, music can be a mode of repression), and his name, while perhaps a term of endearment, is also a term of diminution and perpetual infantilisation. Up until the very end, there is only one Strauss, and it is not him. His task is not necessarily to defeat, replace, humiliate or kill his father – although his father seems locked into this way of melodramatically framing the plot – but to find some way that he can grow into himself. His task is that much more difficult because there are other fathers to contend with: the father of his beloved Rasi, who similarly wants to contain him in a newly configured family that continues the repressive dynamics of the old one; and the father-at-large of patriarchal culture, represented (and also parodied) by the Prince, an intimidating but also comical figure who guards access to love and sex with the threat of his imaginary sword.

Artistically, Schani needs to find a way to express himself musically, in a way that not only separates himself from his father, but that manifests the spirit of exuberance and freedom. Hitchcock's films are traditionally about moral imperatives; this one is his fullest treatment of an aesthetic imperative, the responsibility to be an artist.

Interpersonally, Schani needs to find a way to negotiate a relationship with Rasi that is not based completely on self-sacrifice and compromise. Schani is, I think, always headed towards being part of a couple, and his music and musical activity exemplify interaction, not individual isolation. But it is no easy task to accomplish this – being a creative individual in a relationship – and though Rasi is first seen singing a duet with Schani, for much of the film she signifies the personal and domestic pull to leave the artistic imperative aside. In the face of her ultimatums, he affirms 'I'll not be dictated to', but he aims for an independence that does not preclude connection.

Another related interpersonal problem Schani faces is that of navigating between two rival women as love objects. Much of the film plays with the idea of the romantic triangle, but it is not nearly as central and serious a concern here as it is in, say, *Blackmail* (1929). It is rather a kind of MacGuffin, a contrivance to set certain aspects of the plot going and also to provide Hitchcock with an occasion for some inventive sequences using triangle structures, one of his favourite designs. And although Rasi takes the triangle scenario very seriously, and is jealous and frequently upset, the Countess is perhaps never really a serious option as either a romantic love object or even a dalliance for Schani. She functions, rather, as a practical and magical 'enabling' character for Schani – I am using this term not to call to mind an often negative psychological dynamic but to allude to the almost always positive character in a fairy tale. As an enabling figure, the Countess is a very effective transitional object, and in some respects functions less as a romantic love object than as the mother he never had, an intimation reinforced by casting Fay Compton for this role, strikingly older than the boyish Schani and girlish Rasi.

And finally, socioculturally Schani has to find a way to overcome broader anti-artistic and repressive forces. The culturally defined notion of responsibility is to be an unexceptional family man and cog in the works. Rasi's father bluntly states the options as 'Confectioner or musician', and although the former is invitingly 'sweet' – life with a contented Rasi and surrounded by pastries – the specific danger to Schani is conveyed in an anecdote told by the father: Schubert evidently visited the bakery, and the reason why he never finished the 'Unfinished Symphony' was because he was so taken up by eating cakes. The bakery is allied with the weight of history (that is, previous examples of unsublimated indulgence and capitulation), and is a place of mechanical labour and thwarted creativity, exactly what Schani needs to break from.

All these problems are represented and transformed by music. Of the many examples throughout the film worth discussing, I'll conclude by focusing on the two most important: the composition of the song and then the concluding performance of the 'great waltz' (as the film was alternately titled).

In presenting the composition of the song as an exemplary creative act, Hitchcock, the archetypal model of and spokesperson for the auteur, by no means downplays the role of individual authorship: Schani is the focal point of Hitchcock's dramatisation of the working of the auditory imagination, to use T. S. Eliot's (1933) handy phrase. But the song emerges from other forces beyond his personal needs and determination to assert his independence and creativity. In the ongoing 'story' of the song, Hitchcock shows that its origins are collaborative and social as well as individual. Schani's brooding artistic ferment starts to take definite form when the Countess suggests that he write music for her lyrics. Rasi helps further shape the song by recalling what turns out to be a foundational rhythm and associated lyric. And, in one of the most memorable sequences of the film, the song is grounded in and substantially generated by Schani's playful receptiveness to and ability to reshape the rhythms of the bakery, which otherwise is the hell envisioned for him. The spectacle of the rolls being tossed catalyses one part of the song, and the turning of the dough another. There's Hitchcockian wit, irony and insight in framing the making of the song in such a way that the river, the ostensible subject, is hardly present. The essential task of music (and perhaps art in general) is not representation: Hitchcock shrewdly shows that 'The Blue Danube' in fact has nothing to do with the Danube, which, as one character notes, is not even blue, but 'dirty brown', like used bath water. It is to transform noise – energy, emotion, the clang and clatter of life – into harmonious form, a harmony that is both aesthetic and existential. At the end of the scene of composition, Schani announces 'joyously that "It's all arranged." ' He means the song, not his marriage, but, despite what Rasi believes and says, the one is a necessary prelude rather than obstacle to the other.

Performance completes the song, and reinforces the idea that it is not only an artefact but an action, with real consequences on individuals, couples and groups.

Schani is oblivious to the plot that has been set up for him to conduct his song, and then he is reticent to take the stage and the baton, but finally does so and gains in self-assurance and creative satisfaction as the song builds and builds. This moment is more than a personal triumph: Hitchcock's careful choreography emphasises the way the song moves out from Schani through the orchestra to the audience, which listens attentively, starts to sway and then begins to dance, first one couple, then another, then others. Contagion is a recurrent motif in Hitchcock's films, and it is often associated with danger: the spreading of fear, hysteria, troubling information or emotions, violence, and so on. But the contagion here is pleasurable. The tremendous applause and cheering at the end affirms Schani's achievement and fame, and signal the ascent of the young Strauss. But part of what makes this moment such a triumph is that it is public, shared and communal. (It is counterpointed with the Elder Strauss's performance of an old song to a much more restrained and separated private group.) 'The Blue Danube' is not a complete waltz until it is composed, performed and danced. This sequence, a miniature of the entire film, shows the creation of a work of art, a person, a reputation, a couple and a community.

It is ironic that Rohmer and Chabrol find *Waltzes from Vienna* so distasteful, calling it a 'real disaster', and seconding Hitchcock's own admission that 'I hate this film' (Rohmer and Chabrol, 1979: 37). While it is not at all concerned with metaphysics, morals, guilt, pain, alienation and evil, as they require of a true Hitchcock film, it is intricately structured around a variety of exchanges, an element that they more than any other critics place at the core of Hitchcock's works. Innumerable substitutions and replacements occur throughout the film, including: the switch of one song for another; noise turning to music; dissolves from one woman to another, culminating in the magical switch of the Countess and Rasi that allows for a happy ending; and the exchange of one Strauss for another – which happens, miraculously, without requiring the sacrifice of one for the other. In *Waltzes from Vienna*, these exchanges – not demonic doublings and exchanges of guilt, as Rohmer and Chabrol might prefer, but positive transformations, fairy-tale-like substitutions and switches of both objects and people, and transferrals of potency – revolve around and are facilitated by music. And perhaps the final, most miraculous transformation of all is that full awareness of the therapeutic power of music in *Waltzes from Vienna* brings a hitherto neglected and unappreciated Hitchcock film back from the dead.

Notes

1 It's unclear exactly what Hitchcock is doing with the clock in the composer's room in *Rear Window*, but it may echo a moment in *Waltzes from Vienna* where the plot is advanced by turning back Strauss senior's wristwatch.

2 John Fawell (2001: 98–9) usefully calls attention to how Jefferies 'project[s] his own ideas and biases upon the Composer', identifying him as a kindred spirit, 'another man harried by the institution of marriage'. But Fawell's speculation that the composer more likely might be 'grieving for a lost love by the name of Lisa' is supported only by the fact that

two songs he is associated with ('Mona Lisa', played at the party he hosts, and 'Lisa', the song he writes) include that name (98). While I differ from Fawell on this specific point, his overall analysis supports my main argument that Hitchcock shows that the composition of a song (and perhaps, by implication, art in general) need not rest fundamentally on wish-fulfilment, direct mimesis and simple self-expression, and is not inevitably a strategy of obsession or control.

3 See my essay 'Hitchcock on Griffith' (2005–6), written as an introduction to, and analysis of, Hitchcock's own early (1931) essay on Griffith, 'A Columbus of the Screen', reprinted immediately thereafter.

References

Brown, Royal S. (1982), 'Herrmann, Hitchcock, and the Music of the Irrational', *Cinema Journal* 21:2: 14–49.

DeRosa, Steven (2001), *Writing with Hitchcock: The Collaboration of Alfred Hitchcock and John Michael Hayes*. New York: Faber and Faber.

Eliot, T. S. (1933), *The Use of Poetry and the Use of Criticism*. London: Faber and Faber.

Fawell, John (2001), *Hitchcock's 'Rear Window': The Well-Made Film*. Carbondale: Southern Illinois University Press.

Gottlieb, Sidney (2005–6), 'Hitchcock on Griffith', *Hitchcock Annual* 14: 32–45.

Hitchcock, Alfred (1931; 2005–6), 'A Columbus of the Screen', *Hitchcock Annual* 14: 46–9.

Hitchcock, Alfred (1995), *Hitchcock on Hitchcock: Selected Writings and Interviews*, ed. Sidney Gottlieb. Berkeley and Los Angeles: University of California Press.

Mulvey, Laura (1975), 'Visual Pleasure and Narrative Cinema', *Screen* 16:3: 6–18.

Ong, Walter J. (2002), *Orality and Literacy: The Technologizing of the Word*. New York: Routledge.

Rohmer, Eric and Claude Chabrol (1979), *Hitchcock: The First Forty-Four Films*, trans. Stanley Hochman. New York: Frederick Ungar Publishing Co.

Simmon, Scott (1993), *The Films of D. W. Griffith*. New York: Cambridge University Press.

Sullivan, Jack (2006), *Hitchcock's Music*, New Haven: Yale University Press.

Weis, Elisabeth (1982), *The Silent Scream: Alfred Hitchcock's Sound Track*. Rutherford: Fairleigh Dickinson University Press.

Weis, Elisabeth and Randy Thom (2007), 'The City That Never Shuts Up', in Murray Pomerance (ed.), *The City That Never Sleeps*. New Brunswick: Rutgers University Press, pp. 214–27.

5

A Lacanian take on Herrmann/Hitchcock

Royal S. Brown

Bulgarian-born Lacanian theorist (and psychoanalyst) Julia Kristeva once wrote, 'I dream of an impossible film: *Don Juan* by Eisenstein and Hitchcock, with music by Schoenberg. Invisible. Empty Theaters' (Kristeva, 1975: 77). In this article Kristeva deals with what she calls *le spéculaire*, which I will translate as 'the specular' (literally having the properties of a mirror), and which the author defines as 'the visible sign that calls forth fantasy because it carries with it an excess of visual remnants that are useless in identifying objects because chronologically and logically they precede the famous "mirror stage"' (74) set forth in the psycholinguistic theories of Jacques Lacan. Kristeva refers to these supplementary pieces of information that transform the Symbolic gaze, the Symbolic hearing, into the specular gaze, the specular hearing, as 'lektonic remnants', sights and sounds that precede the formation of Symbolic discourse – 'pulsations, somatic waves, surges of color, rhythms, tones' (73). To other examples of modern art, which include the work of Matisse, Klee and Rothko, Kristeva adds the cinema of Eisenstein because of

> the minute organization of its space, the rigorous positioning of objects within that space, the calculated intervention of each sound and each piece of dialogue, which join to the excessively visual a 'rhythmic', 'plastic' dimension, an enigma that does not explain itself immediately and within which is encoded the filmmaker's *angst*, which elicits the *angst* of the audience more deeply than the referential sign-image is capable of doing. (1975: 74)

Having also noted that 'Everything specular is bewitching because it brings to the domain of the visible the remnants of nonsymbolic agressivity, nonsymbolic drives that are not verbalized and therefore not represented' (73–4), Kristeva goes on to suggest that 'represented horror is the specular *par excellence*', and that Alfred Hitchcock, by 'joining Eisensteinian rhythm to a vision of terror', might very well be a '*cinéaste par excellence*' (75). Don Juan, who transforms 'passion for a silenced mother into a series of mistresses, and his love for the father – into reciprocal murder', becomes 'the ideal specular hero' (77).

Interestingly, in her list of artists who remind us that 'modern art ... found its privileged domain in the distribution of those lektonic remnants at the expense of the image/sign of a referent', Kristeva includes the composers Arnold Schoenberg and Anton Webern. To those who find the music of Schoenberg and Webern austere to the point of being hyper- rather than pre-symbolic, Kristeva's inclusion of them in her pantheon of what might be called 'artists of the specular' may seem rather baffling. But it must be remembered that, for all their intellectual manipulations of the basic music material, Schoenberg and Webern, among others, were actually attempting to liberate the horizontally and vertically elaborated tones of music, plus the timbres, rhythms, textures and what have you from the rigid codifications of a hierarchically structured system that had dominated Western music since the Renaissance. John Shepherd, in his book *Music as Social Text*, notes that

> post-Renaissance, 'educated' men became so aware of the potential for separating the meaning of a word from its referent, and so seduced by the intellectual power this represented in terms of manipulating and controlling the world, that they had difficulty seeing beyond the immediate implications of their own cleverness. In acting as an antidote to this tendency, the very fact of music as a social medium *in sound* reminds us, not so much of what has been lost, but of that of which we have ceased to be publicly enough aware. (Shepherd, 1991: 7)

The equal – one is tempted to say egalitarian – stressing in Schoenbergian atonality of all twelve tones of the Western, chromatic scale, as opposed to the hierarchical valorisation of seven over the other five found in what Shepherd calls 'functional tonality', shifted the emphasis of Western music back towards the area of pre-Symbolic sound. On the other hand the preordained resolutions and progressions of tonal music, with its intense focus on a single tonal centre, had in its own way accomplished in music what the sign/referent split accomplished in verbal language. As Shepherd points out,

> Functional tonal music is about sequential cause and effect – a cause and effect which depends, in the fashion of materialism, upon the reduction of a phenomenon into 'indivisible' and discrete, but contiguous constituents that are viewed as affecting one another in a causal and linear manner. The analysis of functional tonal music often concerns itself with 'showing' how the final satisfying effect of stating the tonic chord is 'due' to previously created harmonic tension. (1991: 124)

Serialisation of other elements of the musical language similarly allows the basic sound of a particular element to assert itself on its own terms rather than remaining subordinated to a quasi-causal structure that artificially creates tension and inevitable resolution. The Webernian *Klangfarbenmelodie*, for instance, effectively isolates the tone colours of the various instruments involved in a given composition as sound rather than subordinating those timbres, rhythms, textures, etc. to broader, quasi-Symbolic harmonic, rhythmic, textural, etc. determinations.

All of which brings us to Bernard Herrmann. I have no intention of suggesting that Herrmann ever composed on what many would call the 'advanced' level of a Schoenberg or a Webern. Even in the area of film music, many composers, both inside and outside of Hollywood – Leonard Rosenman's name comes immediately to mind – have produced scores in a considerably more modernist idiom, at least on a purely musical level, than most of what one can find in Herrmann's music. But I do want to suggest that Bernard Herrmann, in his own way, produced music, particularly but not exclusively in his scores for Alfred Hitchcock, that linked more closely with the full specular potential of the cinema than has just about any other film music ever composed. Herrmann certainly came to the movies via a very different route from the one followed by most. As of the early 1930s Herrmann had embarked on a conducting career that found him championing the music of little-known or unappreciated composers, most particularly American modernist Charles Ives, about whom Herrmann would write in 1932,

> In 1890 Ives was writing polytonality, which in 1920 Milhaud introduced in popu-
> lar garb. In 1902 he was producing poly-rhythms, atonality and tone clusters which
> many years later Stravinsky, Schoenberg and Ornstein received credit for originating.
> Let it be clearly understood that the above composers were not aware of Ives' work,
> any more than Ives had been aware of their compositions, 30 years ago. (Herrmann,
> 1932, quoted in Smith, 1991: 21)

Around the same time Herrmann had also begun to compose his own music. A recently discovered Prelude for piano written on 20 January 1935 already reveals some important tendencies. This brief piano piece, while not crushingly dissonant, has absolutely no tonal centre. Instead, its entire harmonic character revolves, rather in the manner of Russian composer Alexander Scriabin, around the particular sonorous character of the various chords, most of them seventh chords that never approach anything that could be defined as a resolution. We will see further on where this use of unresolving seventh chords as a harmonic focal point will eventually lead the composer. Further, Herrmann's Prelude offers nothing that could be defined as a traditional melody. Instead, several brief motifs, including a three-note figure heard at the outset, provide the Prelude with its only quasi-thematic content. This thematic practice also rhythmically liberates this seventeen-bar piece, which in no way depends on the so-called four-bar phrase (*Vierhebigkeit*) in its overall structure.

Very much the same thing can be said about Herrmann's five-movement Sinfonietta for Strings, also from 1935, portions of which will resurface some twenty-five years later in the score for Hitchcock's *Psycho*. All the way back when Herrmann was only twenty-one years old he was able to translate into very non-conventional, very non-tonal music both the *frayeur*, that pre-Symbolic terror, and the *frayage*, that pre-Symbolic, desiring knowledge of the Other that lead to both aggression and *angst* that are the essential elements of Kristeva's specular. But it was not until 1960, when he composed the score for Hitchcock's *Psycho*, that Herrmann found a form of musical expression that allowed him to fully elabo-rate that strings-only vision of darkness. I would suggest, in fact, that Herrmann needed both the cinema and directors such as Hitchcock and Orson Welles to wholly elicit those specular elements that never found a completely satisfactory place in his concert works. Susanne K. Langer (1957) has dangerously generalised that 'music at its highest, those clearly a symbolic form, is an unconsummated symbol' (240) and that 'what music can actually reflect is only the morphology of feeling' (238). But with the development of such elements as functional tonality and a four-based rhythmic idiom, Western music was able to create, as John Shepherd has suggested, a sense of causality and linearity that cut into that art's ability to function as what Kristeva calls a non-verbal signifying system 'built up exclusively out of the semiotic stage' (1991: 22).[1] Western music, then, has often moved just as comfortably into the illusory sign/referent world of the Lacanian Symbolic as did verbal language and for that matter the linear/realist narrative that is the backbone of Hollywood cinema. It took the Wagners and the Debussys, the Weberns, the Schoenbergs and the Ives and, in his own way, Bernard Herrmann to liberate the musical artwork from the purely Symbolic and to create a set of floating signifiers that serve as a mirror to *suggest* the unsymbolisable.

This is of course precisely what Hollywood, with its penchant for clearly defined, linear narratives and its various means, such as continuity editing, for evoking a pseudo-historic sense of contiguous time and space, did not want – and therefore by and large did not get – from its composers. As Kristeva has suggested, and as we will see further on, Hitchcock, with his use of montage, his thematics of suspense and horror, and his narrative structures, was able to at least partially liberate the cinematic language from the domain of the Lacanian Symbolic. And thus, Herrmann's floating musical signifiers found a comfortable home amidst Hitchcock's floating cinematic signifiers where both, rather than being forced into the artificial consummations of the sign/referent symbology, were free to turn backwards towards the darkness of the pre-Symbolic. One might in fact posit that Herrmann's music needed the figurative nature of the cinema in order to become fully specular, since one can presume, in trying to pinpoint Kristeva's ever elusive terminology, that the specular involves the manifestation of the chora as lektonic remnants in figurative art, which had to at least turn towards the Imaginary in order not to drag the music down into artificial consummations.

Before entering into the figurative domain of the cinema, Herrmann's music actually received a boost towards the specular via the medium of radio drama. Already a staff conductor for the CBS Radio Network, for which he programmed and conducted often unorthodox concerts, Herrmann became the staff composer first for *Columbia Workshop* in 1937 and then, in 1938 and 1939, for Orson Welles's hour-long *Mercury Theatre on the Air*. Indicatively, Herrmann continued working in the radio medium into the 1950s, and he would eventually make contributions to television dramas such as *The Twilight Zone*. Typical of the composer's style for the radio medium is the music he wrote for a radio adaptation of Aldous Huxley's darkly pessimistic, futuristic novel *Brave New World*, broadcast on the *CBS Radio Workshop* on 27 January and 3 February 1956, with Huxley himself providing the narration.[2] Herrmann's musical language here, deployed in extremely brief cues that generally provide a segue from one segment of the radio drama to the next, has practically no linear dimension whatsoever. Almost its entire impact comes from two areas, harmonic and instrumental colour. The instruments, reduced to a small number by budgetary (but also, one rather suspects, for Herrmann, aesthetic) needs, consist of a harp, celesta, timpani and two horns, with the harp and celesta carrying the entire weight in several cues in which the entire harmonic character of the music grows out of a single bitonal chord, heard both broken and unbroken, dominated by the interval of the third.

Interestingly, one rather suspects that the type of cue required by dramatic musical backing, quite brief for the radio and generally brief enough for the cinema, represented a final liberation for Herrmann, even though the time constraints of the cinema have long been attacked by so-called 'serious' musicians addicted to rigorous formal structures. As I have suggested, Herrmann, except in a few works such as the piano Prelude and the Sinfonietta for Strings, never seems entirely comfortable drawing his inspirations out into extended forms such as the symphony, string quartet, or even opera, and he is generally at his least convincing when trying to create themes to fit into the 'classical' forms required by such pieces. On the other hand the non-linear nature of Herrmann's musical vision made the short cue the ideal for his particular style (the second variation of the Sinfonietta's finale is a Webernian four bars long). Although his apparent lifelong ambition was to become a conductor and/or perhaps to write the great American opera, which his *Wuthering Heights* definitely is not, Herrmann acquired his major reputation working mostly within a medium with whose dark, specular side his particular sensibilities were more closely aligned than those of almost any other film composer.[3]

When he moved from the radio to the cinema Orson Welles brought much of his crew from the *Mercury Theatre on the Air* with him, including Bernard Herrmann. Their first collaboration in the brooding *Citizen Kane*, released in 1941, establishes both director and composer as artists of the specular *par excellence*. One need go no further than *Citizen Kane*'s opening sequence. As Gregg Toland's camera moves through the fog hanging over the ruins that surround Kane's mansion, Xanadu, we hear music that is almost all instrumental colour, most of it coming from the lower registers of the bassoons, muted trombones and bass clarinets. Out of this murky darkness emerge, barely, two motifs. The first one, associated with the adult Kane, comes right out of Rachmaninoff's equally gloomy tone poem *The Isle of the Dead* (1908). The second motif is associated with Kane's lost sledge (and mother and childhood …), Rosebud. It is a motif that will rarely extend beyond a bare bar or two (Figure 5.1).

The harmonically ambiguous nature of this modal motif works hand in hand with the movie's narrative, which does not reveal the Rosebud secret until the end of the film, and then only for the audience, at which point the motif will extend to a chromatic fourth bar that stops short in the Prelude but that will loop the motif back in upon itself at the end. The signifier/absent-signified nature of the musical/non-visual motif amalgam deepens our reading of the Rosebud symbolism by extending it to the domain of what Kristeva calls *la mère tue*, the silent or perhaps silenced mother within the aura of whose absence Kane/Don Juan will seduce women and tilt against the capitalist/industrialist/political father. Indeed,

Figure 5.1 Herrmann's Rosebud motif from *Citizen Kane* (Music Sales Group).

the Rosebud motif will reappear, quietly, in a flute solo over a moody accompaniment in the harp at the extremely significant moment in the film when Kane makes up his mind to enter the apartment of his future mistress, who, enjoying a taboo status Kane's wife cannot have, replaces, at least for a while, the hero's silenced mother, whose warehoused possessions Kane was on his way to examine when he runs across Susan Alexander.

It cannot be stressed enough how the general overuse in Hollywood cinema of the leitmotif device, borrowed from Wagner, cheapens the film/music relationship, artificially consummating the musical signifier by tying it into specific elements of the narrative text while the latter in turn becomes hyperexplicated, to use my colleague Claudia Gorbman's (1987) term, via the musical redundancy. Only Erich Korngold, of the leitmotif composers, managed to escape triviality by organising his themes and motifs so ingeniously within the overall fabric of the score that he all but created, as I have suggested in my *Overtones and Undertones* (1994), a new musical form. Although Herrmann did not entirely avoid the leitmotif, his use of it was always sparing, even in his lesser efforts. And in his best work – such as *Citizen Kane* and, as we shall see, *Vertigo* – motivic associations with the narrative are of such a multilayered nature that both the filmic and the musical texts are deepened rather than cheapened. I stress again that Herrmann needed a visionary director and darker subject matter to bring out his best work, and one can only wonder what kind of music the composer would have produced for Welles's two brooding postwar films, the 1946 *The Stranger* and the 1948 *The Lady from Shanghai*. Remembering that near the end of his life Welles suggested that Herrmann's music was 50 percent responsible for *Citizen Kane's* artistic success (see Carringer, 1985, quoted in Smith, 1991: 84), one can only regret that the composer would have to wait for Alfred Hitchcock to find the perfect match for his particular musical vision.

The shape of a typical Bernard Herrmann film score, then, differed from the outset from those of most of his colleagues. Where Hollywood had a penchant for big melodies such as the 'Tara' theme from Max Steiner's score for *Gone with the Wind* (1939), Herrmann generally created whatever thematic material he could be bothered with out of small cells, much more flexible within the overall cinematic context than a genuine melody. As the composer noted to me in an interview a year before he died,

> You know, the reason I don't like this tune business is that a tune has to have eight or sixteen bars, which limits you as a composer. Once you start, you've got to finish – eight or sixteen bars. Otherwise the audience doesn't know what the hell it's about. It's putting handcuffs on yourself. (Brown, 1994: 291–2)

Even when he composed in a mellower, more romantic idiom, as in the title theme for the 1947 *The Ghost and Mrs Muir*, Herrmann's idea of a big theme is a series of four-note cells set to moody, seventh-chord harmonies and repeated sequentially. At the opening of the cue, we have the impression of a melody trying to define itself via those four-note cells. When the main theme, which is still incomplete by traditional standards, finally does break out, it is little more than a compressed variation on the preceding material. Further, where Hollywood composers tended toward a full-orchestra sound, Herrmann often stressed individual timbres, more often than not because of a non-specific, tone-colour concept he would have for a particular film or filmic sequence rather than for some symbolic connection between timbre and situation, certain obvious gimmicks in *The 7th Voyage of Sinbad* (1958) to the contrary notwithstanding. By the time he entered the 1950s he was honing this particular facet of his skills to something of a fine science. Thus, the totally themeless cue for the opening 'Radar' sequence of Robert Wise's 1951 *The Day the Earth Stood Still* is nothing more than a Mendelssohnesque scherzo for two pianos and vibraphone.

And if the composer was not above exploiting the easy association between electronic instruments and futuristic narratives, he all but created the 1950s science fiction sound in *The Day the Earth Stood Still* via the incorporation of two theremins and an electric organ into a bizarre orchestra also including an electric violin, electric bass, four pianos, four harps and a section of some thirty assorted brass. In one cue a young boy has followed an alien named Klaatu (Michael Rennie) to the site of the flying saucer, where Klaatu signals his for-the-moment-immobile robot named Gort with a torch he shines from a distance so he won't be seen, at which point we hear an eerie antiphony between the two theremins in a series of two-note half-steps that descend chromatically over a vague rumbling, probably in the electric bass and electric organ, with likewise eerie timpani glissandi coming in later. Via the theremins, whose timbres fall in some liminal area between the human and the non-human, and via the foregrounding of instrumental timbres that create a musical background substantially different from the symphony orchestras film audiences were accustomed to at the time, the score focuses the ears more on the physical qualities of the timbres than on their integration into the linear, forward movement of the music, thereby moving towards the experiencing of the sounds as those 'pulsations, somatic waves, surges of color, rhythms, tones' that Kristeva describes as lektonic remnants that are an essential element of the specular experience.

But it is with the films of Alfred Hitchcock, and in particular the 1958 *Vertigo* and the 1960 *Psycho*, that Herrmann's music has its deepest specular interactions. I would like to start by briefly summarising a major point in my analysis of the Herrmann/Hitchcock scores in my article 'Herrmann, Hitchcock, and the Music of the Irrational',[4] which I will then enhance with a perception from a Laura Mulvey article much less well-known than her 'Visual Pleasure and Narrative Cinema'. Two of the most characteristic sounds in Herrmann's music are various forms of seventh chords, and passages of parallel thirds. These chords and intervals tend to stand on their own much more strongly in Herrmann than in other Hollywood composers, since Herrmann's non- and/or anti-melodic practices and his predilection for building his music out of short cells isolate them from the linear, quasi-causal resolutions of functional tonality. I need to stress that there is nothing revolutionary per se about these practices. Debussy's music abounds in parallel chords producing very much the same effect as in Herrmann, i.e. the isolating of the sound of the chord as such rather than incorporating it into some kind of resolutional harmonic movement. And the fourth movement (*Schnelle Viertel*) of German composer Paul Hindemith's 1922 *Kleine Kammermusic* No. 2 for wind quintet hammers insistently throughout its brief length on a minor-major seventh chord identical to the Hitchcock chord as heard in *Psycho*, and it is fairly improbable that Herrmann would not have been acquainted with this chamber piece, which was fairly popular during its era. Certainly Herrmann was not composing anything close to the 'experimental, atonal music' attributed to his early scores by Hitchcock biographer Patrick McGilligan (2003: 507). What is revolutionary, if such is the term, is that Herrmann brought these devices – and others – into an art form where the norm was a much more conservative musical language.

At any rate, for whatever reasons Herrmann, from the outset of his collaboration with Alfred Hitchcock in the 1955 *The Trouble with Harry*, came up with a harmonic – not instrumental – sound that he seems to have associated if not with Hitchcock's oeuvre as a whole then at least with the more ominous sides of it, since this harmonic characteristic plays a major role in *Vertigo* and *Psycho*, both of which deal with the murderous misogyny that underlies patriarchal culture. Significantly the Hitchcock chord does not turn up in any of the composer's non-Hitchcock films. (The 1972 *Frenzy* makes up the third panel of the triptych that begins with *Vertigo* and *Psycho*. One regrets not only that Herrmann was no longer on speaking terms with the British-born director by this point but that the apparently very Herrmannesque music originally composed for it by Henry Mancini was rejected by Hitchcock.) The backbone of that harmonic sound is a minor-major seventh chord that I have dubbed the Hitchcock chord. *Major* seventh chords abound in Herrmann's scores, particularly in his later work, and it is because of the pseudo-resolution of this chord into a sixth chord and the sequential repetition of it a step lower that Herrmann acquired later in his career the annoying tendency of constantly flirting with the pop song 'Jeepers Creepers' (Figure 5.2).

David Raksin quotes Arthur Morton, a well-known orchestrator and composer, as saying, 'If that son-of-a-bitch doesn't stop writing "Jeepers Creepers" I'm going to kill him' (Brown, 1994: 288).

But the chord that I am calling the Hitchcock chord invites no such pseudo-resolutions and no such facile melodism. It is formed, reading from the bottom up, of a minor third, a major third and another major third (Figure 5.3). It is this chord that dominates the preludes of both *Vertigo* and *Psycho* and that returns to haunt much of the first half of *Psycho* at various points. But we can hear the possibility of this chord as early as that obsessive, augmented triad that dominates the score for *The Trouble with Harry*. All it takes is the addition of a minor third below that

Figure 5.2 Herrmann's 'flirtation' with 'Jeepers Creepers' (author's notation).

Figure 5.3 Annotation for the 'Hitchcock chord' (author's notation).

chord to get the Hitchcock chord. We can also hear, more strongly perhaps in the Hitchcock scores than in Herrmann's other film music, the tendency to take the interval of the third, that building block of stability in functional tonality, and turn it into what one might call a floating, specular musical signifier by moving it up and down in small parallel steps. This appears most transparently in a cue from the 1956 *The Man Who Knew Too Much* where Doris Day is waiting outside Ambrose Chapel, and in the cue for the long-dead Carlotta Valdes in *Vertigo*, which in places is all but identical to *The Man Who Knew Too Much* cue.

Herrmann, then, is doing in music what Hitchcock is doing in his films, which is to say starting off in the domain of the normal, the causal – one thinks immediately of the town of Santa Rosa, California, in the 1943 *Shadow of a Doubt*, the hustle and bustle of the ad exec's universe in the 1959 *North by Northwest* or, for that matter, the banal lovers' tryst that opens *Psycho* – and moving into the betwixt-and-between domain that Laura Mulvey has described as 'liminal'. 'Hitchcock's heroes', writes Mulvey – and one might certainly add Hitchcock's heroines – 'are plunged into a world turned upside down, in which identity and even name become uncertain, in which the logical expectations of everyday life are reversed in a nightmare universe that also celebrates the pleasure and excitement of liminality' (Mulvey, 1989: 171). But Hitchcock's nightmare adventures generally take place, in an ongoing narrative/visual counterpoint, in ordinary settings generally presented within the confines of the usual movements of continuity editing. The British Museum (*Blackmail*), the Statue of Liberty (*Saboteur*) and Mount Rushmore (*North by Northwest*) are reserved for climactic moments, just as are, for instance, the frenetic editing of *Psycho*'s shower scene or the zoom-in/track-out (and vice versa) shots associated with *Vertigo*'s acrophobia. Similarly, in Herrmann there is always the possibility of resolution in those unresolved seventh chords (although less so in the minor-major seventh Hitchcock chord than in the others), while the parallel thirds always point towards tonal stability without ever quite getting there – indeed, the Ambrose Chapel cue from *The Man Who Knew Too Much* and the Carlotta Valdes theme play over a drone on D (in a habanera rhythm in *Vertigo*) as a kind of ongoing reminder of a lurking normalcy.

In this vein Mulvey's article questions the efficacy of avant-garde filmmaking, since, as she points out, a 'negative aesthetics can produce an inversion of the meanings and pleasures it confronts, but it risks remaining locked in a dialogue with its adversary. Counter-aesthetics, too, can harden into a system of dualistic opposition' (1989: 164). Mulvey instead proposes the generation of a kind of narrative which, 'with the help of avant-garde principles, can be conceived around ending that is not closure, and the state of liminality as politically significant' (175). This will enable the particular art form to 'question the symbolic, and enable myth and symbols to be constantly revalued' (175). It seems to me that it is in precisely this vein that Herrmann, in the interview I did with him shortly before his death, rejects the aesthetics of Pierre Boulez, and why I would suggest that the liminal quality of Herrmann's art makes it more appropriate to discussions of the specular than the atonality of a Schoenberg, a Webern or a Boulez. While Mulvey implies that, in Hitchcock, 'journeys always end in safe returns' (171), this is certainly not the case for *Vertigo* and is only partially the case for *Psycho*, since Norman/Ma ('Norma') Bates' jail-cell monologue followed by a few-second superposition of Norman's face and that of his mummified mother pretty much undoes the psychiatrist's smug post-mortem, as does Herrmann's crushingly bitonal A flat minor/D unison chord that accompanies *Psycho*'s visual non-closure.

Finally, I bring up one other way in which, in *Vertigo*, Herrmann's music and Hitchcock's cinema in essence remain in the domain of Mulvey's liminality through their evocations of the Kristeva specular. It is in fact indicative of just how profoundly complex the Herrmann/Hitchcock amalgam is that this particular perception became reasonably clear to me only after perhaps the fortieth time that I watched and/or taught and/or wrote about Hitchcock's masterpiece, which now has made it all the way to the top of the British Film Institute (BFI)'s 100 Best Films list. The particular issue that I wish to examine here is how narratively, visually and musically the relationships between Scottie Ferguson and 'Madeleine'/Judy, between Gavin Elster and his (soon to be ex-)wife Madeleine, and the unnamed 'man of power' and Carlotta Valdes, represent not the metaphysical 'love death' (*Liebestod*) of *Tristan und Isolde*, even though more than one writer on the subject has heard Wagner's music in Herrmann's score, but rather the kind of 'death love' (*Totenlieb*) that is inevitable in the patriarchal culture of the Symbolic. This becomes apparent as of *Vertigo*'s title sequence, with Saul Bass's stunning animations of Lissajous spirals and Herrmann's music.

But it is communicated perhaps on its deepest level in the remarkably subtle, brief and dialogue-less sequence when, at Ernie's restaurant in San Francisco, Scottie sees 'Madeleine' for the first time. In bad writing about film music the author would be content to simply label the music here as 'Madeleine's Theme' and then proceed to totally literalise, or perhaps linearise, the film/music relationship by pointing out every place in *Vertigo* where this 'theme' reappears. The slightly more perceptive writer would note how the four-note fragment that begins the cue ultimately gets woven into the full-blown, so-called 'love music'. But of course the character we see on the screen is not Madeleine Elster but rather a woman (Judy Barton) pretending to be Madeleine, whence the quotation marks. 'Madeleine' is supposed to be possessed by the spirit of her great-grandmother, Carlotta Valdes. And so we have four different gazes that are attempting unsuccessfully to pin onto this multiply imagified woman a single signified. There is the gaze of Scottie Ferguson set up by the first shot; there is the gaze of Gavin Elster, who is sitting at the table with Kim Novak/Madeleine/Judy/Carlotta; there is the gaze of the spectator; and there is the gaze of Hitchcock himself, prominently represented by the lyrical, semicircular movement of the camera to the back corner of the restaurant before it starts a slow track in on 'Madeleine', thus subverting expectations of a reverse-angle shot seen from Scottie's point of view. The theme might better be titled 'Looking at "Madeleine"'.

Meanwhile Herrmann's musical cue, with its muted-string theme over a soft accompaniment of major seventh chords that partially resolve in characteristic Herrmann downward whole steps (we're almost at 'Jeepers Creepers' here), seems like a lyrical prelude to Scottie Ferguson's eventual tragic love for 'Madeleine', who is basically a floating signifier of a character. Yet the music has deeper secrets. First of all the theme, characteristically for Herrmann, rather than having that classic romantic flow, is initially made up of a series of four-note fragments, each of which establishes its identity apart from the thematic continuity, almost as if each incarnation of the gazed-upon woman has her own piece of the theme. Second, the overall tonality of the cue is an ambiguous amalgam of G major and G minor that ultimately suspends on a D, which is precisely what happens in the much more ominous and much more dramatic title Prelude. If I wanted to be really esoteric I would point out that the 'Madeleine' cue is scored for muted strings only, which is also the case of the 1935 Sinfonietta that gave the composer the springboard for his *Psycho* music, scored almost entirely for mute strings, the most notable exception being the shower scene music and its subsequent reappearances. Just as important, perhaps, is the 6/8 metre in which the cue is written. While it is difficult to feel the 6/8 pulse in this cue, particularly as conducted by Ray Heindorf for the original music tracks, the metre suggests the presence of a hidden waltz, just as do the cut-time triplets of the Prelude. One of the great constants of the 'classic' film score is of course the use of the waltz whenever it is a question of love, thank you Max Steiner et al. Not only does Herrmann seem to be following in that vein, albeit very subtly for a while, he ultimately turns *Vertigo*'s love music into about as full-blown a waltz as it is possible to get. Far from being a dance of love, however, this cue appears for the first time as 'Madeleine' is about to waltz off to the church tower from which Gavin Elster will throw his already dead wife. From the outset the waltz in *Vertigo* is a *Totentanz*, with all that it implies of violence and agressivity.

This, of course, is wholly consistent with *Vertigo*'s extremely dark vision of so-called love in the patriarchal world of the Symbolic. Scottie Ferguson, our Don Juan/Orpheus, ventures out of the world of the Lacanian Symbolic into a liminal domain that is cinematically created by the strongly specular nature of Hitchcock's narrative/visual style and by Herrmann's music style. But it is not just the non-Symbolic agressivity of the Imaginary that does in *Vertigo*'s multiple heroine but rather Scottie's return to the world of the Symbolic. For our Don Juan/Orpheus is not content with 'knowing' a woman sexually. He must 'know' her Symbolically, he must look at her as she emerges from the darkness in order to possess her quasi-eternally as a signifier of death that can exist only through the death of the 'real' woman. Herrmann's music plays a double role in this. It is music that accompanies, in both *Vertigo* and *Psycho*, the repeated, and therefore ritualised, sacrifice of the woman. As Kristeva has noted in another work, 'What is violent is the irruption of the symbol, the putting to death of substance in order for it to signify' (Kristeva, 1974: 73). At the same time it is music that, because it has been liberated from much of that art's musical and cine-musical symbology, suggests pre-Symbolic aggressivity on something close to a pure level, to which anyone who has ever been frightened out of taking a shower by Herrmann's shrieking violins descending in major seventh intervals can attest. The glissandi introduced into repetitions of this figure recall the manner in which the narrator of Thomas Mann's *Doctor Faustus* describes the glissando as 'a naturalistic atavism, a barbaric rudiment from pre-musical days'. The images of terror contained in a work entitled *Apocalypse* by *Doctor Faustus*'s fictitious composer 'offer a most tempting and at the same time most legitimate occasion for employing this device'. Similarly, one might say that the 'represented horror' of Hitchcock's films, rather than the concert hall or the average Hollywood film, offered Herrmann 'a most legitimate occasion' for recasting the shape of film music by partially, rather than wholly (as would atonal or experimental music), stripping that art of many of its equivalents to the Lacanian Symbolic and restoring it to much of its specular potential.

Notes

1 The 'semiotic' is Kristeva's equivalent in language for Lacan's 'imaginary' stage. Kristeva uses the Greek word 'chora' for what might be called the 'semiotic presignifier', which she defines as 'neither a model nor a copy', since it is 'anterior and subjacent to figuration … and can only be compared with vocal or kinesthetic rhythm' (1975: 24).

2 This programme was once available on a long-playing record brought out by Pelican Records (LP 2013) in 1979. According to amazon.com's website, it is currently available on CD on the EI (Cherry Red) label as a Japanese import.

3 More recently, one thinks of Howard Shore, about whom music critic Alex Ross, writing in the *New Yorker*, stated that 'Shore … may well be the most imaginative composer who has worked in Hollywood since Herrmann' (1998).

4 Originally published in *Cinema Journal* 21:2 (Spring 1982): 14–49. Reprinted several times in various sources, including, in a revised version, my *Overtones and Undertones* (Brown, 1994).

References

Brown, Royal S. (1994), *Overtones and Undertones: Reading Film Music*. Berkeley: University of California Press.

Carringer, Robert (1985), *The Making of Citizen Kane*. Berkeley: University of California Press.

Gorbman, Claudia (1987), *Unheard Melodies: Narrative Film Music*. Bloomington: Indiana University Press.

Herrmann, Bernard (1932), 'Charles Ives', *Trend: A Quarterly of the Seven Arts* 1:3: 99–101.

Kristeva, Julia (1974), *La Révolution du langage poétique*. Paris: Éditions du Seuil. [Author's translations.]

Kristeva, Julia (1975), 'Ellipse sur la frayeur et la séduction spéculaire', *Communications* 23: 73–8. [Author's translations.]

Langer, Suzanne K. (1957), *Philosophy in a New Key: A Study in the Symbolism of Reason, Rite, and Art, 3rd ed*. Cambridge, MA: Harvard University Press.

McGilligan, Patrick (2003), *Alfred Hitchcock: A Life in Darkness and Light*. New York: Regan Books.

Mulvey, Laura (1989), *Visual and Other Pleasures*. Bloomington: Indiana University Press.

Ross, Alex (1998), 'Oscar scores', *New Yorker*, 9 March. Available online at Alex Ross: The Rest is Noise, www.therestisnoise.com/2004/05/oscar_scores.html. Accessed 5 May 2014.

Shepherd, John (1991), *Music as Social Text*. Cambridge: Polity Press.

Smith, Steven C. (1991), *A Heart at Fire's Center: The Life and Music of Bernard Herrmann*. Berkeley: University of California Press.

6

Portentous arrangements: Bernard Herrmann and *The Man Who Knew Too Much*

Murray Pomerance

There is little question among scholars of cinematic music and scholars of Hitchcock that the Hitchcock–Herrmann collaboration was, on balance, a profoundly positive one that left us with not only the playful *The Trouble with Harry* (1955) but at least five masterpieces of film – *The Wrong Man* (1956), *Vertigo* (1958), *North by Northwest* (1959), *Psycho* (1960) and *Marnie* (1964) – this not-withstanding the composer's summative recollection to Royal Brown (1994) that he had finally said to the filmmaker, 'Hitch, what's the use of my doing more with you? Your pictures, your mathematics, three zeroes. My mathematics, quite differ-ent' (290). The love affair, if that it was, did not end well, a fact that has materialised in numerous accounts. My understanding is that when he was at Universal record-ing *Taxi Driver* for Martin Scorsese, Herrmann brought his new wife Norma over to the legendary bungalow, along with his brand new copy of François Truffaut's *Hitchcock*, which he expected Hitch would sign for him while also meeting the wife. He knocked on the door and Hitch's assistant Peggy Robertson answered only to say that Mr Hitchcock, unfortunately, was not in at the time. The Herrmanns went away disappointed. Hitch had been standing behind the door.[1]

The cause of this rancour, or embarrassment, was *Torn Curtain*, for which Hitchcock had quite specifically requested that Herrmann write a light score: 'If you will agree to doing a more modern score, up-to-date and so on, you will do the picture. If you refuse, then I'm afraid I'll have to choose someone else.' Herrmann had cabled back: 'DELIGHTED COMPOSE VIGOROUS BEAT SCORE FOR TORN CURTAIN.' (Herrmann to Hitchcock).

The recording sessions were at the Goldwyn Studio (on Santa Monica Boulevard: the former Warner Bros. Hollywood plant). After his lunch on the fate-ful day, Hitchcock was driven there with Peggy Robertson. She saw Herrmann, who said, 'We're going to start with reel one.' What she heard was, by her own account, 'funereal, dirge-like music, where Hitch had wanted the light music. I was horrified and I didn't know what to do':

> And just at that moment the doors opened and Hitch walked in. He came up to me and he said, 'How is it?' So I said, 'Well …' 'What are you doing now?' So I said, 'Reel

two.' He said, 'Well, I'll hear reel one.' So I looked around for Benny and Benny said, 'Don't hear reel one, Hitch. Reel two is the important one.' And he said, 'No, I want to hear reel one.' And he heard it, and then – it was the first time I've ever known him to do it, and the only time – he stopped. He said, 'That's enough, I've heard enough, I don't want to hear anymore.' And Benny said, 'Don't you love it?' So he said, 'No, I asked for light music there, Benny, and I don't want to talk about it any more.' And he went straight to the studio and said, 'Let him go. He broke the bargain that we had, which was for light music.' And that was it. (Hall, 2002: 294)

On 25 March 1966 Herrmann was cabled that his agreement was terminated at the close of business that day.

The music research for the picture had included the Philadelphia Orchestra's recording of Bartók's *Concerto for Orchestra* under Eugene Ormandy and Pierre Boulez's *Marteau sans maître*. Dimitri Tiomkin had wired his desire to score the picture as well (Tiomkin, 1965); other composers given consideration were Kenyon Hopkins (who had written *12 Angry Men*), Riz Ortolani (composer of *Mondo cane*), Maurice Jarre (composer of *Lawrence of Arabia*) and John Addison (who had won an Academy Award for *Tom Jones* and finally got the *Torn Curtain* contract).

The *Torn Curtain* escapade may be regarded as the nadir of the Herrmann–Hitchcock relationship. It was otherwise more than cordial, and entirely productive. Of their successful collaborations, most devotees of Hitchcock's films and Herrmann's music agree that the most consummately and integrally symphonic (indeed, the most Wagnerian) score is *Vertigo*; it has been intensively and illuminatingly discussed by David Cooper (2001). Herrmann's labour on *Vertigo* was complicated by the 20 February 1958 Hollywood musicians' strike, in which the studios' drive to use freelance workers threatened the job security that the American Federation of Musicians was striving to improve. As the score could not be recorded at Paramount, the producer Herbert Coleman made immediate moves to have musicians in London do the work, but in sympathy with their American counterparts the British musicians refused. Muir Mathieson had been engaged to conduct the London Philharmonic, in lieu of Herrmann: 'The contract forbade an American conductor', writes Jack Sullivan, 'One of Herrmann's keenest disappointments in a career filled with acrimony was not getting to conduct *Vertigo* himself' (2006: 232). The company removed to Zurich, whence on 11 March 1958 Coleman cabled the studio that thirty-eight minutes only had been recorded 'before international musicians European in Zurich withdrew all men in sympathy Hollywood musicians' (Coleman, 1958a). By 31 March, the sessions were shifted to Vienna, where the local musical assistant, Max Kimental, offered that a 'heavy bowing' sound in the strings, an 'effect [Mr Herrmann] was after', was 'difficult to get here or [in] England because of the different technique' (Coleman, 1958b).

The desire for a heavy bowing effect in *Vertigo* is only one tiny example of Bernard Herrmann's broadly inventive and thoroughly knowledgeable approach to musical composition, and of his self-estimation as a serious composer (which filmgoers would have discovered by listening to the piano concerto written expressly for, and filmed as a climactic part of, John Brahm's *Hangover Square* (1945)). Herrmann's orchestration is frequently unforgettable, as is discovered perhaps most sharply in *Psycho*, written for strings only and making astounding use of violin downbowing and bass sostenuto. The famous and characteristic slashing sound is derived from a combination of techniques applied simultaneously: vigorous, even violent downbowing *sforzato* jabs on two disharmonious notes, E and E flat, by the first and second violins, all this played with ferocity (*feroce*) on swiftly repeating minims in 3/2 time.[2] Some of what is heard in *Psycho* is produced out of the imagination of Hitchcock, however.

> They got to the part at the end of the picture, in the cellar, when Tony runs down the steps and his mother's skeleton head. And Hitch said, 'Well, Benny, why don't you have that music with all the strings in it?' ... And Benny usually didn't take criticism ... so it was surprising, when Hitch made that suggestion, that he selected it. And of course it *was* a good idea, because those marvelous chords gave so much to the picture'. (Peggy Robertson to Barbara Hall in Hall, 2002: 164)

The Wrong Man has some beautiful Cuban-style dance music under the main title, 'a rather innocuous Latin ditty [alternating] with a more characteristically Herrmannesque motive', and a notable use further on of 'a string bass played pizzicato, giving a mildly jazzy flavour to the music and also reminding us of the protagonist's job' in a house band at the Stork Club (Brown, 1982: 25). Also found here are haunting adagios which set out Manny Balestrero's solitary angst in partnership with Hitchcock's sparse framing, Robert Burks's radiant bath of light, and Henry Fonda's restrained performance. The fandango of *North by Northwest* alone puts the score in musical history, playing jovially as it does on Bernstein's 'America' from *West Side Story* (which gets a notable reference in the film) and, fleshed out with restless 6/8 violin passages and brazen brass work in the Mount Rushmore sequence, producing a sparkling climax to the action of the story. The music for *Marnie* is both tempestuous and conflicted, all of its harmonic glories richly promised and then compromised by doubts and retractions. 'He had been recording MARNIE and his wife walked out on him' (Robertson, in Hall, 2002: 295). *Marnie* is one of Hitchcock's truly great films, and Herrmann's combative, lush, almost schizoid score (copied by the composer four years later for Truffaut's *La Mariée était en noir*) lifts and carries the essentially female, essentially nostalgic line of the story (see Pomerance, 2014). Scholars and film lovers have paid less attention to the musical glories of *The Man Who Knew Too Much*, largely, I think, because, rather than working through and interrelating a coherent set of his own musical motifs, as was his practice in these other films, Herrmann here played a different kind of compositional role.

The Man Who Knew Too Much – Paramount production no. 10336 – was in pre-production as early as February 1955 and was photographed in Marrakech, London and Los Angeles from 13 May to 17 October of that year. On 1 April, Hitchcock responded to a request from James Stevens, about the possibility of being hired, by indicating that Bernard Herrmann had been selected instead to score the film. 'Perhaps you know of him' (Hitchcock, 1995). Herrmann 'started his services in connection with the production activities' on 22 May (Fjastad, 1955b), although on 18 April he was sent, by Herbert Coleman, revisions to Dominic Bevan Wyndham-Lewis's lyrics of Arthur Benjamin's *Storm Clouds Cantata* for verification and acceptance before they were to go for censorship clearance. The phrase 'Yet stood the trees' had been substituted for the pathetically fallacious 'All save the child' and the word 'head' pluralised in one of the solo passages (Coleman to Herrmann). In this way the original

> All save the child – all save the child
> Around whose head screaming,
> The night-birds wheeled and shot away,

a portrait of a lonely victim hounded by nature, was converted to

> Yet stood the trees – yet stood the trees
> Around whose heads screaming,
> The night-birds wheeled and shot away,

an expressivist, even grotesque image in the style of Bouguereau or Friederich. It fell to Herrmann also to consider and approve Ray Evans's lyrics to his composition with Jay Livingston, 'Que Sera, Sera (Whatever Will Be, Will Be)'.

By contract, Herrmann would have four principal duties for this film: according to a letter from Paramount's music director Roy Fjastad of 12 July, he was engaged to 'compose, arrange, orchestrate and conduct' music for the film for six weeks' work (which commenced in fact on 4 November) on an exclusive basis and a further nine weeks on a non-exclusive basis. Herrmann would receive $15,000 for all his work, in addition to first-class transport to London for him and his wife and living expenses on location. (Like Ben and Jo McKenna, he would reside at the Savoy.) His credit card would read 'Music Scored by Bernard Herrmann' (Fjastad to Justin). In fact, however, a fifth duty was added to the list, namely appearing onscreen as an orchestral conductor during the cantata sequence, this appearance even billed within the film on a huge billboard outside the Albert Hall. Royal Brown has made a fascinating interpretation of Herrmann's presence in this capacity, suggesting not only that 'Hitchcock even times certain events to the music' (Brown, 1994: 79; see also Pomerance, 2000),[3] but also that 'As conductor, Bernard Herrmann is responsible for keeping the music moving forward',

> and he thus becomes both Hitchcock's musical (and in this case visual) alter ego and the villains' greatest ally. For the listener/viewer all this has the psychological effect of causing the music to 'leave' the diegetic level and 'rise' to the level of nondiegetic music backing the suspenseful action. This in turn has the effect of transforming the sequence into a (silent) film-within-a-film controlled by the villains via the artistic creation, in this case the music. (1994: 79–80)

Hitchcock turns the screw even further, of course, giving us macro-close shots of the score at two points during the performance so that, in the first instance, the shot of the cymbalist's score, we will see an overall map of the whole event

Figure 6.1 *The Man Who Knew Too Much* (1956, Dir: Alfred Hitchcock). The score for the cantata, descending violin sixteenth-note passages racing ahead (Paramount Pictures/Filwite Productions).

and, noting the juncture at which the murder is to occur, find ourselves able to count down to the climax; and in the second, the shot of the conductor's score with descending violin semiquaver passages racing ahead and leading the eye and consciousness of the viewer quickly into the future (Figure 6.1), we will sense the increasing approximation of the event, as though it is looming toward us on a road.[4] I will return to the *Storm Clouds* below.

Given the range of contributions that Herrmann made to *The Man Who Knew Too Much,* this film presents a particularly revealing view of his collaboration with Hitchcock, and merits far closer study than is evidenced by Patrick McGilligan's disparaging evaluation that 'His score – rising and falling arpeggios – was the least distinctive of his contributions to Hitchcock films' (2003: 521). Pertinent to scholars interested in music, for example, is his arrangement for the screen of already existing music, an activity he described late in his life to Brown as 'stupid' (1994: 291). The music I'm referring to, beyond Benjamin's cantata, is the hymn 'The Portents', which I discuss at length in a 2005 contribution to *The MacGuffin*. This non-denominational standard would most likely have been selected by Herrmann himself from a repertory of available public-domain materials in the Paramount library, then arranged for a small 'choir' of forty-two churchgoer extras, rehearsed with the singers by Herrmann himself on set (since he did not frequently use assistants),[5] and then recorded as live production sound while the camera turned. As one listens to the Ambrose Chapel sequence, one hears in this singing, and especially as the vocal scale climbs up to a woeful dominant, a sharp, unsure and reverberant tone that is not present for any of the rest of the film – or for somewhat similar other filmic hymn sequences, such as 'In the Sweet By and By' or 'Give Me That Old-Time Religion' in Howard Hawks's *Sergeant York* (1941) or Arthur Sullivan's 'Onward Christian Soldiers' in Mervyn

LeRoy's *Mrs Miniver* (1942), both films that would have been known to Hitchcock and Herrmann – this affecting, even slightly irritating directness occasioned by the high-ceilinged set that Henry Bumstead had built on Paramount's Stage 5 for the shooting and direct recording on 9 and 11 July 1955. There is a chilling quality to the sound of these downtrodden parishioners singing that makes for a sharp punctum of realism in the scene; one has 'fallen out of' the high climes of Hollywood romantic drama into the grey and dingy precincts of the 'actual world'. I suspect it is not immaterial to consider how, for Hitchcock, the 'actuality' of this little world far from Hollywood's fragrant glamour found an appropriate setting in a poor district of London.

For realism, however, nothing surpassed the bizarre challenge of the cantata, given to us in what appears to be full performance.[6] As to this celebrated work, taken as a piece of music alone, it here gets the respectful, fully stereophonic recording it deserves (and of which the composer must have dreamed), so that the rather lush productive forces – a full orchestra, a giant choir and a contralto soloist – are displayed without reduction or restraint. Stereo sound reproduction for cinema began around 1937, and was thus unavailable when Hitchcock made his first *The Man Who Knew Too Much* in 1934. In that early film, not only is the cantata less glorious than one would wish as an acoustic experience, but thematic devices are borrowed from it to inhabit the rest of the film, whereas by 1956 Hitchcock had learned to keep the cantata entirely in its place. As his biographer Steven Smith recounts, Herrmann's responsibilities involved slightly expanding the original score, by doubling some orchestral parts and 'adding expressive new voices for harp, organ, and brass' (1991: 196). I should note that a comparison of the original Benjamin scoring (Benjamin, 1955), reported by the composer in a letter to Roy Fjastad, and that of the Herrmann arrangement in my copy of the conductor's score, shows that what Herrmann added to the harp, cymbals and percussion battery already present was one side drum, one additional harp and a second pair of cymbals, the last a specific order from Hitchcock, who in undated, dictated music notes requested that, on the record played for (both the assassin's and the audience's) rehearsal at Ambrose Chapel, the cymbals be 'sweetened'. Arthur Benjamin ('a favourite of Herrmann'; Smith, 1991: 195) not only ceded over to Hitchcock control of all rights in the music but also agreed, as of 24 March, to write about a minute and a half of additional material in time for recording on 20 May, since Hitchcock wished to 'elongate the playing time' (Fjastad, 1955a). For Royal Brown, this protraction of the cantata is rather emphatic: he notes that the running time is 'more than doubled' over that in the 1934 film: 'Whereas in the original version it takes a little over four minutes for the cantata to reach the climactic point where Jill screams … in the remake that same climax-cum-scream comes almost nine minutes into the work.' Without detailing it, Brown notes 'considerable padding added by Herrmann to Arthur Benjamin's original score' and comments that the 'nonvocal introduction comes close to lasting as long as the entire work in the original' (1994: 78–9). In 1934, the first twenty-four bars of the opening Lento section were used as the opening title music and then elided as the cantata performance actually began; whereas, in 1956, Hitchcock incorporated all of the Benjamin score and for his titles used a theme composed especially by Herrmann to suggest ominous portentousness (a theme in which timpani beats dominate a repeated four-note ascending theme in the brass). The culminating *Allegro Agitato* of the cantata is conducted in the remake with notably less haste, permitting a large number of intercut perspectives on Ben entering the Hall, finding Jo, climbing up to the mezzanine, arguing with police officers, and finally going off on his own hunt for the assassin's box. Hitchcock was an inveterate music lover, who in this passage makes it possible for his viewers to join with him in experiencing the thrill not only of Benjamin's music as reconceived by Herrmann but also of the topography of the Royal Albert Hall (opened 1871, with more than 5,200 seats), explored here in shot after shot as the music builds.

In agreeing to the extra writing, Benjamin recommended that Muir Mathieson be contracted to conduct the cantata, but by 3 May Paramount executives were concerning themselves as to whether Herrmann possessed the necessary working papers to conduct in England, an urgent concern, since he would fly *en famille* just after midnight on 5 May, stopping over for a few days at Copenhagen's Palace Hotel (where, ten years later, Michael Armstrong and Sarah Sherman would follow!) and arriving at London Airport at 6.45 p.m. on 9 May.

By 23 April, the Covent Garden choir had been booked, as had the London Symphony and the Albert Hall for the six-day period of 26, 27, 28 and 31 May, and 5 and 6 June. Herrmann is reported by Smith to have had his 'happiest' relation with this orchestra while working on this film. During shooting breaks, he

> entertained the musicians with Hollywood anecdotes and gained their respect with his knowledge of musical minutiae – so much so that at the end of filming, the orchestra presented him with a book on the Symphony inscribed 'to Bernard Herrmann, the Man Who Knows So Much.' (1991: 198)

While non-musical filming of lobby business and audience reactions was taking place in the Albert Hall, the cantata was prerecorded with the symphony and choir (and with Barbara Howitt, selected as soloist by Herrmann on his arrival (Coleman, 1955b)) on 26 to 28 May at the Festival Hall across the river; while, on 31 May and 5 and 6 June, filming with all forces took place in the Albert Hall with the prerecording in use for synchronising the action (Selby, 1955). The production utilised a Westrex magnetic film recorder channel for turning in interlock with the Technicolor VistaVision camera. Vernon Duker, a colleague of Benjamin's, reported to me that he was present at some of the Albert Hall filming and that for some shots not including Herrmann the musical forces were conducted by Richard Arnell. The cantata as we see it onscreen in the film, and in 'performance' at the Albert Hall, is occasionally rendered through a de facto 'pantomime', the 'orchestra and choir under the baton of Herrmann' being in fact the 'orchestra and choir under the baton of Arnell' (Duker, 1995). Live sound recording was not part of the Albert Hall production. Interestingly, then, although we do see Herrmann on the podium at the Albert Hall (Figure 6.2), and the London Symphony and Covent Garden choir devotedly working away under his beat (factoti of the villain, per Brown), the sound that we hear is not completely the result of his conducting

Figure 6.2 *The Man Who Knew Too Much* (1956, Dir: Alfred Hitchcock). Herrmann conducts the LSO in the film (Paramount Pictures/Filwite Productions).

at all. His orchestrational contributions will be undetectable to most listeners, even as his physical presence on the podium would be invisible for those not accustomed to finding him in a crowd and those who did not trouble to read the poster advertising the concert and his role, as Jo made her way into the Hall. Let us say that Herrmann's work in respect of the Benjamin cantata is modest, while, of course, diegetically it is very significant indeed – as is that of the many supporting players viewers do not identify but who culture the film ineradicably. Notably, as many commentators have mentioned, there is no other sound during the cantata performance at all, save, of course, one sound; and indeed Brown quotes Jimmy Stewart's recollection that a dialogue scene between Doris Day and himself was cancelled by Hitchcock, who told them to 'act out' the scene so that his enjoyment of the music would not be interrupted (Brown, 1994: 79).

Herrmann was also disconnected from the composition, scoring, rehearsal and recording of the two Jay Livingston/Ray Evans songs, 'Que Sera, Sera' and 'We'll Love Again', which bracket the action of the film and form a central emotional foundation for the narrative development of the McKenna family. These two songs, positive epitomes of the kind of pop, casual, unreflected music that Herrmann saw as beneath his station, occupy between them a startling nine minutes and twenty-five seconds of screen time (even more, then, than *Storm Clouds*), with the 'Que Sera, Sera' reprise at the Embassy – as the camera moves outside the salon, up the marble stairs, and into the heart of darkness – constituting one of the great set pieces of Hitchcockian cinema (see Pomerance, 2011). If Herrmann didn't write these pop tunes (just as, when *Torn Curtain* came around, he wouldn't write one again),[7] he did have to put up with Hitchcock's desire to have them, and by all accounts he behaved amenably and graciously, notwithstanding that his name would appear in the credits as the scorer of the film and that Coleman's earlier request for his approval of the cantata and song lyrics was a clear indication that Herrmann was regarded as the music director (Coleman, 1955a).

Responsibility fell to Herrmann for composing twenty-one minutes and thirty-five seconds of cues, notably less music than would constitute his typical contribution to other films but work that is nevertheless invariably striking, effective and beautiful as musical composition. Some of the Herrmann composition for this film is eccentric in the extreme: I refer to three Arab trios, scored for chamber group and played onscreen in excerpt at various moments during the Moroccan restaurant scene. David Cooper notes that cultural reference is provided here by a 'portamento string technique and an Arab-sounding mode' (2001: 63). One can go further about this 'Arab sound', I think, by pointing to the distinctly *volkisch* Semitic minor key and the use of accidentals reminiscent of klezmer songs. But even Jewish-born Benny Herrmann had always been at a distance from the popular. His Russian-immigrant father was a *culturatus*, and exposed him from his youngest days to high art.

> 'My father was always insistent that we be aware of the adventures that lie before us and that art could fulfil our lives to a larger degree than life itself,' Benny's brother Louis said, 'We were taken to operas and museums at a very early age – perhaps too early, but who can say? We did not grow up in a permissive attitude. We understood that discipline and obedience were part of the ritual of growing up.' (quoted in Smith, 1991: 11)

In these string compositions one hears a very tight, economical, 'obedient' harmony, and an elegance is derived – even for this background music – through spareness of melodic invention and ornamentation: the music is flavoured 'Middle East' but structured 'Bartók'. A certain patina of verisimilitude is provided to these 'chamber music' cues through their placement: they are preceded by five cues – ranging from eight seconds to a minute and a half – of traditional, sharply rhythmic native music (one by Herrmann, eight lifted from authentic recordings in the Paramount Music Department library) wafting through Marrakech's busy Place Djemaa el Fna as the McKennas' bus arrives from Casablanca; and they are followed by four more traditional cues, ranging from fifteen seconds to two minutes and nine seconds, of similar native music in the marketplace as little Hank is taken by Lucy Drayton to hear the teller of tales (a real figure discovered and filmed on location) and Ben and Jo wander off to argue about how many children they might have. Against the mix of rudimentary, slightly whiny native instrumentals and crowd noise, the plaintively lovely Herrmann compositions in the restaurant scene seem generic and focused and pure.

After his fanfare opening credit music, the principal Herrmann cues for the film include all of the following:

(a) 'Nocturne' (2:42), beginning after Jo and Hank sing 'Que Sera, Sera', when Louis Bernard leads Jo on to the twilit balcony of the hotel suite at the Mamounia to have 'the pleasuring of serving [her] a drink' and enquire

whether she was ever on the American stage, and ending when the mysterious stranger (Reggie Nalder) shows himself at the hotel room door. This
cue has a lulling quality, while at the same time moving eerily up and down
semitones in a harmonic arrangement that suggests tentativeness, emptiness,
anticipation. A music note (undated) dictated by Hitchcock indicates, 'Benny
to consider musical motif for the Assassin. In bedroom scene – Mamounia
Hotel – Assassin coming to door of McKenna suite – we have deliberately left
out any comment on him by the McKennas so that musically we can make a
point about the mysterious reaction of Louis Bernard to this intrusion.' The
balcony moment is enriched by a wondering clarinet, with a tidal breathing
in the woodwinds beneath, as Jo walks across the room and opens the door
to find the cultivated French gentleman we will later meet again with a gun
in his hand.

(b) 'The Chase' (1:03), a frenetic percussive tattoo with a bass clarinet overlaying
    long ominous notes as the police pursue a stranger through the marketplace
    and he receives a knife in the centre of his back. This segues directly into:

(c) 'The Knife' (0:56), shrill piercing trumpet syncopations counterpointed by
    sustained notes in the bass woodwinds as the victim stumbles rightward
    across the front of the screen and heads into the marketplace (the dagger and
    the river of scarlet bleeding it has produced situated neatly between two ver-
    tical rows of indigo dye streaming down his back), falls into Ben McKenna's
    arms, reveals himself as Louis Bernard, and begins whispering that haunting
    mantra, 'A man – a statesman – is to be killed – assassinated – in London –
    soon – very soon. Tell them – in London – Ambrose – Chappell.'

(d) 'Louis Bernard's Death' (0:28), with sustained descending bass notes in the
    strings and bass clarinets as Bernard's helpless indigo-stained hand slips from
    Ben's neck and he expires.

(e) 'The Warning' (0:24), a troubled violin passage, picking its way up and
    down through a treacherous territory of sorts and backed up by hauntingly
    obscure organ chords, as Ben concludes his mysterious telephone call at
    the Commisariat, with the unknown voice commanding, 'Remember! Say
    nothing!'

(f) 'The Alley' (1:12), as Ben watches the man he thinks is Ambrose Chappell
    disappearing under the taxidermy sign in Camden Town and follows him. The
    movement is down a slender alley lined by red-brick walls, and Hitchcock's
    camera takes Stewart's place moving forward. Originating with eerie sus-
    tained descending half-tones in flutes (and prefiguring the opening title music
    Herrmann would later compose for Truffaut's *Fahrenheit 451*, where the chro-
    matic movement is reversed), the cue proceeds with a reprise of the morbidly
    ascending four-note theme from the opening prelude.

(g) 'A Close Call' (0:42), as the real Ambrose Chappell comes out of his office and
    there is a *scherzo* skirmish in the taxidermy shop, ending with the gazing head
    of an observant lion on the wall.

(h) and (i) two brief cues both marked 'Ambrose Chapel' (0:12 and 0:11) as we
    see Jo looking at the outside of the chapel and, back at the Savoy, her guests

surmise that something is 'wrong'. Descending sustained notes in the bass clarinets and subtle pizzicato strings.

(j) 'The Chapel' (1:42), which runs from Jo waiting outside in front to Lucy Drayton inside, adjusting the hymn board and then moving upstairs to check on Hank – Royal Brown notes that this descending four-note motif in D minor – B flat – A – A flat – E – 'strongly resembles' passages from *North by Northwest* and is reused note for note in the *Vertigo* nightmare sequence (1994: 156–7; see also Cooper, 2001: 127).

(k) 'Exit' (0:53) as the assassin leaves the chapel from the rear and is driven away and we hear, as Brown describes it, a 'more dramatic' version of the 'Chapel' cue (1994: 157). The 'drama' emanates from a sharply interfering minor chord *sforzando* in strings.

(l) 'The Fight' (0:16), an *agitato* double-tempo brass variation of the opening credit theme, becoming breathless as the chauffeur comes downstairs at the chapel and tangles with Ben. This ends on a high sustained note as Ben is coshed.

(m) 'Arrival and Embassy' (0.14) as Jo emerges from the phone booth and we see the front doors of the chapel tightly locked. When the police arrive and join Jo outside, there are hopefully rising phrases from muted brass.

(n) Another cue marked 'Arrival and Embassy' (3:49), as we move to the (unidentified) embassy and workers are evacuated from the kitchen. Involving winds with string sostenuto beneath, only the first part of this cue is used in the final cut.

(o) 'Embassy Hall' (0.44) as Drayton and his wife wait anxiously in the lobby of the embassy and then Drayton confesses his failure to the Ambassador: 'Something very unusual happened.' Sustained low notes in celli and basses with syncopated violin and viola pizzicato, creating a sense of tension and time racing.

(p) The sixteen-second 'Finale', as Ben, Jo and Hank come back to the Savoy together and wrap the picture, this made emphatic by the repetition from the opening credit theme but with conclusive amplification of the timpani beats.

In addition to all of these cues composed especially for placement in the film, we hear three (more or less identical) versions of an excerpt from the cantata being used as a rehearsal cue for the assassin. The importance of this rehearsal scene cannot be overstressed, nor can that of the repeated musical excerpts, which build anticipation, involvement and a hint of mystery. Not only the intending shooter but the film viewer as well waits patiently to learn the music – a brilliant dramaturgical device for winding us into the action and affiliating us with the nefarious forces bent on producing murder. If the cymbal crash is intended to 'cover' the assassination, we are put in a position to anticipate it, and thus primed to be 'looking forward' to the killing. As well, of course, we are now sufficiently 'educated' that the specific photography of the cantata sequence has double meaning: a drama is being played out in its own right, but we are marshalling and measuring it bar by bar, because not just dramatically but also musically we know the point to which it is heading. History predicts itself.

Acoustically, then, *The Man Who Knew Too Much* is a kind of temporal quilt, utilising Herrmann's often aching cues, some of which exhibit his typical penchant for using brass choir and emphatic percussion; naturalised local sounds, such as the call of a muezzin or the native music in the marketplace or the sound of Ben ringing the church bell; very sophisticated and formalised symphonic composition, such as the Benjamin cantata and the opening Prelude and concluding Finale composed by Herrmann to work in harmonic association with it (both the Prelude and Finale being self-consciously serious and symphonic in form and orchestration); popular songs, performed in both cabaret and unprofessional, everyday style; artfully composed Moroccan chamber music and native chanting; and artfully placed silence (as 'heard' in Bernard's final, gasping warning). Beyond all this, there are startling acoustic punctuations – much in the style of Stravinsky, yet accomplished by Hitchcock and the editor, George Tomasini, not Herrmann, as we hear with Jo's scream at the Albert Hall and the audience response. The often tempestuous and outspoken Bernard Herrmann is here drawn away from solo composition into a happy, and very beautiful, compliance with Hitchcock's needs. With his skilled cue composition, musical arrangement and orchestration, he becomes for Hitchcock a paragon of helpfulness and loyalty – this in the face of his having already by this time composed twenty motion pictures, including some frequently cited as significant examples of brilliance in the field: *Citizen Kane* (1941), *Hangover Square*, *The Ghost and Mrs Muir* (1947), *On Dangerous Ground* (1951), *The Snows of Kilimanjaro* (1952), *Beneath the 12-Mile Reef* (1953) and *The Egyptian* (1954), to name some. With *The Man Who Knew Too Much* he becomes very much a man behind the scenes, his every move artful, his every sound tragic.

Notes

1 Donald Spoto confirmed to Ken Mogg that Peggy Robertson had told him this story directly, adding, 'She was there. She saw it with her own blue eyes.' Mogg confirmed it to me (personal communication).
2 I am grateful to Jamie Thompson for help in interpreting the score here.
3 In which a case is made for Hitchcock linking his visions to Herrmann's orchestration of Benjamin on a bar-by-bar basis, not just for 'certain events'.
4 An effect Hitchcock would render explicitly at Prairie Stop 41 in *North by Northwest*.
5 During post-production of *Marnie*, the brothers Dick and Donald K. Harris were brought in for music editing work.
6 Excepting, of course, the final chords, to play which the orchestra members appear entirely unwilling in the face of the catastrophe in the Hall.
7 The songwriter Diane Lampert went to some trouble expressing her desire that he use a lyric she had written over his exit music for *Taxi Driver*, intending it for Norma Herrmann to sing: 'Your music is not ordinary and if an ordinary conventional lyric is put to it how do you expect to grab the audience as they are walking out over the end credits.' One verse: 'Pumpkin soft inside/ Under a skin you hide/ You open your heart too wide' (Lampert, 1975). One month afterwards, with Herrmann now deceased, Lampert wrote to Norma, 'Perhaps Scorsese is someone to get this idea off the ground. We could

approach London Records, as they would have the most to gain financially, this being a great promotion for their albums … [Scorsese] said Benny did not give him a copy of the lyric, but must have given it to the music dept. So I sent him a copy' (Lampert, 1976).

References

Note: AH = Alfred Hitchcock Collection, Margaret Herrick Library, Academy of Motion Picture Arts and Sciences, Beverly Hills.

Benjamin, Arthur (1955), Letter to Roy Fjastad, 25 February 1955, *Man Who Knew Too Much* music file 390, AH.

Brown, Royal S. (1982), 'Herrmann, Hitchcock, and the Music of the Irrational', *Cinema Journal* 21(2): 14–49.

Brown, Royal S. (1994), *Overtones and Undertones: Reading Film Music.* Berkeley: University of California Press.

Caffey, Frank (1955), Night wire to Richard Mealand, 3 May 1955, re Bernard Herrmann's work permit for English recording, *Man Who Knew Too Much* music file 390, AH.

Coleman, Herbert (1955a), Letter to Bernard Herrmann, 18 April 1955, re lyrics of the 'Storm Cloud' cantata, *Man Who Knew Too Much* music file 390, AH.

Coleman, Herbert (1955b). Memorandum to Bernard Herrmann, 26 April 1955, re booking of Festival Hall and choir, *Man Who Knew Too Much* music file 390, AH.

Coleman, Herbert (1958a), Cable to Frank Caffey, 11 March 1958, re Zurich recording session for *Vertigo*, *Vertigo* music file 996, AH.

Coleman, Herbert (1958b), Unsigned letter [probably from Herbert Coleman] to Max Kimental, 31 March 1958, re string bowing, *Vertigo* music file 996, AH.

Cooper, David (2001), *Bernard Herrmann's 'Vertigo': A Film Score Handbook.* Westport, CT.: Greenwood Press.

Duker, Vernon (1995), Personal correspondence, 8 September 1995.

Fjastad, Roy (1955a), Letter to Arthur Benjamin, 11 March 1955, re cost and parts for cantata, *Man Who Knew Too Much* music file 390, AH.

Fjastad, Roy (1955b), Letter to Sidney Justin, 12 July 1955, re Bernard Herrmann work commencement, *Man Who Knew Too Much* production file 391, AH.

Hall, Barbara (2002), *An Oral History with Peggy Robertson.* Beverly Hills: Academy of Motion Picture Arts and Sciences.

Herrmann, Bernard (1965), Wire to Alfred Hitchcock, 5 November 1965, re scoring *Torn Curtain*, *Torn Curtain* music file 902, AH.

Hitchcock, Alfred (1955), Letter to James Stevens, 1 April 1955, re scoring, *The Man Who Knew Too Much* music file 390, AH.

Lampert, Diane (1975), Letter to Bernard Herrmann, 3 December 1975, re lyrics, Bernard Herrmann Collection, Davidson Library, University of California at Santa Barbara.

Lampert, Diane (1976), Letter to Norma Herrmann, 5 January 1976, re condolence, Bernard Herrmann Collection, Davidson Library, University of California at Santa Barbara.

Pomerance, Murray (2000), 'Finding Release: "Storm Clouds" and *The Man Who Knew Too Much*', in James Buhler, Caryl Flinn and David Neumeyer (eds), *Music and Cinema*, Hanover, NH: University Press of New England, pp. 207–46.

Pomerance, Murray (2005), 'Why Hides the Sun in Shame?: Ambrose Chapel and *The Man Who Knew Too Much* (1956)', *The MacGuffin*, www.labyrinth.net.au/~muffin/ambrose_chapel.html. Accessed 29 January 2014.

Pomerance, Murray (2011), 'Some Hitchcockian Shots', in Thomas Leitch and Leland Poague (eds), *A Companion to Alfred Hitchcock*, Malden, MA: Wiley-Blackwell, pp. 237–52.

Pomerance, Murray (2014), *Marnie*. London: BFI.

McGilligan, Patrick (2003), *Alfred Hitchcock: A Life in Darkness and Light*. New York: Regan.

Selby, Kay (1955), Inter-Office Communication to Herbert Coleman, 27 April 1955, re scheduling of recording, *Man Who Knew Too Much* music file 390, AH.

Smith, Steven C. (1991), *A Heart at Fire's Center: The Life and Music of Bernard Herrmann*. Berkeley: University of California Press.

Sullivan, Jack (2006), *Hitchcock's Music*. New Haven: Yale University Press.

Tiomkin, Dimitri, Wire to Alfred Hitchcock, 18 November 1965, re scoring *Torn Curtain*, *Torn Curtain* music file 900, AH.

7

On the road with Hitchcock and Herrmann: sound, music and the car journey in *Vertigo* (1958) and *Psycho* (1960)

Pasquale Iannone

Released in 1958 and 1960 respectively, *Vertigo* and *Psycho* are arguably the most famous works in the Hitchcockian oeuvre, celebrated and analysed by generations of scholars. In approaching these two canonical works, therefore, I am deeply mindful of the immense body of literature they have inspired. In terms of sound and music, the films represent the real high point of the Hitchcock–Herrmann collaboration, with both scores, though wildly different aesthetically, featuring some of the most famous pieces in the history of film music. In this chapter, I will examine two key sequences from *Vertigo* and *Psycho* – two early scenes in which the film's protagonist is shown on a car journey, scenes in which sound – in particular, Herrmann's music – contributes heavily to a depiction of troubled, unstable subjectivity.

Characters at the crossroads

It may seem that the characters of Scottie Ferguson (James Stewart) in *Vertigo* and Marion Crane (Janet Leigh) in *Psycho* share very different fates. The former film unfolds almost entirely from Scottie's point of view and he is therefore diegetically ever-present. Marion, on the other hand, famously meets a violent end 47 minutes into *Psycho*'s 108-minute running time.

While few writings on *Psycho* have read the film as a dream/nightmare from Marion's point of view, the temptation to interpret Scottie's story in such a way has been harder to resist. Charles Barr (2002: 32) has picked up on James F. Maxfield's observation that *Vertigo* can be seen as a dying man's dream in the same way as is Ambrose Bierce's 1890 short story *An Occurrence at Owl Creek Bridge* (made into a film by Robert Enrico in 1962). *Vertigo* opens with a breathless nighttime chase. Scottie and a fellow policeman are chasing a suspect over a San Francisco rooftop. Scottie slips on roof tiles and is left hanging from his fingertips. The other policeman gives up the chase to come to Scottie's aid only to fall to his death, leaving Scottie suspended. The viewer never sees

Vertigo's protagonist being rescued or even falling and surviving (unlikely, given the great height he is hanging from). There are no hospital or convalescing scenes; Hitchcock cuts to Scottie in the studio of his friend Midge (Barbara Bel Geddes), apparently near complete recovery and heading for retirement from the police force. In this segment, Scottie explains that he suffers from acrophobia ('I wake up at night seeing that man fall from the roof and I try to reach out to him'). The viewer is therefore given *some* information on Scottie's condition, but the narrative ellipsis creates uncertainty and this has in turn invited speculation on the part of critics and scholars. Indeed, even if we were to disregard the *Vertigo*-as-dying-man's-dream hypothesis, there is no doubt that *Vertigo* is an oneiric film – one man's waking dream – and, as will be discussed further in this chapter, it is Herrmann's music that contributes most to this. *Vertigo*'s Scottie is already at a crossroads in his life – diagnosis of acrophobia, impending retirement – before he is led (and *led* is very much the right word here) to a growing obsession with Madeleine.

Psycho's Marion is at a very different crossroads. At the beginning of the film, she is in bed with her lover Sam (John Gavin) during her lunch break. In *A Long Hard Look at Psycho*, Raymond Durgnat calls their discussion 'conversation and negotiation' (2002: 33) and his analysis is very useful in attempting to make sense of Marion's actions in the later car sequence. 'Even while sensually enlaced and kissing', Durgnat notes, 'Marion expresses her discontent' (2002: 33). She tells Sam that this will be the last time they meet like this – stealing a few minutes in a cheap hotel – and that they should get married. 'Yeah,' he says resignedly, 'and live with me in a storeroom behind a hardware store in Fairvale? We'll have lots of laughs. I tell you what, when I send my ex-wife alimony, you can lick the stamps.' Hitchcock's foregrounding of Sam's financial worries (not only does he have to pay alimony, but he is also paying off his late father's debts) provides the motivation for Marion to steal $40,000 from her employer. The only thing standing between her and Sam settling down together is money; in her mind, the theft solves her problems. 'It is Sam's fault that Marion steals the money, which has no importance for her' notes Robin Wood, 'it is simply a means to an end: sex, not money is the root of all evil' (1989: 143). Wood makes a crucial point here. While both Marion and *Vertigo*'s Scottie are markedly different, it is the stirring of sexual feelings that spur both to transgress. Wood points out that, in these early scenes from *Psycho*, the past has a hold on the present and the viewer 'is led gradually to a situation where present is entirely swallowed up by the past, and life finally paralyzed' (1989: 143). This is something that is even more marked in *Vertigo*; after all, what is Scottie's following of Madeleine if not a journey into the past? While *Vertigo*'s protagonist is drawn slowly and helplessly to a mysterious figure – his car appearing to glide after hers and riding on Herrmann's gently swelling, beguiling themes – for Marion, the feeling is less of helplessness and more of anxiety. While Scottie is being drawn in, Marion is rushing away; on the horizon for both, however, is a final encounter with death.

Hitchcock and the car journey

In his discussion of methods of transport in Hitchcock, Michael Walker argues that 'there are relatively few of his films in which cars are the dominant mode of transport, and these are mostly late in his career. Hitchcock's characters tend to travel quite a lot, but journeys of any length are more usually undertaken by public transport' (2005: 374). Car journeys, however, feature in one way or another in the majority of Hitchcock's films. Some of the most memorable include Cary Grant's treacherous car ride in *North by Northwest* (1959); Grant again, only this time with Grace Kelly at the wheel in *To Catch a Thief* (1955); and, in a more comic register, Bruce Dern with Barbara Harris in *Family Plot* (1976). Rarely, however, have car scenes been imbued with the same intensity as in *Vertigo* and *Psycho*.

In *Drive: Journeys Through Film, Cities and Landscapes*, Iain Borden discusses the representation of driving in film. 'The single most powerful idea attached to urban driving', he argues, 'is that cars and driving are true harbingers of democracy, creating a world where all men and women are equal, where they can go anywhere, do anything, meet anyone' (2013: 17). However, as Borden later admits, 'not all films deal with car driving in an entirely celebratory manner … the freedoms offered by the city are not without complications and contradictions' (31). In his book, Borden explores the psychological states involved in city driving under headings such as 'Signs and Signals', 'Time and Rhythms' and 'Anticipation and Mapping', and, before close analysis of the *Vertigo* and *Psycho* driving scenes themselves, I would like to briefly consider Scottie's and Marion's journeys through some of these prisms.

Borden suggests that mapping in driving 'has been primarily a cognitive activity, through which one knows the city less as an abstract map and more as a local experience' (2013: 62). The seeming 'irrationality' of Madeleine's drive, he writes, 'boosts intrigue and mystery, reducing San Francisco to a stage-set of impenetrable facades and meaningless surfaces' (62–3). While he certainly has a point here, Borden's characterisation of *Vertigo*'s San Francisco is perhaps a little precipitous. In his essay 'Alfred Hitchcock Presents San Francisco: The Master and the City by the Bay', Craig Phillips is nearer the mark when he states that San Francisco 'exists in geography both real and dream-infused' (2013: 49); after all, during the scene in question, there are several clearly identifiable locations. Borden is right when he states that 'mapping in driving is ultimately a matter of maintaining control of the city' (2013: 63), but this is something that Scottie struggles with in his initial pursuit of Madeleine, as it is she who is 'taking the lead'.

The car journey in *Psycho* takes in a wider area (the city and the freeway) but, like *Vertigo*, it blends both real and fictional locations. Marion drives from Phoenix (Arizona) to Bakersfield (California), where she sells her car, but her final destination is the (fictional) town of Fairvale, where she will meet Sam. Unlike Scottie, Marion appears to have greater agency; she knows where she's going. Borden aligns the car journey in *Psycho* with other narratives of 'reconfiguration': 'The car interior during these long drives lies in between pleasures and conflict – a place of joys, emotions and loves but also of troubles, trials and stresses, of challenges and transformation both within and without' (2013: 95). Marion's drive is 'part of a deeper journey into herself, trying to come to terms with what she has done and who she is becoming … an almost imaginary world in which the driver attempts to make some kind of sense out of a highly unreal situation' (96). Borden goes so far as to reference Greek myth in relation to Marion's drive: '[It's] like the final journey by boat across the River Styx in Greek mythology, an in-between state where Marion is almost dead herself but is yet to reach the Underworld' (96–7). If the journey in *Psycho* can be called 'a suspended interlude' (96), then the journey in *Vertigo* is a more of an overture, a scene that serves to lead Scottie (and the viewer) into Madeleine's world.

Hitchcock and Herrmann

The collaboration between Alfred Hitchcock and Bernard Herrmann is justly celebrated as one of the most effective and influential director–composer collaborations. Like the partnership between Federico Fellini and Nino Rota, or indeed Sergio Leone and Ennio Morricone, the work of one is unimaginable without the other. With filmmakers like these, there was never a question of aural wallpapering. Who can imagine scenes in Leone's *Once Upon a Time in the West* (1968) – from the first appearance of Jill (Claudia Cardinale) to the final showdown between Harmonica (Charles Bronson) and Frank (Henry Fonda) – without Morricone's music to add emotion, rhythm and so much more? In his biography of Herrmann, Steven C. Smith argues that,

> while Hitchcock's art was that of the disengaged observer looking into his own suppressed fears, Herrmann's was that of an outspoken participant whose art could be both passionately romantic and psychologically revealing. His musical idiom was the perfect accompaniment to Hitchcock's often detached images, giving them an emotional core and reinforcing thematic purpose. (Smith, 1991: 192)

It is interesting to note that, rather than anything characteristically suspenseful, the Hitchcock–Herrmann collaboration began with a comedy, 1955's *The Trouble with Harry*, a score Hitchcock considered to be Herrmann's best. 'Drolly commentative', according to Smith, '[the score] also contains passages of lyric tenderness and nostalgic beauty unique in his work with Hitchcock (the obsessive romanticism of *Vertigo* being entirely different)' (1991: 193). By the time Herrmann arrived at *Vertigo*, he had scored three Hitchcock pictures. While *The Trouble with Harry* was a dark comedy, *The Man Who Knew Too Much* (1956) was Hitchcock's remake of his own 1934 film about the kidnapping of a young child by assassins determined to prevent her parents from revealing their murderous plans. In both this film and *The Wrong Man* (1956), music becomes a strong diegetic presence. Herrmann himself appears in the latter as an orchestra conductor and the film features singing star Doris Day in one of the lead roles. In the former, Emmanuel Balestrero (Henry Fonda), a jazz musician, is falsely accused of robbery in what remains one of Hitchcock's most formally sober pictures, quasi-documentary in its approach: '[The film] has a dark Poesque claustrophobia and a Kafkaesque night-marishness in its depiction of an innocent man suddenly imprisoned by an all-powerful authority for something he didn't do and doesn't know about' (Sullivan, 2006: 209). In his instructions to his orchestra, Herrmann asked for a 'very cold and very factual approach' (207), the opposite of *Vertigo*, his next Hitchcock picture. Manny, like Scottie in *Vertigo*, is also caught in a web; he too lacks the agency of a conventional Hollywood protagonist, but his story is very different. Apart from the famous jail sequence, there are comparatively few subjective cues for *The Wrong Man*, while *Vertigo*, of course, is full of them.

On the road/'Toward the Within'

The two journey sequences in question are both of a similar length (fourteen min-utes) but are structured very differently. The scenes have been analysed before – notably by Barr (*Vertigo*) and Durgnat (*Psycho*) (both 2002) – but there is very little scholarly writing that compares and contrasts the scenes' use of sound and music.

Occurring some eighteen minutes into the film, *Vertigo*'s car sequence is struc-tured in five parts. From the point when he is seen waiting for Madeleine across from her home to his eventual return to see Midge, Scottie stops off four separate times: at a florist, at Mission Dolores and its adjacent graveyard, at the art gallery at the Palace of the Legion of Honor and finally at the McKittrick Hotel. The longest passage of driving is the first (running at just under two minutes). In his discus-sion of the scene, Barr outlines that, of its fourteen-minute duration, there are '160 separate shots, 57 of which are from Scottie's POV [point of view]' (Barr, 2002: 39). In *Psycho*, the driving passage is also fourteen minutes, but Marion only gets out three times and each individual section is longer. Hitchcock also packs more nar-rative information into each segment.

There is a minimal amount of dialogue in both driving scenes. Barr argues that Hitchcock 'continued to express an allegiance to non-dialogue aesthetics' (2002: 40) in his sound films and that, while '*Rear Window, North By Northwest* and *Psycho* have particularly lengthy non-dialogue sections ... in none of them is the pattern as systematic as in *Vertigo*' (2002: 40). This is a crucial point and differentiates *Vertigo* from *Psycho*, which has far more dialogue (both real and imagined). In narrative terms, the relative absence of dialogue in the *Vertigo* car scene is certainly not unmotivated; after all, Scottie drives alone and converses only briefly with an attendant in the gallery and the owner of the McKittrick hotel. Hitchcock allows Herrmann's music to seep to the surface, to take prec-edence over the image, very much like Leone allows Morricone a free hand in their collaborations from *A Fistful of Dollars* (1964) and beyond. While his filmmaking is a world apart from Hitchcock's, the sound aesthetics of Robert Bresson also seem to link to the methodology of Hitchcock–Herrmann in the driving scenes. In *Notes on Cinematography*, his book of aphorisms on the cin-ema, Bresson writes that 'image and sound should work together in a sort of relay', and that 'when a sound can replace an image, cut the image or neutralise it. The ear goes more toward the within, the eye toward the outer' (1977: 28). Regarding sound in Bresson's films themselves, Lindley Hanlon has noted that 'sound and the absence of sound play a fundamental role in Bresson's films, in the structuring and intensification of visual images and as an independent element of composition and signification. Sound is Bresson's most important source of narrative economy, never duplicating an image's message' (1985: 323). In essence, this is the opposite of the 'Mickey-Mousing' technique and Hanlon's phrase regarding sound as source of narrative economy is especially crucial in relation to *Vertigo* and *Psycho*. In narrative terms, what can we say actually happens in the two driving scenes? Two characters are shown driving various distances, both stopping off on various occasions. As outlined above, what becomes important in the scenes are less the physical journeys and more the psychological or mental processes and these are reflected almost entirely through sound and music.

Sullivan has pointed out that 'Scottie inhabits the Wagnerian realm of romantic passion, self-enclosed and indifferent to reality' (2006: 227) and this is undoubtedly true. Indeed, as Sullivan rightly points out, Herrmann's score is 'unabashedly Romantic, the most Wagnerian score in the movies' (2006: 223). The music used in the car scenes is, of course, not yet on the grandest scale, reflecting as it does only the beginnings of Scottie's attraction to Madeleine, his helpless bewitchment. The music swells slowly and is soft and ethereal, even ghostly.

Although Marion's car journey lasts roughly the same as Scottie's in film terms, it obviously takes place over a longer temporal span. As I have already touched upon, while Scottie is drawn *toward*, Marion is rushing away. She would therefore appear to be the more active character. She has, like Scottie, transgressed, but she has got away with her theft and, at least at the beginning of her journey, she has a greater sense of purpose. This is supported by Herrmann's own observations on the scene: 'What you actually see is a very good-looking girl driving a car. She could have been driving it to the supermarket, to her mother-in-law's, she could have been just going for a ride before going back to work' (quoted in Smith, 1991: 239). Herrmann argued that, even with the addition of subjective sound, there was no real sense of foreboding in the car sequence. Director and composer then decided to return to the music from the opening of the film. Herrmann added that 'this tells the audience, who don't know that something terrible is going to happen to the girl, that it's *got to*' (quoted in Smith, 1991: 239). Once again, as with *Vertigo*, Hitchcock allows Herrmann's music to convey his protagonist's inner reality. The composer's stark, strings-only score is radically different to the full-bodied romanticism of *Vertigo*. While the individual themes swell slowly and blend hypnotically into one another in the earlier car scene, in *Psycho*, Herrmann's music, despite being less of a presence quantitatively, jags on to the film's soundscape with greater force and insistence. While Scottie only briefly interacts with another

Figure 7.1 *Vertigo* (1958, Dir: Alfred Hitchcock). Scottie begins his pursuit of Madeleine (Alfred J. Hitchcock Productions/Universal Pictures).

character, Marion is forced into interaction with several characters including a motorcycle policeman and a car salesman, both of whose suspicions are aroused by her hastiness and apparent anxiety.

Tracking Scottie and Marion

In the first shot of *Vertigo*'s car journey, we see Scottie reading a newspaper in his car. He glances round at the apartment block across the road as Madeleine gets into her car. After starting with languid woodwind, the strings swells up gradually, following the camera's trajectory as it glides up the building. When Scottie sets off slowly after Madeleine, the woodwind again comes to the fore in an undulating pattern over a series of shot-reverse-shots of Scottie (Figure 7.1) and the road in front of him.

The music's rhythm is in tune with Scottie's state of mind (intrigued, curious) and the movement of his car (slow, smooth movements), but also with the weather. It is a sunny, crisp day – in stark contrast to the darkness and heavy rain in *Psycho*. When Madeleine takes a turn into an alleyway and comes to a halt, Scottie follows, stopping just far enough behind that he isn't noticed. She enters the side door of what we learn is a flower shop and Scottie follows. The woodwinds take on a darker hue as Scottie enters the dark backshop. The strings then swell slowly up to the famous reveal in which Hitchcock shows Scottie edging open the door into the flower shop with a horizontal wipe (left to right). The wipe is synchronised with a plaintive violin as we see Madeleine shopping for flowers. Scottie then slinks away back to his car and his tailing of Madeleine continues. The journey from the flower shop to Mission Dolores is covered in less than 40 seconds, with Hitchcock compressing time through ellipsis. Though present, the woodwinds take a back seat to the strings here and, when Scottie stops outside the Mission, eerie, insistent organ notes surface. When he enters the chapel, all other sounds are flooded out apart from the organ theme, which appears to have now become diegetic. When

Scottie comes out into the adjacent graveyard, the darkness of the chapel gives way
to the hazy, dreamlike atmosphere. 'When James Stewart follows Madeleine to the
cemetery', Hitchcock told François Truffaut, 'we gave her a dream-like, mysterious
quality by shooting through a fog filter. That gave us a green effect, like fog over
the bright sunshine' (quoted in Truffaut, 1984: 244). The accompanying romantic
melody is played on strings with the woodwind adding small pulses of mystery.
When Madeleine leaves, Scottie goes to investigate the tombstone at which she
has laid flowers. The sharp cut to the tombstone is accompanied by the sound of
three bells and ominous, low woodwind. 'Whether this fateful bang is a real bell
or Herrmann's score is deliberately ambiguous', notes Sullivan; 'bell sonorities continue ringing throughout the movie – tolling at Carlotta's grave, clanging forlornly
from the streetcar in the foggy San Francisco night' (2006: 230). The following two
driving passages – from Mission Dolores to the Legion of Honor and from there to
the McKittrick Hotel – are short and functional, with no music to accompany the
shots of Scottie and the road in front of him. There's a real sense of Madeleine's grip
on Scottie tightening and he's now becoming impatient to find out more about her.
In the scenes in the Legion of Honor gallery, we watch Scottie watch Madeleine as
she gazes at the portrait of Carlotta Valdes. Here, Herrmann introduces arguably
his most mystery-drenched cue, 'Carlotta's Portrait'. The camera assumes Scottie's
point of view as it draws into the small bouquet of flowers beside Madeleine and
then up to Carlotta in the painting, who holds the same bouquet. Hitchcock cuts
back to Scottie and then we get another point of view, this time drawing into the
back of Madeleine's head, her hair curled up in a bun. The camera returns to the
painting and we see that Carlotta's hair is in the same style.

When Scottie arrives at the McKittrick Hotel, he watches Madeleine walk up
to the door and enter. As he approaches the hotel, Herrmann's strings darken and,
in the window of a room on the first floor, we see the blind slide up to reveal
Madeleine as she removes her jacket. The shot is a repetition of the reveal in the
florist; but where that scene used a horizontal wipe, here it is a vertical reveal. Also,
just as Herrmann synched the music with movement within the frame in the florist scene, here he uses a few ethereal vibraphone notes as the blind glides upward.
When Scottie enters, the landlady admits to a certain Carlotta Valdes staying in
the hotel, but that she hadn't been in that day. Scottie insists on seeing her room
but, as the landlady says, the room turns out to be empty. Scottie looks out the
window and sees that Madeleine's car has gone, too. The viewer is as unsettled as
Scottie; the hotel scene is the first indication that everything is not quite as it seems
in Madeleine's story.

Scottie's journey ends with him stopping briefly by her apartment block again
(he sees her car parked with the bouquet on the dashboard) and then returning to
see Midge. In these fourteen minutes of screen time, it is Herrmann's music that
has done most to give a sense of Scottie's burgeoning obsession. The shifting colours and tones of the music evoke mystery, attraction, bewitchment and something
altogether darker, too. Aside from Herrmann's music, Hitchcock does little with
the sound design to suggest Scottie's state of mind. In many ways, the soundscape

Figure 7.2 *Psycho* (1960, Dir: Alfred Hitchcock). Marion Crane drives away from the policeman (Shamley Productions/Universal Pictures).

is full, compelling and powerful enough without further embellishment. The same cannot be said for *Psycho*, where Hitchcock adds to Herrmann's brooding yet comparatively minimal, strings-only cues with Marion's 'inner voices'.

As she begins her journey from Phoenix, Marion is framed in exactly the same way as Scottie in *Vertigo* (classic frontal medium close-up at the wheel). Instead of introducing Herrmann's music immediately, however, Hitchcock introduces the first internal voice – her lover Sam. 'Marion? What in the world? What are you doing up here?' he says, ''course I'm glad to see you, I always am. What is it Marion?' As Michel Chion observes in *The Voice in Cinema*, the quality, the texture of these internal, acousmatic voices take on an unreal quality through filtering and reverb: 'How do we understand that these voices resonate "in her head" and not that they are voices calling up images of her as they talk about her? Because they conform to audio conventions that establish a sound as subjective, making it unrealistic' (1999: 52). Hitchcock's protagonist stops at a crossing and lifts her left arm to rest on her temple. In the first few seconds of the journey – manifested both 'mentally' and physically and even before Herrmann's music is introduced – we already get a sense of Marion's unease. We then get a reverse shot from her point of view looking out the windscreen as pedestrians stream by. A cut back to Marion and she is seen nervously, impatiently biting her forefinger. We then return to the pedestrians and, in chilling silence, we see Marion's boss walk past. She is taken aback and smiles nervously but another shot tells us that he has recognised her. Herrmann's strings slash on to the soundscape and establish a thumping rhythm, a reflection of Marion's heart pounding in fear. She drives away and the sharpness of the strings persists in shots of an emotionally rattled Marion. In *Psycho*, unlike the car journey in *Vertigo*, Marion's anxiety becomes more and more visible through her facial expressions as she drives (Figure 7.2). She bites her lip; her hands appear restless on the wheel; far more is relayed through the image than in *Vertigo*, where Scottie's facial expression rarely goes beyond the quizzical.

The following scene – of Marion stopped by the side of the road and her encounter with the policeman – unfolds entirely without extra-diegetic music and it is all the more effective for its use of silence; if anything, it makes the sudden surge of Herrmann's strings all the more terrifying and anxiety-inducing. 'Herrmann wrote plenty of anxiety into the score [for *Vertigo*] but also romantic passion and glimmers of light', argues Sullivan. '[In *Psycho*,] everywhere the music suggests enclosure' (2006: 256–7). Once again, the same theme re-emerges as Marion sets off, continuing as she drives and dissipating as the policeman disappears from her rear-view mirror. When Marion stops off to sell her car, a softer, more romantic *Vertigo*-esque theme is used as she walks the lot. It returns again in the ladies' room as she counts out the money.

The final part of Marion's journey features both internal voices and Herrmann's score as Hitchcock's protagonist imagines what various characters must be making of her behaviour. Durgnat has referred to the scene as 'a silent film carrying a radio play' and said that Marion's expressions serve to link image- and sound-tracks (2002: 90). She first imagines an exchange between the car salesman and the policeman. Once again the voices retain the same texture as the earlier episode: an otherworldly feel, removed from reality (for instance, there are none of the diegetic sounds one might expect from a car lot on a busy street). Then Hitchcock presents a wider range of voices, including her boss, his secretary and the client from whom Marion has stolen. At first, without it been explicitly stated – no sounds of ringing or putting down receivers, for instance – we are presented with a telephone exchange between boss and secretary, then one between boss and client, before finally coming to a face-to-face confrontation between the latter two. With this final passage, 'we're inside and outside Marion. We hear her mind, we see her face … The voices make her "interior monologue" (but not a "stream of consciousness"; they're too focused, too themed, which streams of consciousness are not)' (2002: 90). While acknowledging Chion's comments on the unrealistic nature of Marion's inner voices, Durgnat's assessment seems more convincingly nuanced: 'As the audio-scenes are in her imagination, and that's in a jumpy state, we can doubt their veracity. But their general tenor is so reasonable, plausible, probable, one can also interpret them as "realism"' (2002: 90).

When critics and historians talk of the oneiric, dreamlike quality of *Vertigo* or the stark, unsettling nature of *Psycho*, Bernard Herrmann's contribution is impossible to overestimate, a fact that Hitchcock was only too aware of, as a filmmaker who had always paid particular attention to his films' soundscapes. Indeed, as early as 1933, just a few years into the sound era, he observed that

> It is in the psychological use of music … that the great possibilities lie. It makes it possible to express the unspoken … The basis of the cinema's appeal is emotional. Music's appeal is to a great extent emotional, too. To neglect music, I think is to surrender, willfully or not, a chance of progress in filmmaking. (Hitchcock, in Gottlieb, 1995: 243–5)

On the surface, the respective car journeys of Scottie and Marion offer little in terms of conventional action, but both scenes are imbued with unease, with mystery and anxiety. As I have shown, Herrmann's music and Hitchcock's use of subjective, internal sounds play a pivotal role in charting the vicissitudes of the characters' emotions, and there can surely be no doubt that, to quote Chion, they add precious value to the image.

References

Barr, Charles (2002), *Vertigo*. London: BFI/Palgrave Macmillan.

Borden, Iain (2013), *Drive: Journeys Through Film, Cities and Landscapes*. London: Reaktion Books.

Bresson, Robert (1977), *Notes on Cinematography*. New York: Urizen Books.

Chion, Michel (1999), *The Voice in Cinema*, trans. C. Gorbman. New York: Columbia University Press.

Durgnat, Raymond (2002), *A Long Hard Look at Psycho*. London: BFI/Palgrave Macmillan.

Gottlieb, Sidney, ed. (1995), *Hitchcock on Hitchcock*. London: Faber and Faber.

Hanlon, Lindley (1985), 'Sound in Bresson's *Mouchette*', in Elisabeth Weis and John Belton (eds), *Film Sound: Theory and Practice*. New York: Columbia University Press, pp. 323–31.

Phillips, Craig (2013), 'Alfred Hitchcock Presents San Francisco: The Master and the City by the Bay', in Scott Jordan Harris (ed.), *World Film Locations: San Francisco*. London: Intellect, pp. 48–9.

Smith, Steven C. (1991), *A Heart at Fire's Center: The Life and Music of Bernard Herrmann*. Berkeley and Los Angeles: University of California Press.

Sullivan, Jack (2006), *Hitchcock's Music*. New Haven: Yale University Press.

Truffaut, François (1984), *Hitchcock by François Truffaut*. New York: Simon & Schuster.

Walker, Michael (2005), *Hitchcock's Motifs*. Amsterdam: Amsterdam University Press.

Wood, Robin (1989), *Hitchcock's Films Revisited*, New York: Columbia University Press.

8

A dance to the music of Herrmann:
a figurative dance suite

David Cooper

Prelude

My earliest encounter with the music of Bernard Herrmann was in the early 1970s, as a teenager growing up in Belfast who was interested in contemporary music and always on the lookout for the scores of new pieces I could afford to buy. I discovered by sheer chance the music for Bernard Herrmann's *Echoes* for string quartet in Tughan-Crane's music shop, a somewhat surprising piece for them to have in stock. It was some time later that I found a coupling of the work on LP with Rubbra's 2nd String Quartet played by the Amici Quartet, which the veteran critic and composer Malcolm MacDonald had reviewed in *Gramophone* in October 1967, several years before I came across it. Perhaps only half reading the sleevenotes of the record, MacDonald remarked that

> If eminently serious music seems right for the string quartet this is due partly to the conditioning of history. The number of ballets, on the other hand, written in the first place for string quartet is likely, you would think, to be a very small one. However small it may be it was in 1965 increased by one when Bernard Herrmann wrote *Echoes* (arguably a sextet? – it is for two dancers and string quartet). The echoes danced out by the two participants on stage are those of a series of nostalgic emotional remembrances; the score underlines this mood with great skill and very substantial continuity. Indeed its very concentration on variants of the one mood is perhaps a limitation as far as the work's effectiveness as a concert score is concerned. The quartet repertory, however, is surely badly in need of pieces which are something other than fully serious large-scale works; here is such a piece, and it includes many passages of real beauty into the bargain. (MacDonald, 1967: 213)

Echoes clearly owes much to Herrmann's film work and in particular has resonances with his scores for *Vertigo* (1958), *Psycho* (1960) and *Marnie* (1964). However, nowhere in this review does MacDonald mention that at the time Herrmann was one of the most significant and influential film composers in the world and arguably at the summit of his career.

If MacDonald was perhaps being deliberately coy about his knowledge of Herrmann's primary musical activity, I was simply ignorant when I first laid my hands on the score for *Echoes*. I initially presumed that Herrmann was a contemporary art-music composer and, indeed, probably a British one in the cast of Gerard Schurmann or John McCabe, given that the score was published by Novello. Such a misapprehension would, of course, be cleared up in a few milliseconds nowadays, courtesy of an internet search engine, or the indefatigable IMDb, rather than several years, as was the case for me. Clarification came somewhat later by way of conversation with a musicology Ph.D. student at the University of Leeds, and through him the discovery that Herrmann was in fact a very successful and very American film composer, albeit one who was a musical and cultural Anglophile. This may be indicative of the status of the film composer at that time.

The second aspect of my personal attraction to Herrmann's music was through my tendency towards gephyrophobia and an irrational fear of driving on long suspension bridges. I found in the Scottie of *Vertigo* a character who I could relate to through his acrophobia and height vertigo. But, more importantly, I could hear in Herrmann's music a potent ability to support the film's narrative development subtly and make manifest sonically its underlying psychological thrust without the need to resort to slavish and literal translation and therefore reduplication of the visual into the aural and musical.

I could also discern a composer who was concerned with structural unity and demonstrated Leith Stevens' pedagogical dictum that a 'score should be planned as an entity, as a complete unit so that it will have a beginning, a middle and an end'. Later in the same lecture from which this quotation is drawn from, and which was delivered at UCLA to aspiring film composers, Stevens remarked that

> this is not just haphazard writing of music to fit scenes. The score must make musical sense from one end to the other. It must develop logically and should not depart so far over the length of the picture that you lose identity with the original. (2006: 349)

The discussion thus far brings two particular issues to the fore: first, the long-standing dichotomy of the film composer as either an 'artist' or an 'artisan'; and second, the specific characteristics of Herrmann's music which encouraged Hitchcock to allow it at times to entirely dominate the aural landscape and indeed to replace dialogue entirely for significant periods. The former of these issues is addressed in detail by Bill Rosar in his extended editorial titled 'Bernard Herrmann: The Beethoven of Film Music?' in the 'Herrmann Special' edition of the *Journal of Film Music*. Rosar notes the MGM composer Herbert Stothart's prediction 'that composing for films would ... take its place as a legitimate form of art music in time' and an implication 'that it might ultimately be *the* art music of the future' (2003: 122). By contrast, the view expounded by Leonard Rosenman (the composer of, among many other films, *Rebel without a Cause* (1955) and *Fantastic Voyage* (1966)) was that 'basically it doesn't function as music, because the propulsion is not through the medium of musical ideas. The propulsion is by way of literary ideas. [I]t's almost music, but not quite' (2003: 123).[1]

A subsequently influential and oft-quoted examination of the role of music in film appeared in 1938 – the same year as Welles's infamous radio version of *The War of the Worlds*, the music for which was Herrmann's responsibility – in

Footnotes to the Film, edited by Charles Davy. A polemical chapter written by the French composer Maurice Jaubert argued that the function of music in film was:

> to deepen and prolong in us the screen's visual impressions. Its task is not to explain these impressions, but to add to them an overtone specifically different – or else film music must be content to remain perpetually redundant. Its task is not to be *expressive* by adding its sentiments to those of the characters or of the director, but to be *decorative* by uniting its own rhythmical pattern with the visual pattern woven for us on the screen. (Jaubert, 1938: 111)

In an idealistic vision of the potential score he argued with considerable passion:

> Let film music, then, free itself from all these subjective elements; let it also like the image, become realistic; let it – using means strictly musical and not dramatic – support the plastic substance of the image with an *impersonal* texture of sound, accomplishing this through a command of that mysterious alchemy of relationships which belongs to the essence of the film composer's trade. Let it, finally, make physically perceptible to us, the inner rhythm of the image, without struggling to provide a translation of its content, whether this is emotional, dramatic or poetic. (1938: 112)

And he concluded with the comment that music 'ought, like the script, the cutting, the décor and the shooting, to play its own particular part in making clear, logical, truthfully realistic that telling of a good story which is above all the function of a film' (115).

A similar tack was taken at the end of the following decade, at roughly the time Herrmann was scoring Joseph L. Mankiewicz's *The Ghost and Mrs Muir* (1947), by the Hungarian writer and film theorist Béla Balázs (who had written the libretto for Bartók's opera *Duke Bluebeard's Castle* and the scenario for his ballet *The Wooden Prince*). He noted in a chapter which examines the 'Problem of the Sound Comedy':

> Thus the sound film in its most recent development no longer seeks to illustrate the passions seen in the pictures, but to give them a parallel, different, musical expression … It is natural for music to accompany the main turning-points of the action of the film, but it need not translate its every motive into rhythm – such servile following of the action would lend the film a ballet-like or pantomime-like quality. (Balázs, 1952: 236)

Of course, one might argue that the most familiar musical gesture in Herrmann's entire film output, which accompanies the shower scene in *Psycho*, involves precisely the kind of redundancy alluded to by Jaubert and Balázs. However, such instants of very tight synchronisation between music and image in his scores are balanced by an overall tendency towards allusion rather than description that helps lay bare the image's 'inner rhythm'.

When I was invited to submit a proposal for the second volume of the innovative *Film Score Guides* series by Greenwood Press, there was no doubt in my mind that the film had to be by Hitchcock and the score by Herrmann (see Cooper, 2001). For me, *Vertigo* was the most perfect of the collaborations between these two artists and I found its subject matter of particular personal relevance. The Greenwood Press series of guides, which was subsequently taken over by Scarecrow Press, was unusual at the time, in that it provided the opportunity to study an individual film score in considerable technical musical detail, employing musicological analysis of music and examining its mode of production, as well as placing it within the broader framework of the film. It was presumed that a film score was potentially as appropriate an object of intellectual scrutiny as any autonomous musical composition, albeit that it was enmeshed within the other narrative components, and it functioned, at least in part, by means of conventional musical communicative processes. That is to say, film is a medium in which signifiers are potentially compound, whether the discrete visual and sonic elements (including music) are apparently mutually reinforcing, contradictory or neutral in their relationship.

Pas d'action

In a diary entry of January 1955, later published in his wonderfully titled book *Musician: A Hollywood Journal of Wives, Women, Writers, Lawyers, Directors, Producers and Music* (1987), the English film composer Lyn Murray (1909–89), who was born as Lionel Breeze and brought up in Barrow-in-Furness before his family moved to the United States when he was in his mid-teens, remarked that:

> Hitchcock is shooting another picture, *The Trouble with Harry*. He told me he doesn't have a composer for it yet. I now make what is probably the biggest mistake of my life. I recommend Herrmann for it. Hitch does not know Herrmann. I introduce them. (Murray, 1987: 152)

Murray, who had scored Hitchcock's *To Catch a Thief*, released in September 1955, was of course absolutely correct in his judgement about the error he had made, for the relationship between Herrmann and Hitchcock would span the period between *The Trouble with Harry* and their break-up over *Torn Curtain* eleven years later and include some of Hitchcock's most successful and iconic films. According to William H. Rosar, it was Murray who apparently suggested the use of Gounod's 'Funeral March for a Marionette' as Hitchcock's theme tune for the TV series *Alfred Hitchcock Presents*, which was first screened in 1955, and he is said to have remarked that 'Benny could make a shower curtain look like a tapestry' because of his sensitivity to timbre and orchestral colour (Rosar, personal communication).

As is very well-known, and often remarked upon, Herrmann was unusual in Hollywood because of his tendency to orchestrate his own scores. There may well have been a financial as well as artistic advantage to this – Murray reports that he was contracted for the film *Tender is the Night* (in June 1961) by 20th Century Fox for $10,000, but that Henry King had actually wanted Herrmann (Murray, 1987: 224–6). Murray was eventually pulled from the film when Herrmann persuaded executive producer David O. Selznick to take him on – in Murray's account, this involved tears from the notoriously emotional Herrmann. Selznick actually wanted a popular music theme tune of the type that Herrmann was incapable of writing and was antipathetic to, and therefore hired Sammy Fain to compose this. According to Murray, Herrmann (who had apparently tried to write a pop theme, but it was rejected) eventually agreed to the use of Fain's song and cut his normal fee of $17,500 – a level which included orchestration – to $15,000 for this film.

Hearing Herrmann's Hitchcock scores in the light of Murray's music for *To Catch a Thief* is revealing. Murray had come under the influence of Herrmann as a contractor, mentor and friend since the 1930s, when Herrmann had called on him to help with arrangements of popular music for his radio work. By 1955, Murray had scored at least nine films, many radio programmes and had made a huge number of musical arrangements, not least for his own chorus, the Lyn Murray Singers.[2] He would go on to a particularly successful television career, writing scores for TV series such as *Gun Law* (1955–75), *The Virginian* (1962–71), *Dragnet* (1951–59) and, most relevant to this chapter, at least eighteen episodes for *The Alfred Hitchcock Hour* between 1962 and 1963. Given that by this stage Herrmann had become so closely associated with Hitchcock, his contributions to this series may be indicative of some level of stylistic coherence between Murray and Herrmann: Murray's approach in *To Catch a Thief* is perhaps a little more heterogeneous than that of his sometime friend (they fell out as a result of a remark that Herrmann made about Murray's wife in June 1961), and a significant proportion is diegetic, drawing strongly on jazz and popular music, while at the same time looking to influences such as early Britten and Prokofiev. There are some quite remarkable sonorities, however, and the early montage describing the robberies and the padding of the cat over the rooftops, with its musical cross-cutting matching the visual changes and its striking use of bass flute and novachord, involves writing that suggests Herrmann at his best. Indeed, there are passages in *To Catch a Thief* that almost seem to prefigure Herrmann's score for *North by Northwest* (1959), for example, in the chase sequence eight minutes into the film, where the police pursue a car they assume to be driven by the former cat thief John Robie though it turns out that his housekeeper is actually at the wheel.

Murray was recording the score for *To Catch a Thief* at the same time that Herrmann was recording *The Trouble with Harry* (1955), he offers an interesting insight into the politics of studio life and Hitchcock's method of interaction with Paramount executives, but also about the potential of music to make more explicit the encoding of sexuality deemed unacceptable under the terms of the Motion Picture Production Code (which was notionally in force until 1968). In a journal entry for 10 March 1955, Murray remarks:

> We rescored a couple of scenes today. In the firework scene with Grant and Kelly I had [tenor sax player Georgie] Auld playing the tune in a very sensuous manner. The front office brass wanted the whole scene toned down and Hitch thought if I rescored it in a more conventional way, like with strings, he might get to keep it. Hitchcock amazes me. He has an innocuous scene where two French plainclothes policemen are staking out a villa hoping to catch the thief. It is a long shot and they are looking at what one imagines are dirty French postcards – a wry Hitchcock

touch. Don Hartman, one of the studio brass, objected and Hitch took it out. I said, 'Why would you take that out? It's charming.' He said, 'The picture doesn't stand or fall on one little shot. Besides, if I take that out they won't complain so much about the fireworks scene.' (1987: 153)

Murray had studied composition and orchestration with the pedagogue Joseph Schillinger, an expatriate Ukrainian musician and artist who influenced many composers through his franchised course published posthumously in 1946 as the *Schillinger System of Musical Composition.* His students included, most famously, George Gershwin, Benny Goodman, Oscar Levant and Glenn Miller, but also studio composers such as Leith Stevens, George Duning, Nathan van Cleave, Eddie Lawrence Manson and Fred Steiner. It appears that John Barry was an advocate of the Schillinger system (Rosar, personal communication).

Schillinger's approach was materialistic and objective – indeed, one of the media on which music was generated in his exercises was graph paper – simple arithmetical and geometrical operations and transformations being used to derive rhythmic and melodic figures. Arguably the system was, in part, a kind of analogue algorithmic music generator before the widespread development of computers, assisting the composer whose imagination was flagging to at least create significant quantities of music that was coherent if not inspired. Schillinger saw his system as being of particular advantage to the radio and television composer because of its ability to craft cues of a specific length with a strong shape. If there is a sense in which some of the music produced by Hollywood composers in the 1950s and 1960s has the character of wallpaper, this perhaps owes a little to the effect of Schillinger. That being said, it can be difficult to trace the specific influences that his method might have had on Murray, though according to Bill Rosar there are apparently some sketches from which the application of the 'system' may be inferred. The only reference I have found was in Murray's journal entry for 11 May 1955, a couple of months after completing his score for *To Catch a Thief,* in which he writes that 'I have been dipping into Schillinger again and am agonizing a piece using some of his devices. It certainly is slow work. (You have to make graphs.) Well, back to the drawing board' (1987: 156).

Now, while Herrmann had a very great enthusiasm for the American experimental tradition exemplified by composers such as Charles Ives, Carl Ruggles, Henry Cowell and Charles Seeger (a supporter of Schillinger), he seems not to have been attracted by Schillinger's 'system'. Though he often employed a protominimalist technique of repeating musical units which was well regarded by editors because it made cutting to the score an easier task, I would suggest that it is very likely that he would have regarded Schillinger's approach to melodic and harmonic writing with a certain degree of suspicion and scepticism. Nevertheless, in 1934 he conducted Oscar Levant (another Schillinger student) performing the Variations on 'I Got Rhythm', a work written by Gershwin under Schillinger's tutelage, and he greatly admired *Porgy and Bess,* also written during Gershwin's period of systematic study.

In the composer Vernon Duke's description of one aspect of Schillinger's influence on film composers, however, a close and important parallel with Herrmann can be found. He remarks that

> Schillinger pupils are without exception peerless and much-sought-after orchestrators. A score by a Schillinger pupil can be recognized not only because of its previously unexplored sonorities but also by reason of the peculiar lucidity of its texture and the effective economy of its orchestral language. These combined qualities present a truly 'integrated' image to the listener's ear. (1947: 104)

There is a common misapprehension that because many high-profile film composers do not have the time to lay out the notes in the full score, they do not consider the orchestration of their music in detail. This is, of course, far from the truth, for even in a short score composers necessarily identify much in the way of instrumentation and voicing, and there is usually a continuous dialogue between composer and orchestrator(s) in the preparation of the full score. Nevertheless, for Herrmann, the absence of such mediation meant that he was able to exert a very fine degree of control in translating his musical ideas into notation, and often find exactly the right timbre to fit the narrative situation and sonically gel with the rest of the soundtrack, allowing minimal interference during mixdown.

Murray's cue number 2B, 'Parle Anglais', from *To Catch a Thief* offers a useful demonstration of his orchestral palette and its relation to Herrmann's. His employment here of bass flute, cor anglais, low register clarinet and bass clarinets, sometimes seen as almost trademark timbres in their use by Herrmann in the Hitchcock films, can be seen as part of a more widely found sonic repository (albeit that Murray's previous working relationship with Herrmann is likely to have influenced his technique). Similarly, the seventh-based harmonies and parallel chordal voicings and progressions all betoken a common and shared musical substrate.

Pas de deux

In an interview with Ted Gilling in *Sight and Sound*, published in winter 1971–2, Herrmann considered his relationship with directors in general and with Hitchcock in particular. He offers here a significant insight:

> Nearly all the directors I've worked with had some feelings about the kind of music a picture should have, or if they didn't, the producer might. In the end, I don't think they have definite ideas. The best you can get out of a director is some of his sensitivity about collaborating with a colleague on making a film. Hitchcock, for example, is very anxious for you to tell him when you see a rough cut where you plan to use music, because if you're using music, he'll cut it differently. A scene without dialogue may seem endlessly long by itself, but appears to shorten with the music. *Psycho* has many scenes like this which seemed to take place in a few seconds, yet the sequences are quite long. The opposite happens with the shower murder, which only lasts about

ten seconds. People will tell you that it goes on for ever, but it's the intensity of the music which makes it seem so.

You always work with Hitchcock from the beginning, from the time of script. He depends on music and often photographs a scene knowing that music will complete it. If that is the case, he may eliminate dialogue completely. When we worked on *Vertigo*, he said when we came to the famous recognition scene, 'If we're going to have music, we won't have one word of dialogue; we'll just have the camera and you.' (1971–2: 38)

Unlike *To Catch a Thief*, a comparatively minor position is assigned to diegetic music in *Vertigo*. While such music tends to reinforce the 'grounding' of the narrative, Scottie's detachment from reality, a narrative premise of the film, is literally underscored. He is either intolerant of (or insensitive to) music and his inability to face reality, of which his vertigo is a symptom, is mirrored by his rejection of music in the 'real' world. His musings and sensations are encoded by Herrmann's score, and thus, rather than Scottie as Orpheus the musician (and we recall that *Vertigo* has at its roots reworkings of the themes of both Orpheus and Eurydice, and of Tristan and Isolde), this role is usurped by the composer Herrmann who sonifies him; only we, in the Elysian Fields of the cinema or living room, can hear the music through which his drama progresses, and which projects his dreams and his longings.

I would argue that, although Herrmann's score for *Vertigo* is conceived and executed very much as music for film, we can find residual traces of the influence of both music theatre and dance in his approach: it has points of reference that are operatic, and musical-dramatic methods of working that invoke ballet and more popular forms, both explicitly through the employment of rhythms derived from genres such as the waltz, tango and habanera and implicitly through the interrelations of the visual and the sonic. These elements and approaches support the filming and editing techniques that draw upon them and reinforce the narrative development in ways that are both expressive and decorative, arguably helping make perceptible the 'inner rhythm of the image' that Jaubert alluded to and provide for them what in Balázs's terms are 'a parallel, different, musical expression'.

Herrmann brought a significant and specific subsidiary layer of intertextual musical meaning to *Vertigo*, through reference to Richard Wagner, and in particular to his opera *Tristan und Isolde*, which was completed in 1859. This influence is realised on three levels, by the use of:

- an abridged Wagnerian leitmotivic technique specifically to signify Madeleine and her supposed alter-ego Carlotta Valdes
- specific melodic, harmonic, formal and textural devices that parallel those of Wagner
- thematic material that is modelled specifically on Wagner, such as the magic fire music from *Die Walküre*.

A key referential sonority in *Vertigo* that is drawn from *Tristan und Isolde* is the so-called Tristan chord, one of the most widely discussed and analysed

Figure 8.1 The first phrase of the Prelude to Act One of Richard Wagner's opera *Tristan und Isolde* (public domain).

harmonic units in Western music theory because of its influential position in the breakdown of tonality (Figure 8.1). It lies at the heart of a leitmotif that initiates the Prelude to the first act of the opera, a figure which commentators have seen to unite musical encodings of Tristan (the rising minor sixth and falling minor second connoting yearning and sorrow) and Isolde (the chromatic rise suggesting desire). The point of elision of these two sub-motifs is an ambiguous dissonant chord, which can enharmonically be read as a half-diminished seventh (F – A♭ – C♭ – E♭). When its upper note (G#/A♭) rises in the expectation of resolution, it lands very briefly on a further dissonant chord – a French sixth, which itself initially fails to resolve.

As a complete musical idea, while arguably on one level (recalling Stravinsky's dictum about the essential inexpressiveness of music) it may be an empty sign, on another it encapsulates yearning through its continual failed attempts to musically resolve. To invoke Nattiez (1993: 292–7), it is androgynous and as a single sonority it is liminal, both connecting and separating its two elements, looking forwards and backwards, Janus-like. It is also a chord type that is described by Arnold Schoenberg as 'vagrant' and, through its role in the transformation of tonality in late nineteenth- and early twentieth-century Western art music, signifies dissolution and breakdown. Remembering that Maurice Blanchot's novel *Thomas the Obscure*, another reworking of the Orpheus myth, was published in 1950, four years before Boileau and Narcejac's *D'Entre les Morts*, it can be argued that it symbolises what he might have characterised as an Orphic moment.

Wagner finds a number of different ways of 'resolving' this chord, or at least moving from it onto other harmonic units in the course of *Tristan und Isolde*. These include progressions back onto the chord itself, onto other dissonant chords, and sometimes in more conventional ways, as for example at the beginning of Act Three, during the prelude that leads to the discovery of the unconscious Tristan, where it is reoriented and is repeatedly treated to a series of underlying plagal resolutions.

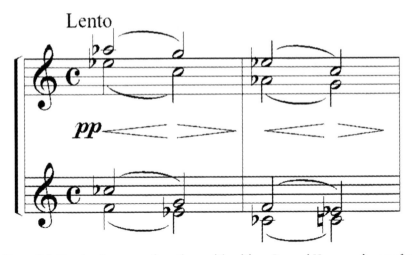

Figure 8.2 The chord sequence from the cue 'Sleep' from Bernard Herrmann's score for
Vertigo (Sony/ATV Music Publishing/Famous Music LLC).

In *Vertigo*, the half-diminished-seventh 'Tristan' chord makes its first appearance as a significant referential gesture in the sequence of musical cues called
'Sleep', 'By the Fireside' and 'Exit'. In narrative terms, Madeleine has just made her
'suicide' attempt by jumping into the sea near the Golden Gate Bridge and has
been 'rescued' by Scottie. Set in his apartment the scene opens with a four-chord
cycle involving two resolutions of the Tristan chord (enharmonically notated, but
in exactly the same configuration of pitches as employed by Wagner), alternatively
alluding to two forms of closure (first plagal, then perfect), but both ending on the
same chord of C minor, extending the chord's liminality by metaphorically achieving and undermining resolution in a cycle of descents from the musical heights to
the musical depths (Figure 8.2). We note especially the two final pairs of chords
at the culmination of the slow leftward pan taking in Madeleine's clothes hanging
out to dry in Scottie's kitchen (signifying her nakedness), the point of view of the
pan being ours, not Scottie's: the first lingering Tristan chord is heard against the
shot of Madeleine and it resolves on the midshot of Scottie; the second as he stands
to consider her confused murmuring, resolving on the shot of Madeleine lying
in bed, framed by the open doorway. This final resolution is in fact itself a transgression of the established pattern, because the closure is adjusted so that it falls
from 'bare' fifths on Eb to fifths on C, the cue simultaneously closed and left open.
Music accompanies and supports, the gazes of both Scottie as protagonist and us
as external observers: as our eyes scan across the apartment, we are fused musically with him.

Sally Silk notes that, for the French author Maurice Blanchot, 'The transgressive act essential to the inspired moment makes possible a rapport between death,
desire, and art because the desire to see the forbidden is what produces the *oeuvre*'

(1994: 540). The transgressive act is a complex in this scene's narrative: Madeleine's apparent ethical transgression, Scottie's implied sexual transgression and, arguably by the standards of the day, Hitchcock's moral transgression. The Tristan chord is itself transgressive, simultaneously opening up and closing the musical space, at once replete and empty of meaning. As such it is a highly appropriate musical structure given the themes of the film, and symbolises most powerfully the 'convergence of art, desire and death' in this 'Orphic moment'.

In 1944 Salvador Dalí developed his designs for Leonide Massine's ballet *Mad Tristan: The First Paranoiac Ballet Based on the Eternal Myth of Love and Death* (*c.* 1944) shortly before he worked on the dream sequence for Hitchcock's *Spellbound* (1945). By this stage Dalí was notorious in the USA, as a detailed biographical 'Close Up' written by Winthrop Sargeant which appeared in the 24 September 1945 edition of *Life* demonstrates. This article includes a discussion of the Wagner ballets, including *Mad Tristan*, where they are described as becoming 'the sensations of the ballet'. While Hitchcock may well have been aware of Dalí's design, I would not suggest any correspondence, other than the purely circumstantial, between it and *Vertigo*. Nevertheless there is something quite striking about Dalí's background study for the set and it curiously seems to foreshadow and summarise several of the main visual themes of the film: the vertiginous tower, the stables and the sea.

I have discussed in some detail both in my monograph on *Vertigo* (1991, 87–102) and in an article on the relation between film form and musical form published in the *Journal of Film Music* 'Herrmann Special' (2003), a twelve-minute segment from the early part of the film where Scottie sees Madeleine for the first time. In this, subsequent to his meeting with Gavin Elster, he tails her as she passes from Ernie's Restaurant to the McKittrick Hotel, with a soundtrack using Herrmann's non-diegetic score broken only by traffic noise and a brief exchange between Scottie and the art gallery attendant. This is around ten minutes of almost continuous music – built from ten discrete but related cues that together create a hybrid of double variation and rondo forms.

It is possible to construe in this sequence of scenes and series of ten cues a figurative duet (I would not be quite so crass as to describe it literally as a pas de deux) between Scottie and Madeleine/Judy in which she leads and he follows. It is ballet in which the choreography (that is, the onscreen action) is necessarily antecedent and initiatory. In a sense the music dances to the rhythm of the visuals which then appear to move to the rhythm of the music. The formal cohesion and integration of the score and the avoidance of close synchronisation with the images (except for the chiming of a bell while Scottie stands at Carlotta's grave) certainly limits any sense of pantomimic imitation, but the equal partnership between music and action (and one recalls Herrmann's comment quoted earlier, that Hitchcock 'depends on music and often photographs a scene knowing that music will complete it') prevents the score from seeming subservient or located on a 'background' level.

Two key scenes towards the end of the film draw even more literally on music as the counterpart and signifier of dance. In the scene in which Judy returns from the

Elizabeth Arden Salon, wearing the replica of Madeleine's dress from Ranshoff's store, with her hair now dyed blonde, the motif encoding Scottie's obsessional feelings for her reaches its apotheosis as a waltz – closely related to music heard in the cue 'Farewell' that appears near the end of the first half of the film – in a sequence that is matched scenographically by the turntable shot of their kiss at its climax. And in the scene mentioned by Herrmann in his *Sight and Sound* interview, Scottie's recognition that the necklace he has just helped Judy to fasten is identical to the one that appeared in Carlotta's portrait is matched by the habanera rhythm that accompanied its first appearance.

It seems significant that this same habanera rhythm, which musically encodes Carlotta in *Vertigo*, should play such a central role in the score for *Echoes*, and this returns us to the opening of this chapter and the connections drawn between the concert work, dance and film. According to the sleevenotes for the original recording, *Echoes* 'had its origins in an idea for a ballet for two dancers and string quartet' and it was later performed with the title *Ante-Room* on 9 June 1971, by the Royal Ballet Touring Company with choreography, costume design and scenography by Geoffrey Cauley. Just as several of Herrmann's scores for Hitchcock film do, it draws substantially on popular dance rhythms, and as well as the habanera we find allusions to the tango, the waltz and the barcarole, each with its chain of musical, terpsichorean and narratological associations.

George Balanchine, whose choreography for Stravinsky's ballet *Orpheus* predated the production of *Vertigo* by a decade, remarked in 1958 to the Mexican dancer and choreographer Gloria Contreras, when she was a student at the School of American Ballet in New York City and was showing him some of her work, 'Don't compose over the melody. Harmony. Rhythm. This is the atmosphere, the richness over which you should develop your inventions' (Horosko, 1996). Reversing the direction of the relationship, one might argue that Herrmann took an equivalent approach in his scoring of films and television shows for Hitchcock, his harmonic and rhythmic invention being inspired and motivated by the richness and atmosphere of the audiovisual choreography.

Notes

1 Rosar is citing an interview with Rosenman by Pat Gray in Bazelon (1975: 186–7).
2 It is an interesting side note that the Lyn Murray Singers performed in the eighth Experiment in Modern American Music, in the Christmas Day Concert of 1938, held in the Carnegie Hall, with Paul Whiteman among many others (AllMusic, n.d.).

References

AllMusic (n.d.), 'Carnegie Hall Concert: December 25, 1938 – Paul Whiteman | Credits', AllMusic. www.allmusic.com/album/carnegie-hall-concert-december-25-1938-mw0000349896/credits. Accessed 8 February 2011.

Balázs, Béla (1952), *Theory of the Film: Character and Growth of a New Art*, trans. Edith Bone. London: Denis Dobson Ltd.

Bazelon, Irwin (1975), *Knowing the Score: Notes on Film Music*. New York: Van Nostrand Reinhold.

Cooper, David (1991), *Bernard Herrmann's 'Vertigo'*. Westport: Greenwood Press.

Cooper, David (2001), *Bernard Herrmann's 'Vertigo'*. Westport, CT.: Greenwood Press.

Cooper, David (2003), 'Film Form and Musical Form in Bernard Herrmann's Score to *Vertigo*', *Journal of Film Music*, 1:2/3: 239–48.

Dalí, Salvador (*c.* 1944), *Projecte per a 'Tristany foll'*, in *Salvador Dalí: Catalogue Raisonné of Paintings (1910-1964)*, www.salvador-dali.org/cataleg_raonat/resized_imatge php?obra=580&imatge=1. Accessed 17 February 2016.

Duke, Vernon (1947), 'Gershwin, Schillinger, and Dukelsky: Some Reminiscences', *Musical Quarterly*, 33:1: 102–15.

Gilling, Ted (1971–72), 'The Colour of the Music: An Interview with Bernard Herrmann', *Sight and Sound*, 41:1: 36–9.

Horosko, Marian (1996), 'Balanchine's Guide to a Young Choreographer – Excerpts from Diary of Choreographer Gloria Contreras about Conversations with Choreographer George Balanchine', *Dance Magazine*, http://findarticles.com/p/articles/mi_m1083/is_n12_v70/ai_18905905/ Accessed 8 March 2011.

Jaubert, Maurice (1938), 'Music on the Screen', in Charles Davy (ed.), *Footnotes to the Film*. London: Lovat Dickson Ltd, pp. 101–15.

MacDonald, Malcolm (1967), 'Herrmann: Echoes for String Quartet. Rubbra: String Quartet No. 2 in E Flat Major, Op. 73', *Gramophone*, 45: 533: 213.

Murray, Lyn (1987), *Musician: A Hollywood Journal of Wives, Women, Writers, Lawyers, Directors, Producers and Music*. Secaucus: Lyle Stuart Inc.

Nattiez, Jean-Jacques (1993), *Wagner Androgyne*, trans. Stewart Spencer. Princeton: Princeton University Press.

Rosar, William H. (2003), 'Bernard Herrmann: The Beethoven of Film Music?', *Journal of Film Music*, 1:2/3: 121–51.

Silk, Sally M. (1994), 'The Orphic Moment and the Problematics of the Signified in Blanchot', *Neophilologus*, 78:4: 537–47.

Stevens, Leith (2006), 'Film Scoring: The UCLA Lectures', annotation by Mark Brill (ed.), *Journal of Film Music*, 1:4: 341–88.

9

The sound of *The Birds*[1]

Richard Allen

Having attacked people at a gas station, setting off a conflagration, birds begin to gather over Bodega Bay, accompanied by an electronic hum that sounds like the grinding of two large stones or perhaps like the wind. This electronic hum recurs at the film's conclusion, as we anxiously wait to see whether the Brenner family and Melanie Daniels (Tippi Hedren) will make their escape from their besieged homestead. Hitchcock himself described this electronic hum as a 'brooding silence' that 'should give us the feeling of a waiting mass' (Hitchcock and Truffaut, 1962). The sound epitomises the experimental quality of the soundtrack of *The Birds* (1963). The sound accompanies the birds and is caused by their presence but is not quite of the birds, at least not the natural creatures we are familiar with. It suggests their objective presence, yet evokes something alien, something larger than, or beyond, nature. Furthermore, if we follow Hitchcock's train of thought, there is a subjective aspect to this sound, as if it is coloured with anxiety and expresses the internal 'noise' that a fearful, acutely sensitive, self-consciously sentient listener might 'hear'.

It is well-known that Hitchcock did not use a conventional film score for the film, and sourced or diegetic music is heard only twice. Melanie Daniels plays Debussy's *Arabesque No. 1* when she is invited to stay at the Brenner house for dinner, and later the children at the school sing the nonsense song 'Risseldy Rosseldy' just before the birds attack. The rest of the soundtrack consists of dialogue and other human noises, and sound effects. Prominent among the sound effects are the sounds of the birds themselves, which were created on an electronic instrument called the Mixtur-Trautonium, devised and played by Oskar Sala. The Mixtur-Trautonium was a more sophisticated, 'solid state' version of an older valve instrument called the Trautonium, invented in 1929 by Sala's mentor, Friedrich Trautwein.

In this chapter, I shall explore the role of electronic sound in *The Birds*. My goal is primarily a critical one: to evaluate exactly how we are to understand the nature of Hitchcock's aesthetic experiment and to assess the role played by electronically composed sound effects in the director's overall conception of the work. For Hitchcock, stylistic innovation was always tied to technological innovation, and his readiness to use electronically composed sound effects in *The Birds* should be seen against the background of his self-conscious effort, in the wake of his criti-cal lionisation by the journal *Cahiers du cinéma*, to make a film that pushed the boundaries of his art. His embrace of electronic sound can be seen as part of the particularly open mindset with which he approached the production of the film, one that allowed for the self-conscious emulation of the strategies and techniques of Italian art cinema.[2] However, I think we should be careful not to read too much into the electronic nature of the electronically produced sounds in the film, as some critics have done, following Truffaut's widely cited remark that the sound effects function like a score. It is instructive in this context that Hitchcock did not initially intend to use an electronic score, but only decided to use it when he was contacted by Sala's collaborator, American composer Remi Gassmann, during the production of the film. Thus, I shall argue that, while Hitchcock's use of electronic sound is certainly experimental in the sense that it is pushing the boundaries of how sound is used and conceived in cinema, it is mistaken to think that Hitchcock used the electronic sound in *The Birds* primarily because it was electronic. Rather, Hitchcock enthusiastically embraced electronic sound because it allowed him to create the dense layering of sound effects that he wanted for the film, one that anticipates modern sound design. The purpose served by electronic sound in this respect is not fundamentally different from the purposes that underlie Hitchcock's approach to sound design in other works: the electronic soundtrack of *The Birds* serves to augment and enhance the representational and expressive possibilities of sound in film.

Musique concrète or sound effects, histories and contexts

On 18 April 1962, when *The Birds* was already well into production, Gassmann got in touch with Hitchcock at the suggestion of Saul Bass and advised him that the bird sounds he wished to create in the film could be made on Sala's instrument, the Mixtur-Trautonium. In 1959, Gassmann had visited Sala in his studio in Berlin and they had collaborated in writing an electronic ballet score that premiered at the Berlin Festival in 1960 and was subsequently picked up by the New York City Ballet for a new work entitled *Electronics* that premiered in 1961 (Wierzbicki, 2008: 14–15). Gassmann clearly saw the opportunity for creative collaboration on a soundtrack with a celebrated director on a major film. 'For the first time', Gassmann wrote to Hitchcock,

> We have at our disposal, through electronic generation, what has aptly been called 'the totality of the acoustical.' Familiar sounds – from common noise to music and esoteric effects – as well as an almost limitless supply of completely unfamiliar sounds, can now be electronically produced, controlled, and utilized for film pur-poses. (Gassmann, 1962a)

For a director who enthusiastically embraced new technology and approached the filmmaking process with meticulous care, the opportunity to create a soundtrack in this manner must have been immensely appealing, and at the end of the year

Bernard Herrmann, who is credited as sound consultant on *The Birds*, made a trip to Berlin, along with Hitchcock and his editor George Tomasini, in order to oversee the creation and spotting of the electronic-sound elements created on Sala's machine. James Wierzbicki's detailed research on the origins of the soundtrack makes clear that the main composer of the sounds was Sala himself, with Gassmann's role restricted to coming up with the idea, successfully pitching it to Hitchcock, and acting as the production manager for the project.

Hitchcock's innovative use of electronic sound in *The Birds* lies at the convergence of two developments in twentieth-century electronic music: *musique concrète* and electronic music. *Musique concrète*, or 'concrete music', was pioneered by composer Pierre Schaeffer, who in 1951 founded the Groupe de Recherche de Musique Concrète with the engineer Jacques Poullin and the composer and percussionist Pierre Henry at the studios of Radiodiffusion-Télévision Française (RTF). The group was dedicated both to creating musical works out of recorded sounds and to exploiting and augmenting the transformation of the source sound inherent in the recording process itself. It was Schaeffer who (following Jérôme Peignot) coined the term *acousmatique* (acousmatic), borrowing a concept from Pythagoras, to mean 'a sound that one hears without seeing the causes behind it', which was later made famous by film-sound theorist Michel Chion (Chion, 1994: 71–3; Schaeffer, 1967: 91–9). Schaeffer was interested in abstracting sounds from their sources in order that they might be heard as pure sounds. The studio initially worked with microphones, variable record players, a mixing desk, filters and mechanical reverberation devices that, carefully used, allowed a range of effects that became associated with more advanced electronic equipment: playing sound at a different speed, looping sound, extracting small sound segments and filtering that eliminates frequencies in such a way as to preserve the source sound but may render it unrecognisable as such. Tape recording added to these effects the possibility of cutting and editing, superimposition and multitrack recording. Many composers of the period, both young and established, came to work at the group's purpose-built music studio, including Olivier Messiaen, Pierre Boulez, Karlheinz Stockhausen, Edgard Varèse and Arthur Honegger (see Brindle, 1987: 99–103).

The term 'electronic music' refers not to a type of music but to music created by electronic means. The first purely electronic sound device, a forerunner of the modern synthesiser, was the theremin, invented around 1919 by Leo Theremin, which was performed by moving one's hand in the vicinity of the instrument in a manner that created not only pitches but glissandi (movement between pitches). The Ondes Martenot created in 1928 by Maurice Martenot, and widely heard in the theme to *Star Trek*, extended the principles of the theremin, allowing controlled glissandi. The original Trautonium, first exhibited in the 1930s, had a fingerboard that consisted of a resistance wire that was positioned over a metal rail marked with the chromatic scale and hooked up to a neon-tube oscillator, an electrical circuit capable of producing a repetitive signal that was in turn connected to an amplifier. By pressing the wire, the performer touched the rail, completed the circuit and created a sound. Established and emerging composers alike worked with the theremin (Dmitri Shostakovitch, Bohuslav Martinu, Percy Grainger), the Ondes Martenot (Messiaen, Arthur Honegger, Darius Milhaud, Pierre Boulez, Edgard Varèse) and the Trautonium (Paul Hindemith, Harald Genzmer, and others). A modified version of the Trautonium, the monochord, was installed in the first electronic-music studio, which was established in 1951 at the Westdeutscher Rundfunk, Cologne, under the directorship of Herbert Eimert. Its first broadcast in 1954 included compositions by Eimert himself, Henri Pousseur, Karl-Heinz Stockhausen, Karel Goeyvaerts and Paul Gredinger (see Cope, 1989: 211–18; Holmes, 1985: 28–54).[3]

Initially, the philosophy and practice of *musique concrète* were sharply distinguished from those of the proponents of electronic music in Germany. While the rationale of *musique concrète* was to abstract sounds from their sources, the aim of electronic music was to create compositions by purely electronic means. However, in practice the distinction was hard to maintain, since the sound manipulations that Schaeffer wished to make – which involved reverb, filtering, pitch manipulation and looping – were not only readily achievable but actually enhanced by electronic means, and sounds created by the manipulation of source sounds were found to be not readily discriminable from sounds created by purely electronic means. Eventually, Schaeffer incorporated electronic equipment into his studio.

As Philip Brophy (1999) points out, abstracted from the image, the organisation and layering of the sounds from the birds make them sound like a *musique concrète* composition. However, at the same time, the way in which they were created is in fact reminiscent of electronic music, as the soundtrack was not, *pace* Brophy, created by the electronic manipulation of the taped sound of birds. In his interview with Truffaut, which Hitchcock conducted during the summer of 1962, the British director speaks enthusiastically of combining natural and electronic sounds with reference to creating the noise of a truck that sounds like a human cry. The published interview suggests that is in fact what took place: 'We were really experimenting there by taking real sounds and then stylizing them so that we derived more drama from them than we normally do' (Truffaut, 1983: 296). In the recorded interview, however, it becomes clear that Hitchcock is only speaking of his hope that this will be accomplished; in the final film, while the sound and movement of the truck are arguably expressive of Lydia's anguish, the intended electronic distortion of the truck's sound to mimic a human cry is not to be heard. In the recording of the interview, Hitchcock also expresses a desire to augment electronically the natural bird sounds in the final bird attack in the attic. And the published interview seems to confirm this: 'We inserted the sound of wings, but we stylized them so as to create greater intensity' (Truffaut, 1983: 297). However, as the cue sheets in the Gassmann archive (1962b) – as well as Sala's own testimony, as uncovered by Wierzbicki – make clear, aside from the sounds of the birds in the early sequence in the pet shop, all the sounds of and made by the birds (plus certain other sound effects) were created on Sala's machine.[4] Nevertheless, it still may be possible that other sound effects used in the film were created by electronic manipulation of actual sounds in the manner that Hitchcock suggests. For example, in the sequence where the children are being pursued by the birds that seem to emanate from the same schoolhouse that the children have just left, a child turns to face the on-rushing birds and screams, her voice sounding very much as if it has been processed electronically.

Ultimately, from the standpoint of the listener, the distinction between the bird sounds being sourced electronically and their being unsourced is less important than most of them having been electronically produced so as to have a referential relationship to the presence of birds. However, any interpretation of the role of electronic sound in the film as made by or associated with the birds themselves is complicated by the fact that Hitchcock used sound in four different ways. In the first approach, electronic sound takes on the character and quality of something that, while it is associated with birds, has no clear naturalistic referent, such as the aforementioned electronic hum. In the second, not always easily distinguishable from the first, the sounds of the birds are rendered as flutters, squawks and screeches. In the third, the sound of objects that the birds strike, such as panes of glass and wooden doors, are mimed. In the fourth, electronic sound is also used to render sound effects associated with human beings. This is particularly true of the sequence portraying the massive bird attack on the Brenner house, near the conclusion of the film. Presumably because this sequence required substantial bird sound effects but had little in the way of visual special-effects work (the birds being largely offscreen), Hitchcock sent this reel (reel 12) via Gassmann to Sala to work on over the summer of 1962 prior to sending the other significant reels of film. Sala returned reel 12 to Hitchcock with an electronic rendition not only of the bird sounds and bird-associated effects but also of all the noises made by the humans beings in the sequence, most noticeably the sounds made by Mitch Brenner (Rod Taylor) as he moves logs of wood on to the fire, blocks a door with a coatstand and bangs it in with nails to prevent the birds from knocking it down.

The Birds was not the first film to use electronic instruments in crafting sound design. Composers with whom Hitchcock had worked had already used the theremin to add an eerie or discordant atmosphere to film orchestration: Franz Waxman in *Rebecca* (1939), and Miklós Rózsa in *Spellbound* (1945), *The Lost Weekend* (1945) and *The Red House* (1947). Most salient here is Bernard Herrmann's use of the theremin in *The Day the Earth Stood Still* (1951) to motivate the sound of science fiction following its use by Ferde Grofé and Kurt Neumann in their score for *Rocketship X-M* (1950). Herrmann's score for *The Day the Earth Stood Still* called for not only two high and low theremins but also an electric violin and an electric bass. For the scene in which the alien Klaatu stops electric power worldwide, Herrmann created a montage of electronic sounds. Steven Smith has revealed that, 'after recording a long cue of brass and vibra-phone dissonances, Herrmann augmented the piece with music tracks played backwards'. He then completed this sound with 'the process of oscillator testing, usually used to set studio sound levels' (Smith, 1991: 165). Furthermore, in the tradition of electronic sci-fi, the electronic soundtrack of *Forbidden Planet* (1956) is a particularly important precursor to *The Birds*. The score was written by avant-garde composers Louis and Bebe Barron, its production outsourced to their studio, and the result seamlessly combined electronic musical accompaniment with sounds that are sourced in the film (see Wierzbicki, 2005).[5] The soundtrack for *The Birds* thus belongs not only to a general history of electronic film music but, more specifically, to the established association of the electronic score with the evocation of the strange, dreamlike, exotic and discordant.

Oskar Sala went into business as a specialist composer of electronic sound effects and scores on his Trautonium, and before *The Birds* he had scored over 100 movies, including numerous industrial films and a mixed bag of feature films such as Erich Kobler's *Snow White and Red Rose* (1955), Veit Harlan's last film, *Das dritte Geschlecht* (*Bewildered Youth*, 1957), Rolf Thiele's *Das Mädchen Rosemarie* (*Rosemary*, 1958) and Fritz Lang's *Das indische Grabmal* (*The Tomb of Love*, 1959), the second instalment of his Indian epic. Gassmann thus introduced to Hitchcock someone who was very familiar with working with the medium of film and ideally suited to the task of producing a rich texture of bird sounds for the film (for a fuller list, see Davies, 1968).

Given the affinities of *The Birds'* soundtrack with *musique concrète* and Sala's background as a composer of electronic scores – as well as the fact that sounds that Sala created on his machine were used in place of a conventional score in the film – it might seem appropriate to analyse the film as providing a self-contained score. This is the motivation for Wierzbicki's ingenious breakdown of a fifty-five-second segment from the scene of the bird attack on the Brenner household, in which he organises the soundtrack into 'pure sounds' that are labelled according to their aural contours as chirps, yelps, barks, flutters, wooden knocks, strangle sounds and breaking glass, each with its own mark. He then and plots them together with volume markings and a rough ordering of pitch into something that resembles a musical stave (Wierzbicki, 2008). Of course, it is possible with sufficient abstraction to analyse any soundtrack in this way and render it as a score. Furthermore, both the complexity of the soundtrack and the electronic origins of this particular sequence render the section particularly amenable to this kind of analysis. Yet it seems to me that to conceive the soundtrack in this way as a piece of *musique concrète*, an autonomous work of pure sound design, is to denature those sounds from the context in the film within which they are to be understood; namely, one in which they largely function as sound effects, with a quite specific denotative function, and thus as sounds that possess a very different status than a sound accompaniment does. In my own analysis, I wish to acknowledge the inherently mixed nature of these sounds – the way they both function as 'aural objects' with their own sensory contours (partly indicated by musical notation), as bearers of narrative reference, and organise narrative information.

In his interview with Hitchcock, Truffaut also suggested that the soundtrack of *The Birds* functioned like a score: 'There's no music, of course, but the bird sounds are worked out like a real musical score' (Truffaut, 1983: 295). His published comments are actually a response to something that Hitchcock said during the original interview. While the gist of these remarks is reproduced in the book, they are worth quoting in full because they provide a clearer sense of the analogy

Hitchcock intended between the soundtrack of *The Birds* and a film score. Having stated that he wants Herrmann to supervise the soundtrack, Hitchcock continues:

> You often hear musicians, when they compose or they orchestrate, they talk of making sounds, which is what they really do. If you take several sections of an orchestra, and they play one note but they are all harmonizing with each other, it becomes a sound you see. Now I intend to use this sound for the whole of the picture. No music. (Gassmann, 1962a, 1962b)

At the same time, Herrmann stated that there was 'no attempt to create a score by electronic means'(Smith, 1991: 254), and it is easy to see why. The bird sounds are clearly designed to be diegetically anchored and motivated as sounds that emanate from the world of the film; they have neither conceptual nor structural independence from the story and what is taking place within it. Herrmann conceived his task as one of 'matching' the sounds created by Sala on the Trautonium to the visuals of the film, similar to the way in which Hitchcock added sound effects to all his pictures, although it is not clear how much of that 'matching' was actually carried out by Herrmann himself. At any rate, Hitchcock's analogy is thus actually quite limited. It refers to the way in which the different bird sounds are organised and synthesised in *The Birds*. In the absence of music they function as the only organised element of sound.

The one place in the film where, arguably, the sound effects of the birds actually function like a movie score is the credit sequence, but it is the exception that proves the rule (see also Brophy, 1999: 7). The electronic sounds in this sequence are distinctive because the credit sequence is a place where we would conventionally expect to hear music and instead we hear the electronically created bird sounds. They are also distinctive because of the way in which Hitchcock shoots the visuals. As the film opens, we see blue credits appear on a white background of sky, and as black shapes flit across the scene the credits seem to be pecked into oblivion. Accompanying the fluttering are echoing squawks and screeches, but they are detached from what we see, as if sound had been added to the image to create a visual montage. The Hitchcock archive contains a detailed set of instructions by the director for the soundtrack of the film, dated 23 October 1962, which describes how sound should be used. Hitchcock's notes on this sequence hint at both the 'abstraction' in the representation of the birds in this sequence and his awareness that the bird sounds here are replacing a conventional score:

> Title backgrounds as will be seen behind the titles, we have silhouetted flying birds. These will vary in size, start in very close. In fact, so close that they will almost take on abstract forms. For the electronic sounds we could try just wing noises only with a variation of volume and a variation in the expression of it in terms of rhythm. We could also consider whether we have any bird sounds such as crow or gull sounds or their electronic equivalents, or a combination of both wing and bird cry sounds.
>
> Whatever sounds we have in behind the titles the question of volume should be carefully gone into in view of the fact that we are not using any music at all. So therefore in a sense the volume is a very important factor here. (Gassmann, 1962a, 1962b: 5)

The aural orchestration of the bird attacks: three examples

In this section I shall analyse the nature and function of sound in three key bird-attack sequences from the film. In these scenes electronic and man-made sounds are densely layered and interwoven, and they illustrate a progressive escalation in the manner in which Hitchcock represents the auditory assault of the birds. Graphs provide illustrations of the soundtrack during the three bird attacks. The first graph pairing (Figures 9.1 and 9.2) illustrates the second attack on children as they leave the schoolhouse. The first attack on the children takes place at the party of Cathy Brenner (Veronica Cartwright); this second attack is a continuation and amplification of the first. The second set of graphs (Figures 9.3 and 9.4) charts the attack on Melanie, who is isolated in a glass phone booth, after the birds have caused the fire at the gas station. The third graph pair (Figures 9.5 and 9.6) depicts the attack of the birds on the Brenner homestead, where Mitch (Rod Taylor), Lydia Brenner (Jessica Tandy), Melanie, and Cathy have been holed up in preparation for their assault. In the second of each graph pairing, I have broken down the sounds into their various component parts and tracked their duration and (very roughly) their volume and pitch. In the first of each pairing, I provide an accurate guide to the sound contour of the sequences where decibel levels are measured on a comparative scale, with the loudest sound registering as 100 per cent and silence as 0. The charts are correlated with one another so that the overall sound contour of the sequence can be read in conjunction with the interrelationship and changes between the discrete sounds.

Hitchcock's written instructions for the schoolhouse attack sequence are quite precise. However, while they indicate that the sounds in the sequence are both electronic and natural, with particular reference to the natural sounds of the children singing 'Risseldy Rosseldy' preceding the bird attack, they do not make clear the relationship between the bird attacks and the sounds made by the children in the attack sequence itself. Gassmann's cue sheets indicate an electronic score only for the bird attacks, but, as I have already mentioned, some of the children's screams appear to be electronically processed and, arguably, the sound of the children's feet are also either electronically created or processed. This is not simply an academic point, because a key effect of this sequence comes from the manner in which the bird sounds are entwined and embedded with human sounds and the manner in which they are made to sound at once like human sounds and distinct from them.

These are Hitchcock's instructions:

> We should have silence with an odd flapping or two of the wings because we assume the children will tiptoe out. Suddenly we hear the running feet of the children. Immediately there is a tremendous fluttering of wings as the crows rise. In the long shot we see the crows coming over the top of the schoolhouse and for the first time we hear the distant massing electronic sounds of growing anger as they descend upon the children [this latter phrase is underlined by Gassmann in his copy of Hitchcock's notes because he obviously recognized it as a key element in the dramatic tenor of

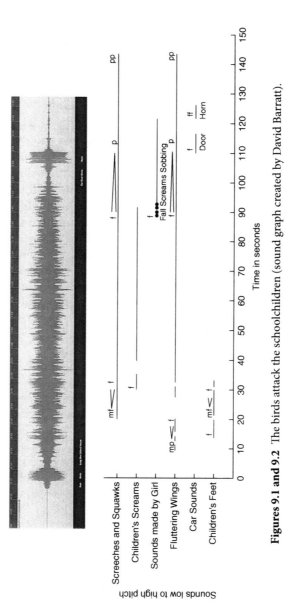

Figures 9.1 and 9.2 The birds attack the schoolchildren (sound graph created by David Barratt).

the piece]. The sound increases now for the rest of the running sequence. We hear running feet, the odd screams of the children which should not be reduced by the croaking of the crows but should be continuous, but possibly not excessive so we do not get a monotonous humdrum all the time. All this continues until the distant screams of the children are heard going down the street, while Melanie picks up Michele and hurries her across to the station wagon. Once they are inside the wagon and the window is wound up, we hear the banging and flattening of wings and the groans all around the station wagon but with a reduced volume. Finally, the croaking dies away as do the screams of the children and Melanie drops her head on the wheel in complete silence. (Gassmann, 1962a, 1962b: 5)

Although Hitchcock does not make it explicit, his insistence that we do not first see the children but hear the running of their feet followed by the flapping of wings suggests the way he is seeking to build an aural parallel or counterpoint between the birds and the children. Because we don't initially see the children, we might easily take the sound we hear to be that of the birds taking flight, since the rumbling of feet is uncannily close to the flapping of bird wings and has a similar density or aural curtain effect. Furthermore, once the sequence of pursuit unfolds, we no longer hear the children running, though we see their running feet in a number of shots. So it is as if now their running is accompanied by the fluttering of the birds, or even as if, like the birds, they are 'flying' down the hill. As the sequence unfolds, the children's screams are in dense counterpoint to the squawking of birds, rendering them birdlike. This parallel between the cries of the children and the squawks of the birds was already established in the attack on the party, where individuated children's cries and avian squawks are paralleled. In his notes on this earlier sequence, Hitchcock states: 'It will be very necessary to watch that the screams of the children and the screams of the gulls do not sound the same' (Gassmann, 1962a, 1962b: 4). Clearly, if the audience could not discern the source of the different sounds and they all blurred into a cacophony, the effect of the parallel between birds and children would be lost.

In this sequence, the aural counterpoint of squawks and screams is closely tied to the visual organisation. Medium shots taken of the birds swooping down on the children from behind are interspersed with close-ups of birds pecking at the children from the front. Hitchcock follows this montage with three paired point-of-view shots and reaction shots of the birds attacking the children. This six-shot sequence is initiated by the piercing, electronically processed scream of a girl in a green sweater, followed by a point-of-view shot of the birds, in which their fluttering looming presence is emphasised over their shrieks. It should also be noted that the relationship between bird and child is further reinforced both through the jerky movements of Melanie and the children that parallel those of the birds, sometimes in sequences that are speeded up, and through the outline of birds that supervene upon and are juxtaposed with the faces of the children. Since birdlike cries seem to also issue from the children, and since bird and child are paralleled visually in the frame, the question arises as to whether the horrific birds are not something alien to the human, to which the humans are reacting, but something that inheres within the human, of which they are a part.

Through both volume and texture, the bird sounds in this sequence are clearly horrific, and yet, compared with what is to follow, the effects of the aural assault are somewhat mitigated (Figures 9.3 and 9.4). First, from the opening of the sequence at the jungle gym, the sounds of the birds are firmly anchored in their visual representation in a way that helps to reclaim our sense of the size and scale of what we hear and to relate it to what we see. Second, while the bird sounds are intense in this sequence, the human sounds are not ceded to the sounds of the birds but compete with them as the children seek to fight the birds off, although, to be sure, the children's screams also contribute to the overall sense of chaos. Third, while the subjective experiences of the bird attacks are individuated perceptually and aurally, we are not strongly aligned with a single character during the assault and Melanie herself, the adult, still seems relatively in control. When Melanie and the two girls finally find refuge in the car and we are restricted to what Hitchcock liked to call the 'subjective viewpoint' as we look with Melanie at the birds pressing against the car window, the birds do not attack; the noise of the birds is reduced, and the sounds of the human world become differentiated from the bird sounds. Furthermore, Melanie successfully 'fights back' with sound by tooting her horn – as much a symbolic gesture that seeks to blot out the bird noise with noise from a man-made machine as a cry for help.

The competition between bird- and man-made sounds continues to be developed during the bird attack on the gas station that concludes with the assault on Melanie in the phone booth. Here there is an intensification of auditory impingement and a kind of auditory conspiracy between bird sounds and man-made sounds. The phone-booth attack commences with the celebrated overhead shot of the birds looking down on Bodega Bay that renders the world of the human so insignificant. This literal realisation of the bird's-eye view is accompanied by the extraordinary slowly pulsing low-frequency electronic hum that recurs at the film's conclusion. In fact, the hum is a constant low frequency that is overlaid by pulsing, rhythmic surges. These pulsing surges have a close affinity with other, louder, environmental sounds, many of them man-made, that serve to amplify and augment the auditory impingement upon the senses of both Melanie and the spectator: the whoosh of the flames, the whooshing jets of water from the firemen's hoses, and finally the careening out-of-control horse and cart that seem lifted directly from Hitchcock's childhood imagination or experience. In this way, in terms of the auditory landscape, high-pitched bird screeches and lower-pitched flutter curtains and whooshes now conspire with various man-made whooshes to drown out the shouts and cries of the human voice.

All of these environmental sounds are linked to an attack on Melanie Daniels's visual field. She is trapped like a bird in a cage, Hitchcock suggests, in a glass telephone booth, such that her view of the surrounding chaos serves as a surrogate for that of the cinema spectator. What might have been a source of refuge, as the car she entered in the previous sequence had been, becomes a chamber of horrors.

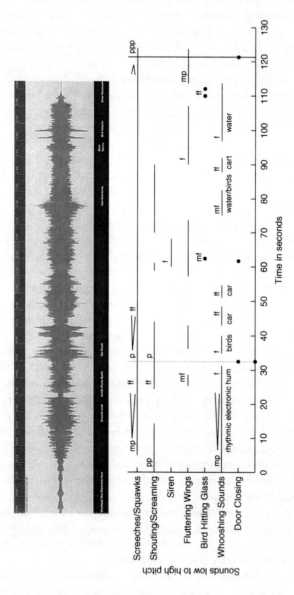

Figures 9.3 and 9.4 The birds attack Melanie in the phone booth (sound graph created by David Barratt).

She and the spectator are momentarily relieved from aural impingement as she enters the glass booth and closes the door (indicated on Figure 9.4 by the first vertical line), but this enclosure only becomes a pretext to stage a frontal assault on her senses and those of the spectator. The assault culminates in a direct attack on the phone booth registered as loud, glass-shattering thuds. Melanie, it seems, has lost the battle of sound that had scarcely begun and is saved only by Mitch, who escorts her to the silent sanctuary of the Tides Restaurant, where inhabitants cower in fear.

Hitchcock's notes on this sequence are much less detailed, but they do reveal, like his notes on the credit sequence, his concern that the volume of the soundtrack of *The Birds* be carefully proportioned and motivated relative to the spatial position and point of view of Melanie, and provide a profile and proportion to the overall arc of sound of the sequence. The volume rises when the birds appear, plateaus when Melanie seeks sanctuary, rises again when she loses that sanctuary, and finally lowers again once they reach the Tides Restaurant and the birds become quiescent.

> Before the mass of gulls appear in this high shot we should begin to hear them o.s. [offscreen], faint but the volume growing. It should start to mount as we see the gulls appear in the f.g. [foreground] of our high shot and then increase as their numbers increase. The volume should increase until our screen is covered with descending gulls. This naturally should be all electronic. When we are below on the ground, we should increase our volume much more and then once Melanie is in the phone booth we should drop it only a little, just enough so that we do not lose impact [sic] of the screams of the birds but merely make the audience conscious that Melanie is enclosed. This volume should continue until she emerges and the volume should rise again until Mitch and Melanie get into the Tides Restaurant. Then it should drop considerably so we get a sense of being cut off from the outside. (Gassmann, 1962a, 1962b: 6)

In the final attack on the Brenner house (Figures 9.5 and 9.6), the motif of aural assault, envelopment and entrapment is dramatically intensified. The Brenner house, an enclosed space, might seem less likely to be penetrated than the glass of the phone booth, and therefore less of a trap than the cage of the phone booth. However, we experience it as far more confining, for now the fluttering of wings and the screeching of birds register as an unseen enemy. In this way, characters and spectators alike are free to imagine the monstrous dimension of the gathering horde, whose entire force seems to be expressed by the impact of a single bird that crashes against the glass of the window, its thud announcing the beginning of the attack. The invisibility of the source of the sound to the characters and the viewer-listener renders it acousmatic, in Michel Chion's sense of the term, a sound that exists offscreen, lacks a visual reference and has the potential, as it does here, to seem all-enveloping and all-threatening.

As in the phone-booth sequence, we are closely aligned with Melanie and the Brenner family, who are trapped within the space, but now our emotions are also

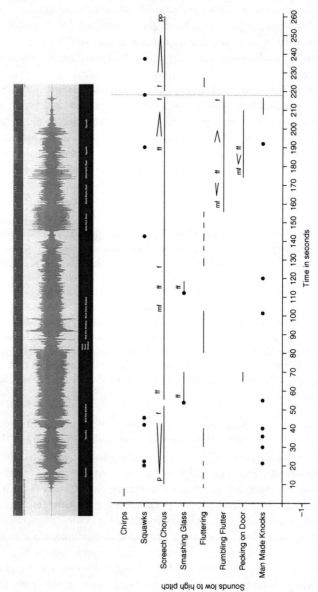

Figures 9.5 and 9.6 The birds attack the Brenner homestead (sound graph created by David Barratt).

influenced by the emotional contagion of fright and panic created among the female characters, which helps to induce feelings of fear in the viewer. Predictable gender differentiation allows Hitchcock to represent both flight and fright responses to fear. While Melanie and Lydia recoil in mute horror, Mitch responds to the first bird by slamming closed the shutter and then combating subsequent pecking attacks by hammering, even more loudly, a coatstand to the door with nails. However, here Mitch's actions create no respite from the bird attacks, with the aural assault in particular proceeding without diminution in loudness or intensity. After he shutters up the window, an intense and unnerving rumbling sound augurs a further attack, one that comes in the form of a ferociously loud pecking on the door. When Mitch blocks the door to protect Melanie from the relentless assault, his action might seem to have caused the birds' attack to abate, were it not for our suspicion that, far from being defeated by Mitch, they have been called off by a lead bird whose squawk, which seems to elicit a responding shriek, creates a momentary suspension of the sound of the birds, as a prelude to their departure.

As in the prior sequences, the aural assault crescendoes, plateaus and then abates, but in this segment the sounds that characterise the assault are more differentiated and undergo development. The initial screech of the birds changes in timbre as they approach and changes again when the assault on the house begins. The sound of shattering glass augments the grating texture of the birds' screeches. The fluttering and screeching sounds are further layered towards the conclusion of the assault, with the rhythmic pecking of the birds on wood accompanied by a low-frequency rumbling sound, which to my ear has an affinity with the sound that earlier accompanied the bird's-eye view but with a coarser-grained texture. This sound could be diegetically explained, perhaps in terms of the birds' pressing against the wood in numbers, but, again, it is really a noise that defies a straightforward diegetic explanation. Together with periodic, isolated squawks, a veritable symphony of bird sounds is created in this sequence.

The attack on the Brenner house lacks a detailed commentary from Hitchcock, presumably because the scene had been scored already by Sala and Gassmann in the 'summer dub'. One wonders, indeed, whether Hitchcock penned his detailed notes in order to wrest some control back from Sala and Gassmann, who had proved themselves so adept at creating the full soundtrack independently of his direction and supervision. The presence of the 'summer dub' undoubtedly also helps to explain the complex layering of the electronic sounds, which combine the initial summer dub with the work that Sala did at the end of the year when Hitchcock and his team came to Berlin to work on the soundtrack. Gassmann uses the term 'vocal curtain' to characterise the dense texture and blanket-like effect of the sound design, which, it should be noted, Hitchcock and his collaborators had created years before the idea of 'sound design' was applied to Walter Murch's contribution to the soundscape of *Apocalypse Now* (1979, Francis Ford Coppola).

Electronic sound and aural expressionism

There are two ways of understanding the role of electronic sound in *The Birds*: its nature as electronic noise and its use. I do not wish wholly to discount interpretation of the role of electronic sound in the film based upon its nature as electronic music. Even as the bird sounds actually mimic the squawking and fluttering of birds, there is a recognisable electronic supplement to the sounds; the hisses, squeaks and whooshes do not sound wholly naturalistic. However, as I have noted, in other places electronic sound is used just like any other sound effect in a film – for example, when electronic sound represents the birds smashing into glass or pecking at wood. Here electronic sound effectively mimics, in a manner that is precisely controlled, sounds that are more or less naturalistic, which here of course means not sounds that we actually could have heard but sounds that we expect or imagine that we would hear in such a situation. The audience of the film is clearly not intended to hear these as electronic sounds, but I do not believe the audience is intended to hear the sounds made by the birds primarily as electronic sounds either. All Hitchcock's comments on the film point to the fact that he turned to electronic sound to augment the expressive possibilities of sound creation and design. As he says in the Truffaut recordings: 'If this electronic sound means anything it's going to give an extra use of dramatic device' (Gassmann, 1962a 1962b). The main purpose of electronic sounds in *The Birds* is to be found in how those sounds are used.

Electronic sound affords amplification and intensification of the tone, timbre, and pitch of the bird noises. The screeches are high-pitched, piercing and grating, and they combine with the low-pitched sound of flutters and rumbles. All this creates an aural assault on both character and spectator that is strange, intense and unnerving. But, while the sounds are highly singular, the soundtrack also represents the birds as a force that is much bigger than what can be represented visually. The birds are small creatures combined together, but their sound renders their massification into a singular screeching unit a monstrous entity. The monstrous quality is enhanced by a detachment of sounds from images: though individuated bird screeches may occasionally be represented visually, the actual screeching of the bird mass is unrepresentable in visual terms.

At the same time, the electronic sound has an expressive function that goes beyond the intensification and sharpening of sounds to discordant and disturbing levels. Of central importance to the way we hear the sound of the birds is the pervasive echo effect that characterises their squawks and screeches. This echo effect is used quite generally to bestow a richer sound upon the electronic signal in electronically created music, but in the context of the electronic sounds of *The Birds* it takes on, together with the manipulation of volume, an expressive resonance that heightens the powerful sense of threat attached to these creatures, as if we perceive human fear or anxiety in the sound.

This expressive resonance is a function not of electronic sound per se but of the way that this sound is used, as can be seen by reflecting upon how Hitchcock achieves such an expressive use of sound in a context that is not dependent on electronic scoring. I am thinking of the celebrated scene where, unknown to Melanie, the birds gather on a jungle gym by the schoolhouse accompanied by a nursery rhyme, 'Risseldy Rosseldy', sung by the schoolchildren. We are initially introduced to the children singing as Melanie goes to warn Annie, the schoolmistress, about the possibility of a bird attack. When Melanie leaves the school and sits down in front of the jungle gym, the sound of the children's voices is rendered offscreen. In one sense, this offscreen sound takes on the musical functions of a score. Insistent repetition of the same tune, the 'mechanical' singing of the children and the repetition even of the words of the song evoke a clockwork sense of rhythm that underscores the passage of time and serves to register the suspense that is created by the relentless build-up of the birds. However, the children's voices are not a score; they are diegetic offscreen sounds. That they are relatively detached from their source and characterised by a sense of volume and an echo effect in the otherwise silent outside world creates, as Chion argues, a kind of acousmatic envelope.[6] We are focused in the scene most of all on Melanie's increasingly agitated movements – because we know, and she does not, that the birds gather behind her, her movements provide a mimetic cue for our own mounting sense of anxiety. Cutting between Melanie's agitation and the gathering of the birds, the sound of the children's voices appears to express her fear to the point where we might imagine that what is being represented here is a mental landscape, as if the song is in Melanie's head and that, in her anxiety, as it is expressed in the song, she is actually conjuring the birds into being as an external projection of that anxiety. The children's song no longer seems simply an accompaniment to the birds, but now appears to be *of* the birds, as they too become a feature of her mental landscape. Of course, this is not what is literally depicted; the birds are real enough. But the sound provides an intensely expressive psychological layer to the scene and, in doing so, it deepens the audience's sense of unease about the impending bird attack.

The electronic sounds of the birds share two important qualities with the sound in this sequence, as both feature heightened volume and, even more importantly, echo. The echo effect is relatively muted in the song 'Risseldy Rosseldy', but in the electronic sounds of the birds it is much more pronounced. The schoolhouse sequence demonstrates how Hitchcock creates this effect elsewhere in the film in two ways: he filters our perception of intensified and augmented sound through the point of view of characters in the film, in particular Melanie; and he draws our attention to the sound of the birds by placing the sound offscreen, thereby enhancing the detachment between the visual representation of the birds and the sound of them. The two strategies cohere, for to the extent that the sound emanates from offscreen while we visually focus on the reactions and responses of Melanie, the sound of the birds seems to express her fears, especially as she begins to break down under the strain of the assault.

For example, at one point during the attack on the Brenner homestead, as Mitch battles with a seagull, we view Melanie in overhead shot as she gets up from her seat and presses back against the wall in terror. In a subsequent low-angle shot, she rolls against a crushed lampshade and across a wall to a fireplace with a look of panic. Accompanying her movement are the loudly echoing screeches and scratching sounds of birds that are wholly offscreen. The bird sounds, as Mitch's action makes clear, represent an objective threat, but, as Melanie struggles mutely and helplessly in the face of this overwhelming aural assault, the sounds seem less an aspect of her objective environment than an expression of her mental anguish. Again, the point is not that they are really a mental projection but that the orchestration of Melanie's responses to the birds as we hear the sounds cues us to perceive them as laden with her emotional distress.

The mental quality that is thereby attached to the sound of the birds is a refined and naturalised version of the more overtly expressionist techniques Hitchcock experimented with earlier in his career, the most well-known of which is the celebrated knife scene in *Blackmail* (1929), where the heroine, Alice (Anny Ondra), upon hearing the word 'knife' uttered several times, begins to obsess over the word in her imagination, and the ordinary sound of the word becomes amplified and distorted in a way that expresses her psychological state. The difference in *Blackmail* is that here the subjective nature of the expressionist technique is overt and overwhelms the representation in a manner that draws attention to itself. In *The Birds*, by contrast, Hitchcock's expressionist sound techniques are seamlessly integrated into the verisimilar world of the film. The dominant idiom is representational realism, into which expressive connotation is sewn.

The visual organisation of the scenes of the bird attack at the phone booth and the Brenner house reinforce the expressionist interpretation of the sound of the birds. If the phone booth, where Melanie squirms in fear, is a cage, it is a particular kind of cage, a glass cage that allows her both to hear in slightly muted tones all hell breaking loose around her and to perceive various objects coming towards her without actually hitting her. In an obvious way, she is looking outward upon and hearing the objective world around her. But two aspects of the scene are peculiar. First, everything in the scene seems directed towards her and staged for its impact upon her, and by extension the film spectator. A runaway car and horse cart, hose water and birds all bear down upon her, as if the whole world is conspiring against her. Second, the phone booth operates as a kind of screen upon which these events are presented like pictures, thereby analogizing Melanie's point of view to that of the film spectator. Because of this screen, Melanie is able to experience these events perceptually and aurally while nonetheless not feeling the full force of their tactile reality. Like the film spectator, she is removed from the space. For these reasons, it is possible to consider the events that she witnesses as a product of her mind's eye – the transparent phone booth functioning like the membrane of her consciousness upon which the events of the world are projected. The chaotic world around her appears as a paranoid fantasy, a hallucinated world in which everything 'out there' seems to exist only for the purpose of impinging upon and threatening the self. Opening the door threatens complete chaos and Melanie's destruction until Mitch rescues her. Again, I am not arguing that this is the way in which Hitchcock wants us to understand the film; rather, that in orchestrating the scene he sews in connotations of paranoia to augment the sense of anxiety attached to the character and to the experience of the spectator.

A similar argument could be made about another enclosed structure – the Brenner house. But here the absence of any physical representations of the birds, save for the bird that breaks through a window and the beaks that attack Mitch's hand, creates a fantasy that is primarily aural in nature. I have already mentioned the idea that the sound of the birds, at the commencement of the sequence, suggests a concentrated force that is located entirely on the tip of the beak of the bird that smashes through the window, but in this context what more absurdly paranoid fantasy could one imagine? Of course, in this scene, along with a dramatisation of Melanie and Lydia's sense of psychological impingement, we have Mitch heroically fighting the birds. As we have seen, the dual protagonists in this context allow for different kinds of emotional response to fear to be represented. However, Mitch's practical, action-oriented response can be considered as no more based in reality than Melanie's paranoid anxiety. For, if indeed these creatures, imaginary and impossible in their nature, are *not* a paranoid projection, Mitch's pragmatic, stolid heroism is equally instinctive and no more effective than Melanie's catatonic response; it is at best a brief postponement of doom and might even serve to perpetuate the antagonism. If anything, it is Melanie's distinctive, perhaps characteristically 'feminine', kind of agency that saves the family. Throughout the film, Melanie has been unusually attuned to the presence of the birds, and when she hears something in the attic while the others are sleeping she exposes herself to the risk of the unknown, the risk indeed of self-annihilation, recognising perhaps that they are a force whose nature requires a different kind of response, a wholesale giving of the self that is Christ-like in character.

By abandoning the use of a traditional score, which tends to bathe the world of the film in sound when protagonists are not speaking, *The Birds* uses sound in such a way as to highlight the expressive significance of muting and silence that often last for an uncomfortably extended period of time. The muting of the human voice can often be read as expressive of human impotence in the face of the birds' assault. Melanie, shut behind the closed window of the Tides Restaurant, is unable to warn the man who is about to light a match, because her voice is muted; again, her position in relationship to what she sees doubles for that of the spectator in the film, who, in Hitchcock's own description of the suspense situation, yearns to intervene in the story and rescue a character under threat but of course cannot. In a scene commented upon by Hitchcock in his conversations with Truffaut, the hysterical Lydia Brenner is rendered mute at the sight of the birds and emotes in silence. Later, a hysterical muteness is collectively represented in the silent accusing stares at Melanie of the women who take refuge at the Tides Restaurant as the departing birds are barely audible in the background. As Elisabeth Weis points out, silence also functions more specifically to create the anxiety associated with suspense in relationship to the birds themselves (Weis, 1982: 140). At the conclusion of the phone-booth attack, the protagonists walk up to the school in silence as they observe the now quiescent birds. The children's nonsense song underscores the silence of the birds as they gather on the jungle gym. In the attack on the Brenner house, the human beings cower in silence, waiting for the birds to come. In this way, the scoring of the bird sounds without musical accompaniment helps to amplify the expressive role of silence in articulating their menace.

What, then, of the role of the electronic sounds in and of themselves? I have suggested how much is achieved by electronic sounds irrespective of their specifically electronic nature, but I do not wish to discount the representational and expressive impact of the electronic sounds themselves. As I have suggested, while we associate the electronic-made sounds with the birds, there are moments when their electronic resonance is clearly audible, and this creates an uncanny and disconcertingly alien quality to the sound that we hear. This electronic supplement bestows upon the sound of the birds what I would characterise as an intrinsically offscreen or acousmatic quality; that is, even when we see the birds, the electronic sound, though it aurally embodies their presence, cannot simply be attributed to the source that is visually represented onscreen. This contributes further to our sense of the monstrous quality of the birds, ensuring that, even when they are represented onscreen, they have a quality that goes beyond anything that could be actually represented or depicted. More specifically, this electronic resonance further augments the expressive, psychological valence of the sound. To my ears, the electronic hisses and whooshes are at their most heightened in the aforementioned scene when the cowering Melanie backs against the lampshade, evoking, at that moment, in their uncanny discordance, less an external monster than a state of mind.

The association of the birds with electronic sounds in the film gives rise to a network of interpretative meanings and associations that links the birds not to nature but to sounds associated with electronic machines. The unnatural, pervasive and insistent character of the electronic noises made by the birds connects them to something that sounds repetitive and relentless, like an electronic mechanism, something that expresses the unyielding and deadly quality of the birds. Hitchcock himself describes the menacing electronic hum that is associated with the birds as 'like an engine that's purring' (Hitchcock, quoted in Truffaut, 1983: 297). The beating of the birds' wings, especially in the final assault on Melanie in the attic, has the sonic solidity and rhythmic pulsing of a machine, like a whirling helicopter blade. The electronic nature of the soundtrack lies, as Elisabeth Weis argues, at the centre of a dense network of cross-references linking birds, machines and humans. The opening of the film overlays the bird wings with 'the almost imperceptible sound of a truck motor' (Weis, 1982: 143). And we have already noted the relationship between bird sounds and machine (or machine-made) sounds, in the assault on the phone booth. Melanie noisily swoops down like a bird to Bodega in a sports car. The sounds of screeching tyres and changing gears as she corners are visually associated with the swaying of the lovebirds in their cage. She continues her trajectory to the Brenner house in a boat accompanied by the putt-putt-putt of its noisy black engine, with which her head is uncannily doubled in the image at the moment of the first bird attack. Later in the film, the noise of Lydia's truck seems to give expression to the emotional state of Lydia upon her discovery of

Dan Fawcett's peck-marked corpse in a way that she, reduced to muteness, cannot. Thus, as Weis concludes, birds sound like machines, humans sound like birds, and machines sound like both birds and people.

Weis also notes that we may associate this monstrous and deadly mechanisation of nature with the filmmaking process itself. More precisely, it is associated with the visual and aural orchestration of the bird attacks that combines the electronic score with visual special effects. In the main, the shots depicting the bird attacks are sequences of what Hitchcock termed 'pure cinema' (cinema without dialogue), which characteristically interrupts the flow of his stories and threatens to undermine the possibility of heterosexual coupling, reproduction and futurity (see Allen, 2007: 140–63; Edelman, 1999). In *The Birds*, it is as if Hitchcock is ranging his mastery of the entire cinema machine, embodied in the relentless mechanistic avian assault, against the characters of his film. If, as Slavoj Žižek suggests, the naive or spontaneous viewer does not tend to link the attack of the birds to the psychology of the family, but awaits the onslaught of the bird attacks against 'an undifferentiated tissue of everyday incidents', then *The Birds* becomes less a film about this family, and its continuation or not, than a film that takes the conventional melodrama of family renewal and subjects that mode of storytelling itself to an act of sabotage (1992: 105–6). *The Birds*, then, appears as incipiently modernist, a work that stages the potential end of narrative cinema itself. In this context, the electronic soundtrack may be understood not only for its thematic and diegetic resonances that render bird noises machine-like (and vice versa), but also for its origins in musical modernism, with its abandonment of the octave and its relentless attack on melody, which is, as it were, the narrative of music. If the opportunity to use an electronic soundtrack came by chance, what better means could Hitchcock have had at his disposal for staging an assault upon storytelling in film?

Notes

1 Thanks to Hector Rodriguez and Steve Fore for their comments on this chapter when I presented it at the School of Creative Media, Hong Kong, and to Allen Weiss for bibliographic suggestions. I am grateful to Jack Sullivan for alerting me to the existence of Hitchcock's notes on the film and giving me access to his copy of them. Special thanks to David Barratt for creating the sound graphs for this chapter and sharing his wisdom about sound design.
2 For a detailed investigation of Hitchcock's approach to filming *The Birds*, see Krohn (2000: 236–63). On the influence of art cinema, see Allen (2013).
3 For a more technical analysis of the different forms of electronic instrument, see Davies (2002).
4 An unmarked copy of this document is also contained in the Margaret Herrick Library, Academy of Motion Pictures Arts and Sciences, Los Angeles.
5 This book provides a comprehensive history and analysis of the making of this score, as well as a survey of its precursors.
6 Chion comments on the acousmatic nature of this sound and some of its functions in *Film, A Sound Art* (2009: 165–71).

References

Allen, Richard (2007), *Hitchcock's Romantic Irony*. New York: Columbia University Press.

Allen, Richard (2013), 'Hitchcock and the Wandering Woman: The Influence of Italian Art Cinema on *The Birds*', *Hitchcock Annual* 18: 149–94.

Brindle, Reginald Smith (1987), *The New Music: The Avant-Garde Since 1945*, 2nd ed. New York: Oxford University Press.

Brophy, Philip (1999), '*The Birds*: The Triumph of Noise Over Music', www.philipbrophy. com/projects/sncnm/Birds.html. First published in Alessio Cavallaro et al. (eds), *Essays in Sound 4*, Sydney: Contemporary Sound Arts. Accessed 25 October 2013.

Chion, Michel (1994), *Audio-Vision: Sound on Screen*, trans. C. Gorbman. New York: Columbia University Press.

Chion, Michel (2009), *Film, A Sound Art*, trans. C. Gorbman. New York: Columbia University Press.

Cope, David (1989), *New Directions in Music*, 5th ed. Dubuque, IA: William C. Brown.

Davies, Hugh (1968), *International Electronic Music Catalog*. Cambridge, MA: MIT Press.

Davies, Hugh (2002), 'Electronic Instruments: Classifications and Mechanisms', in Hans Joachim Braun (ed.), *Music and Technology in the Twentieth Century*. Baltimore: Johns Hopkins University Press, pp. 43–58.

Edelman, Lee (1999), 'Hitchcock's Future', in Richard Allen and Sam Ishii-Gonzalez (eds), *Alfred Hitchcock Centenary Essays*. London: BFI, pp. 239–62.

Gassmann, Remi (1962a), Remi Gassmann papers, University of California, Irvine, box 19, folder 1, letter by Gassmann to Hitchcock, 18 April.

Gassmann, Remi (1962b), Remi Gassmann papers, University of California, Irvine, box 39, folder 1, memo by Hitchcock, 'Background Sounds for the Birds', 23 October, p. 5.

Hitchcock, Alfred and François Truffaut (1962), 'Alfred Hitchcock and François Truffaut (Aug/1962)', www.hitchcockwiki.com/wiki/Interview:_Alfred_Hitchcock_and_ François_Truffaut_(Aug/1962). Accessed 13 October 2013.

Holmes, Thomas B. (1985), *Electronic and Experimental Music*. New York: Charles Scribner's and Sons.

Krohn, Bill (2000), *Hitchcock at Work*. London: Phaidon.

Schaeffer, Pierre (1967), *Traité des objets musicaux*. Paris: Seuil.

Smith, Steven C. (1991), *A Heart at Fire's Center: The Life and Music of Bernard Herrmann*. Berkeley: University of California Press.

Truffaut, François (1983), *Hitchcock/Truffaut*. New York: Simon & Schuster.

Weis, Elisabeth (1982), *The Silent Scream: Alfred Hitchcock's Soundtrack*. Teaneck, NJ: Fairleigh Dickinson University Press.

Wierzbicki, James (2005), *Forbidden Planet*. Metuchen, NJ: Scarecrow Press.

Wierzbicki, James (2008), 'Shrieks, Flutters, Vocal Curtains: Electronic Sound/Electronic Music in Hitchcock's *The Birds*', *Music and the Moving Image* 1:2: 14–15.

Žižek, Slavoj (1992), *Looking Awry: An Introduction to Lacan Through Popular Culture*. Cambridge, MA: MIT Press.

10

Musical romanticism v. the sexual aberrations of the criminal female: *Marnie* (1964)

K. J. Donnelly

*M*arnie has an unerringly romantic orchestral score by Bernard Herrmann, which upon reflection seems slightly at odds with the film. The score's character does not quite seem to fit the film's dark heart and it is tempting to imagine that Hitchcock and Herrmann diverged to a degree in their conception of the film.[1] Upon initial release, *Marnie* was less of a success than Hitchcock's previous films, although the film's critical stature has grown since 1964 and it has come under some sustained yet contradictory critical scrutiny (McElhaney, 1999: 87).[2] Yet not for its music, however, which has received far less attention and arguably appears less celebrated than many of Herrmann's scores.

Marnie looks back to earlier Hitchcock films, and indeed in some ways it appears retrogressive. It certainly retreads some older ground. For instance, the film investigates a woman (like *Vertigo* (1958)), contains a race track scene (like *Notorious* (1946)) and has a narrative based on the freeing of a suppressed memory (like *Spellbound* (1945)). After the experimentation of *The Birds* (1963), *Marnie* seems strikingly static, overreliant on dialogue scenes and perhaps even traditional in aesthetic terms.[3] As for the music, it appears to mix a *Vertigo*-like romanticism with *Psycho*-style explosions from the unconscious, alongside the consistent use of a *Spellbound*-like agitato.

With the poster tagline 'A Suspenseful Sex Mystery', the film concerns a female thief who is suffering from the symptoms of a childhood trauma retained as a repressed memory. An employer victim blackmails her into marriage but sets himself to cure her of her psychotic turns and sexual frigidity. Starring Tippi Hedren and Sean Connery, much is made visually of Hedren's bleached-out beauty and vulnerability, while Connery's powerful presence includes a controversial rape scene. Hitchcock had originally wanted Grace Kelly for the title role and ended up with a very public argument on set with star Hedren. While Donald Spoto suggests that Hitchcock lost interest in the film, this appears not to be borne out (McElhaney, 2006: 88; McGilligan, 2004; Moral, 2005; Spoto, 1983: 475–6). The film espouses a Freudian explanatory framework. Marnie has problems with the colour red and storms, while distrusting men and being 'handled' by them. Her kleptomania is explained by surrogate psychoanalyst Mark as: 'If a child can't get love. It will take whatever it can.' Marnie dismisses her sexual frigidity by berating Mark: 'Oh, men. You say no to one of them and, Bingo! You're a candidate for the funny farm.' To aid his wooing of Marnie, Mark refers to a (spurious) book called *The Sexual Aberrations of the Criminal Female*. The film is far from a straightforward love story in any accepted sense of the word, despite the romantic trappings.[4] Perhaps the principal element of these trappings is the sumptuous orchestral music. Like *Marnie* more generally, Herrmann's music appears more sophisticated and nuanced with each hearing. Like the film, its complexities do not reveal themselves instantly.

Presences in and out of the film

Some address a film *and* its music – as if the latter simply is a bolt-on to an already coherent and finished object. While this notion has its fundamental problems, to a degree I want to begin from that position. What is the music's idea of the film of *Marnie*? How far does the music stand on its own? The current availability of two CDs suggests that it stands up well without the rest of the film. Is it possible to get away from the big magnet of Hitchcock's personality and 'authorship' to ascribe a notable status and agency to the film's music? The key thing to keep in mind is that the music (and music in general) is not the same as the film (and film in general). This is not a grand declaration of musical independence; merely an heuristic strategy to attempt to understand a perplexing film better.

Perhaps we can approach Hitchcock and Herrmann's relationship as personalities manifested in the film, although not simply 'reading off' the film. Hitchcock appears onscreen near the start, exiting from a hotel room. It is intriguing to think that in a similar manner Herrmann's music manifests his presence 'in the film'. During *Marnie*'s production, Herrmann was interviewed for the CBS TV programme *Telescope*, stating, 'I'm brought in at the very beginning of the idea of the film, and by the time it has gone through all its stages of being written and rewritten and the final process of photographing it, I'm so much a part of the whole thing that we've all begun to think one way' (Rosar, 2003: 143). The two formed a synergy on a remarkable series of films. Although they clearly got on extremely well for a long period, they were of markedly different character. However, by the early to mid-1960s, Hitchcock's standing was diminishing and he was becoming more obviously egotistical, while Herrmann was devastated when his wife left him (Smith, 1991: 259; Spoto, 1983).[5] In *Marnie*, if we believe Evan Hunter, Hitchcock apparently was most interested in, perhaps even obsessed with, the film's disturbing rape scene.[6] On the other hand, Herrmann appeared most interested in the fox-hunting sequence, which clearly gave him most scope of any part of the film for sustained scoring and musical development. Perhaps improbably, Hitchcock saw himself as being like an orchestral conductor, expounding the notion that a trumpet solo might be taken as the equivalent of a close-up shot and a long shot might be construed as muted orchestral accompaniment (Truffaut, 1984: 335).

Herrmann, of course, was conductor of the CBS Symphony for fifteen years and saw himself more as a conductor than composer. In the 1963 article 'On Style', Hitchcock wrote: '[Film construction] to me, it's like music. You start with your *allegro*, your *andante*, and you build up' (Hitchcock, 1995b: 298). Is this an instance of staking a claim to the most significant contribution to his films that was beyond his control? One might argue that it was his own particular conception of what music was, but we might also wonder if he confused the nature of music and the nature of film, and perhaps his own relationship to music. Nevertheless, Hitchcock was persistent in his interest in music: eight of the central protagonists in his films were supposedly musicians.

Like the more famous case with Hitchcock and Herrmann's next film, *Torn Curtain* (1966), there was a desire for a hit song as counterpart to the film.[7] We should never neglect to remember that music functions for film not only as a psychological agent (within the context of the film), but also has always been a commercial partner (for sales outside the film). By the 1960s, this was intensifying. In a 1972 lecture at the National Film Theatre in London, Herrmann declared:

> A patient goes to the doctor because he isn't well. That's what music is – music is part of helping a picture. And the patient gets well and goes back to the doctor and says, 'Well, you know I got well, but you didn't make me rich!' Today a composer must not only write a film score, he must also make everybody rich. (Herrmann, 1972, quoted in Smith, 1991: 274)

Herrmann appears to be referring to his relationship with Hitchcock and the bust-up over the 'popular beat score' he failed to deliver for *Torn Curtain*. Yet musical commerce had long hung over Hitchcock and Herrmann, much as it had the rest of the Hollywood studios. 'Que Sera, Sera' had been a massive hit from *The Man Who Knew Too Much* (1956), and even *Vertigo* had the song 'Madeleine' made from its music.[8] 1964 saw the Beatles' success in *A Hard Day's Night*. Unsurprisingly, executives were envious of a film that had gone into profit before its release due to pre-sales of the soundtrack album. While the contemporaneous *Marnie* was never going to be remotely like that, there was a desire to have a clear commercial imperative to some of the music, although it is unlikely they imagined Herrmann would produce a big hit. After all, he had never done this before. A December 1963 memo at Universal/MCA said that Hitch wanted to know some pop song composers – he was actually interested in the theme songs for advertisements (including Tareytown cigarettes and Glendale Federal's Savings and Loans) (Moral, 2005: 136), and there was pressure from Lew Wasserman, who wanted a return to Hitchcock's big 1950s thrillers as well as a big hit record promoted synergetically with the film.[9] An impressive deal for a tied-in song for the film was arranged by Universal. Nat King Cole sang on a recording and had his face on the sheet music of 'Marnie', but the song was a commercial failure (Smith, 1991: 276). Also, Decca released an album at the time of the film's release in 1964, which included some music from the film. The publicity slogan was: 'Nat the King sings the beautiful lyrics of the tune inspired by the brilliant Alfred Hitchcock production for the

Capitol Records label' (Moral, 2005: 139). The song, built on Herrmann's romantic melody from the film, was co-credited to Peter Jason and Gloria Shayne, and the words sound more Nat King Cole than Hitchcock: 'Moon and mist make rainbows in your hair. When I see your smile there's sunlight everywhere. But your world is lonely, Marnie ... Only love can save you. Please be mine. I love you Marnie. Please be mine.' The song consists of the main melody of the film's main theme (the first nine notes followed by the same a whole tone lower in pitch), but then diverges with a flourish for 'But your world'. The overt romanticism of this love song has an ambiguous relationship with the film. The song is firmly *outside* the bounds of *Marnie*, but then in some ways Herrmann's score is partly outside the film, too. Its non-diegetic status means it is outside the world depicted onscreen, it had a release on disc, and makes some sense following a musical logic rather than one solely based on the film's structure and exigencies.[10]

Score

The musical score for *Marnie* broadly corresponds with Herrmann's habitual musical style. His style regularly retained an interest in tone colour (timbre). Herrmann always did his own orchestration (and skilfully wielded the orchestra as a sonic mixing palette), although his fantasy film scores in particular were arguably overreliant on colouristic effects. His musical trademark was the use of ostinati (loops, repetitive sections), which often proved highly effective in tense sequences. However, in other instances Herrmann evinced a great sophistication with respect to music directly matching the image (although eschewing crass 'Mickey-Mousing' or direct thematic usage).

There is a schism between 'romantic music' (a particular style dominant in orchestral classical Hollywood film scores) and 'romantic' in the popular sense of 'characterised by the expression of love'.[11] However, romantic music regularly articulates and represents romantic aspects of mainstream films. *Marnie* has an extremely romantic orchestral score (in the musical sense), dominated by strings and woodwinds. This means a 'soft' sound with little brass employed, something that was uncharacteristic for many of Herrmann's scores. For the 130-minute film, 47 minutes of music was written. The score is dominated by the simple alternation of two main themes, often running in succession, while technically Herrmann's music often used short cells of musical material being 'sequenced' – quite crudely moved upwards or downwards in pitch. After a fashion, the score might be deemed 'minimalist'. William Rosar notes that,

> given the obviously self-imposed structural limitation Herrmann followed ... he was intentionally striving to make often-meager musical content more interesting and dramatically effective through his imaginative and often highly novel use of instrumental color, textures, and coloristic use of harmony. (2003: 140)

In some ways, Herrmann's score involves quite traditional 'development' of musical material: cutting down, varying motifs and harmonies. The overwhelming majority of the film's music is derived from a small amount of material (most clearly small units of melody) being put through minimal melodic variations – although its texture is varied more, perhaps. For instance, the cue called 'The Homestead' on recordings has a truncated version of a bar from the main theme – as half a bar – as its repeated basis, leading to an oboe version of the melody. Indeed, Herrmann tends to use small cells of music which are then 'sequenced' (moved upwards or downwards in pitch) and subject to statement and juxtaposition rather than melodic and harmonic development, setting up a structure of comprehensible 'compartments' of material.

Rosar (2003: 136–7) elaborates Herrmann's 'module technique', which composer and scholar Fred Steiner had discussed with Herrmann in the middle of the twentieth century. Herrmann claimed to use a specific temporal structure when writing film music, which allowed for maximum flexibility. This involved two-bar units which added together to make an eight-bar phrase, allowing for easy cutting of music to fit the requirements of the images.[12] Such an approach encourages the constant use of ostinato (loops of musical material) and repeated phrase, and yields a structure of temporal fragments rather than centring melodic or harmonic structure. According to Rosar, 'the basic pattern is obviously something Herrmann consciously employed as a kind of specialised musical form. This formula readily lent itself to symmetry, since any part of a cue was usually divisible by two' (2003: 136). This is reminiscent of later minimalism in art music. The cellular structure, based on short melodic phrases, is not conducive to lyrical melody and in many ways appears contrary to the dominant tendencies in Hollywood film music and orchestral concert hall music. In the wake of *Torn Curtain*, Lionel Newman, who had just succeeded his brother Alfred as head of music at 20th Century Fox, declared that Herrmann was 'a marvelous orchestrator, but he couldn't write a tune to save his ass' (Smith, 1991: 275). Yet this approach aims at something different. The premise of small musical cells leads to an art of moments, but with an overall organic unity derived from the coherent strategy and systematic use of minimal material. Therefore, the overall score structure is derived only partly from the film's exigencies, and more from an internal logic that makes a cohesive whole from a number of related components, their minimal variations and various permutations. In *Theory of Film Practice*, Noël Burch points to a cellular relationship of material and structure in *The Birds*, which he equates with serial music (1981: 142–3). The tight and logical structuring of musical material is a principal characteristic of serial music, with the same succession of pitch relations being moved upwards or downwards in pitch as well as run backwards ('retrograde'), and mixed vertically (as chords) as well as horizontally (as melody). Although Herrmann certainly did not use this compositional technique, there are similarities in his rigour when dealing with material.

Used as a structuring principle, leitmotivs (representative themes) render something of a skeletal structure of the film, paralleling narrative and on screen developments. Royal S. Brown (2004) noted that, apart from with *The Trouble with Harry* (1955), this was not a usual practice for Herrmann, although it was the dominant strategy in Hollywood film scoring. Famously, Eisler and Adorno (1994) decried the use of leitmotifs in Hollywood film scores as removing the musical essence from the themes and making them into empty signs of something else. Indeed, strict leitmotif scoring has been characterised as an often artless strategy, only a step or more up from the roundly dismissed 'Mickey-Mousing' of matching image action with mimicking sonic equivalents. In other words, as the audience sees a particular image, it hears a particular theme associated directly with it. At its worst, this can illustrate Hollywood's pleonastic economy of crass simplicity in aesthetic terms. However, on the other hand, there is something significant about the degree of welding image and musical motif in many classical Hollywood films that manifests one of the most distinctive aspects of cinema as a form. There is the expectation of musical 'filling out' of the image's (and the character on screen's) 'flatness', but significantly this also manifests a form of psychology. Particular music accompanies – becomes an integral part of – particular characters onscreen, furnishing part of their voice, sonic aura and overall presence. Herrmann's score uses leitmotifs representing emotional states more than character, although the film's main theme is associated very directly with Marnie. Most of the other themes are related to this and, indeed, the small handful of themes are derived from a limited amount of musical material and are closely related in a dense tapestry.[13]

The main theme appears constantly throughout the film and is associated with *Marnie*'s eponymous character. This principal theme itself appears accessibly tonal but not based on tonal harmony's logic of development. Instead sections are cut up, have their pitches altered and are alternated. The two-bar opening statement is then simply repeated at a pitch two semitones lower. This lacks the feeling of 'going somewhere' that is evident in the majority of classical and romantic art music. Instead, harmonic movement does not 'progress' but tends to remain static. Brown (2004: 105–6) makes an extensive discussion of seventh chords in Herrmann's film scores, focusing in particular upon what he calls 'the Hitchcock chord' (a minor triad with an added major seventh). This is a type of chord that is ambiguous within the system, is static and disconnected, not moving towards any resolution as such. Here, instead of a minor with major seventh, the chords are a major seventh alternating with a half-diminished seventh on the same root note. This is a far more romantic-sounding structure, although moving from a more consonant to a more dissonant chord, and in both cases being chords that are not uncommon in jazz and popular music. The two chords accompany the same pitch and the effect of the change is one of 'shrinking away', dropping two pitches by a semitone from the first to the second chord (known in music as 'diminishing').[14]

There are a handful of particular themes in Herrmann's score. The clearest and most prevalent is that associated with Marnie herself, and which is closely tied to a theme that seems to represent 'trauma', which is an agitato that appears at the start. These two themes are woven together into the musical fabric that envelops the film. There is a further theme that seems to represent Mark, appearing only a couple of times – in his office and travelling to his home. This theme mixes with Marnie's theme when the two of them kiss at Mark's office and at the stables.

Perhaps surprisingly, Herrmann includes a small theme for Lil, Mark's sister-in-law, as well, cementing her importance in the film. He also supplies distinct extended cues for the hunt and rape sequence. The music for the rape scene has a melodic line which appeared later in Herrmann's Clarinet Quintet 'Souvenirs de voyage' (second movement: 'Andante [Berceuse]'). It includes a dramatic high-interval jump, which expresses a sense of extreme emotion.[15] On an initial listen, the score sounds very repetitive, although there is more variation of material than one imagines. In *Marnie*, the degree of correspondence of leitmotif and image is beyond Herrmann's norm, and makes the music seem extremely – almost untenably – repetitive.[16] In other words, they remade the 'score' as a recording through removing one of its key characteristics: its repetition. In a way, Herrmann's score ought to be understood as 'disciplined' austerity, rather than self-indulgent free-ranging flourishes.

Artistic plagiarism and authorial presences

It is perhaps not difficult to characterise the *Marnie* score as retrogressive. In comparison with the experimentation of *The Birds*, the music is very traditional. There is some basis to the notion of Herrmann's 'self-plagiarism', where broadly the music is dominated by a *Vertigo*-like romanticism allied with a *Psycho*-like agitato. Herrmann often reused his music (see Wrobel, 2003),[17] as well as 'borrowing' from other sources, especially his and other people's concert hall music. Seven notes of the *Marnie* main theme appear almost directly taken from the opening of the prelude of Herrmann's score for *The 7th Voyage of Sinbad* (1958, also sequenced as in *Marnie*); however, the nine-note melody also bears a remarkable resemblance to part of Leonard Rosenman's title music for *Rebel Without a Cause* (1955). Apparently, Hitchcock considered Herrmann's score for *Marnie* to be self-plagiarism (Smith, 1991: 264; Sullivan, 2008: 276). While arguably self-plagiarism comprises an important part of any sense of 'thematic and stylistic consistency', many composers – perhaps most particularly in film scores – will reuse musical gambits that have worked particularly well already, leading to accusations of limited creativity.[18] *Marnie* sounds like one of his most traditional scores, so it is hardly simply a retread. Indeed, one might argue that its 'normality' is in some ways novel for Herrmann.

But maybe Hitchcock was under the impression that *he* was being plagiarised – as the music was so much a part of his films. Perhaps Hitchcock was so 'large' as an artist that he was increasingly unsure of what was 'him' and what was not. Indeed, Herrmann had already rearranged the score from *The Trouble with Harry* as 'A Portrait of Hitch', so the music in his films already embodied him literally. After *Marnie*, Hitchcock told his assistant Peggy Robertson that Herrmann was using music in other films that rightfully belonged to his films. (He was talking of *Joy in the Morning* (1965) and its notable musical similarity to *Marnie* (Smith, 1991: 268).) This appears to mix a confusion over ownership of the music, with perhaps a psychological confusion over 'self'. Did Hitchcock resent Herrmann, as suggested by some?[19] The 'Hitchcock sound' overwhelmingly was defined by Herrmann, and it may have been a problem that, for many of his audience, an absolutely essential aspect of 'Hitchcock' was Herrmann.

A further problem is that Herrmann's music was – at least to a degree – uncoupled from the film. The music was not absolutely particular to *Marnie*. It was later partially reused in his concert hall music. Although one might argue that repeated musical ideas are an essential part of personal style, the music is not absolutely specific to its accompanying images and ideas. It is thus more of itself, more autonomous, as well as having its own structure based on Herrmann's modular technique, which supplies its *own logic* perhaps almost as much as does the film itself. Furthermore, we might think of musical quotation as the equivalent of a physical cameo appearance. Herrmann is quoting himself to assert his presence in the film.

The film's red-tinted sequences are the clearest examples of authorial presence in *Marnie* in that they break the naturalistic and largely 'invisible' film style for moments of extreme character subjectivity. Indeed, they are the most striking sequences in the film (containing loud music with almost no diegetic sound) and having a startling colour infusion to the diegetic images. These dramatic points of abstraction are aesthetic manifestations of the 'abnormal', of aesthetics as mental state, through exploiting technical strategies *beyond* the 'everyday' for film narration. This is less a situation of aesthetic elements indicating abnormality than manifesting it in themselves, and is closer to strategies such as extreme moments in horror films. These articulate a mode of flashback but also embrace a form of direct 'point of view' embodying disturbed character psychology in the present; they are also psychotic interludes. They mark narrative clues, but also shocking jumps to an *outside* of the temporal flow of the narrative and point outside of the film's established diegetic world. These 'red sequences' manifest possibly the strongest 'personality in the text' moments in the film. Rather than approaching these sequences as unified, perhaps we can understand them as Hitchcock and Herrmann vying to assert their presence in the film through their own artistic métier: *visual* storytelling and a *musical* flourish.[20] At this point, Hitchcock demonstrates his silent cinema background, with a strong visual impetus and dialogue marginalised.[21] For Herrmann, such sequences supply an opportunity for full-on emotive blast, being allowed his musical 'head', as it were. Hitchcock once stated:

> The truth is that with the triumph of dialogue, the motion picture has been stabilized as theatre ... One result of this is a loss of cinematic style. Another is the loss of fantasy. Dialogue was introduced because it is realistic. The consequence was a loss of the art of reproducing life entirely in pictures. (Hitchcock, 1995a: 214–15)

This echoes the famous 'Statement on Sound' made by Eisenstein, Pudovkin and Alexandrov (1988: 113) at the dawn of the talkies. As Siegfried Kracauer noted in *Theory of Film: The Redemption of Physical Reality*, early attempts at integrating sound film elements had one thing in common: 'they play down the dialogue with a view to reinstating the images' (1998: 106). Indeed, this became a mainstay of film technique. What might be described as 'cinematic aphasia' takes place at moments where dialogue disappears and sound and images have a more free play of activity as they adopt the foregound unambiguously. This is *not* the 'talking cinema' that swept the world in the late 1920s and early 1930s. Indeed, Hitchcock's oeuvre is one of the most clear examples of the persistence of the silent film aesthetic in that many key sequences clearly are visual in impetus rather than based on talking.

The images are red and relatively static, a clear part of what Robin Wood (1989: 176) sees as the film's non-naturalistic drive.[22] In contrast, the music is energetic, 'stormy' and kinetic, manifesting an agitato which is associated with trauma across the film. The sequence as a whole is premised upon abstraction, more precisely the dis-integration of film into static imagery (in terms of formalised compositions), primary colour and dominant non-diegetic sound (music).[23] How far are music and image disconnected in these sequences? There is certainly something of a divergence between the seen and the heard here.[24] After all, we have already heard the 'trauma' agitato beforehand, well before it receives the distinctive visual 'accompaniment' that makes up the red sequences. These sequences manifest aesthetics as mental state and psychology. In terms of representation, they are central to 'acting out' events for the sake of the film's narrative (linking them to the central character's 'abnormal' psychology), but they are also crucial to manifesting an important degree of abstraction, where they make a more general sensual and psychic release or discharge. This arguably embodies a form of aesthetic death drive where the film 'reverts' to disintegrated components.[25] It is the point where film as illusory world collapses into its component parts, although it does not appear chaotic but more an over-aestheticised rupture in the body of the film that the narrative will work hard to try to explain and heal. These express Marnie's psychological state but might also tangibly express Hitchcock and Herrmann's aesthetic personalities in the film, or at least allow them to declare their hand in the film's construction.

While these red sequences are crucial clues, they also involve a 'step outside' of the film's flow of time and space, as well as its audiovisual style. Music can achieve this regularly in films (which is arguably one of the central characteristics of its status outside the diegesis). It is not the only element with this tendency. *Marnie* consistently reminds us of books, if not the original source book for the film. There are book-like title cards and Mark is a publisher (which he is not in the original book). In the source book, one man is made into a woman (Lil), two men vie for Marnie's affection and a psychiatrist analyses her. The film condenses three into Mark. Mark was conflated with psychiatrist. However, rather than being an 'amateur psychologist', he has some training in animal behaviour. This moves the film's psychology away from Freud and more towards behaviourism. Consequently, this also moves concerns away from the mind and towards a focus on the body and the physical, most evident in the sex and violence upon which the narrative depends.

Marnie incorporates a strange amalgamation of schools of psychology. The film condenses the book's two main male characters into one (Mark incorporates a psychoanalyst, who 'comes through' as a doppelgänger from his unconscious). This is highly apparent in what appears to be a clear psychoanalysis session, incorporating free association and Marnie dismissing Mark's approach as, 'You Freud, Me Jane?' The figure of the psychoanalyst arguably is played for laughs in *Psycho* – yet Hitchcock clearly was interested in the subject, as illustrated by a number of his films. *Marnie* encompasses a melange of different psychologies, which arguably do not fit together. The book *Sexual Aberrations of the Criminal Female* does not exist, you might not be surprised to find. Yet, Mark recommends Jung's landmark book *The Undiscovered Self* (1958) to Marnie. Yet, rather than being a text of psychoanalysis, this defines a competing school, that of analytical psychology. Furthermore, Mark trained as an animal behaviourist and still 'dabbles' (getting Marnie to type up a paper of his).[26] Marnie is equated with 'Sophie the Jaguarundi', paralleling Mark's 'project' with behaviourist Konrad Lorenz's groundbreaking investigations of animal behaviour.[27] All of these elements do not seem to quite add up – on the one hand suggesting a crucial level of reality behind (underneath) everyday appearances, but on the other making for a troubling and confused theoretical backdrop. But then this is due to all psychologies being reduced to a single emotional register and reconfigured as an aesthetic object for the film. All psychologies are rendered narrative keys to get behind appearances as a consequence of casting psychological problems as entertainment.

While it might easily be argued that these fragmented psychological elements do not need to 'add up' for the film to be convincing, they seems to mirror the film's fragmentation on an aesthetic level that is perhaps most clear in the relationship of image (narrative) and music. The film's condensed emotional tone and melodramatic outbursts are intensified by the degree of disjunction between film elements, which articulates a pool of potent affect beneath the thin surface of rational exterior of both the characters and the film itself.

Conclusion: disagreeable music?

One by-product of the intentionality fallacy is a realisation that, not only is the author's intention not what the film ends up meaning, but that any intention might be rerouted by context and the meaning end up a long way from initial desires of the producers. Robin Wood wrote that Hitchcock did not face up to what he was doing when he made *Psycho*.[28] Indeed, Hitchcock was prone to contradictory rhetoric that mixed some self-deprecation with perhaps more self-aggrandisement, and expert self-publicity. He spoke of his films as if they were in no way collaborations.[29] Indeed, some collaborators were distinctly underplayed by him. Thus he managed to embody so fully the figure of the 'romantic artist' in a popular sense, carefully creating *his* vision.[30] But we have been told – by Hitchcock and others – that *all* of each film was Hitchcock's doing. He was the boss. The film was 'already made in his head' before shooting started. In such a situation, how far could Herrmann have an impact?

It is clear that sonic addition can 'reroute' visuals (Donnelly, 2014; Vroomen and de Gelder, 2000). Furthermore, during his career Hitchcock rarely rejected film scores brought to him – except for *Torn Curtain* and Henry Mancini's score for *Frenzy* (1972) (see Hubai, 2011). Indeed, he also evidently changed his mind on occasions. Composer Herrmann 'knew better' with the *Psycho* shower scene, which Hitchcock originally wanted without music.[31] I would argue that Herrmann's music *reconfigured* films to a degree, and quite possibly against Hitchcock's intention. If Herrmann's score for *Psycho* made it horror rather than comic horror,[32] and his (collaborative) music for *The Birds* made it more like experimental art than an exploitation 'creature feature', then what did Herrmann's music make of *Marnie*? Its intense romanticism *hid*, or at least obscured, an utterly unromantic film.[33] It misdirected and ameliorated, took emphasis away from the loveless romance at the heart of the film. Indeed, the 'romance' consists of Mark's sexual blackmail of Marnie (he evinces little tangible romantic attitude towards her), added to her rape (and subsequent suicide attempt).[34] Add to this the sordid and devastating revelations about her mother's sexual life. Marnie remembers that 'men in white … want in' (her mother's sailor 'johns'), and the mother caps this by telling Marnie she was the product of her wanting 'Billy's basketball sweater'. Yet, in contrast with this tawdry extremity, the music in the film is intensely romantic. *Marnie* most definitely is a 'sex mystery' (as it was billed), but the music oscillates between and romance and stormy thriller. It *misdirects* the audience, so we don't notice the film's unsavoury aspects quite as much as we might, as this is a compelling yet appallingly brutal film. In *Composing for the Movies*, Eisler and Adorno (1994: 75) note that romantic music in the cinema is a palliative, hiding the terrible truth that we might see, of the reality of the illusion of film and our spurious relation to it.

Steven C. Smith notes: 'To Herrmann, *Marnie*'s most serious liability was not its lack of a pop theme but Tippi Hedren (an opinion that could hardly have endeared him to Hitchcock)' (1991: 260). At the start of the film, Marnie washes out her hair dye. This is first time we see her face. Music builds, but climaxes early – emphasising her blonde hair, a moment before we see her face. Is this Herrmann removing emphasis from the fetishisation of Hedren, or perhaps suggesting she is merely a generic blonde, or perhaps again even suggesting Hitchcock's interest in her (archetypal blonde) hair rather than Hedren as an individual? In the rape scene, the music begins with the emotional theme which represents Marnie and Mark's romance, then moves to a variation on the 'Marnie' theme. This implies that the event might be something less than rape – that there is a certain tenderness there – and that the music wants to de-emphasise the actualities of the unsavoury sequence. Only with the camera's movement to the porthole does the music turn to the trauma theme.

The final sequence of *Marnie* is ambiguous. The dialogue suggests the possibility of working towards a cure, but the images seem unremittingly bleak (like the inert ship in port at the end of the road). However, the music finishes with a flourish, giving a positive sheen to an ambiguous conclusion, indicating more strongly the probability of a cure for Marnie. Seeing the situation as hopeless, Slavoj Žižek describes the large ship as 'just a mute embodiment of an impossible jouissance' (1992: 7). Yet this is certainly not mute; Herrmann's music animates the ending. In the symmetrical 'pull-out' shot, we are shown the car driving off, illustrating that the cul-de-sac is not a dead end. Herrmann's music ends on a positive and resounding major chord cadence, which not only supplies a sense of closure for the film, but also makes the ending seem more optimistic.[35] Although there was a film tradition of using a major chord as the final cadence in a film, Herrmann certainly did not make a habit of finishing his scores with a major chord. In this instance, and in the face of the devastating revelations shortly beforehand, this final gasp of positivity appears more optimistic than the images and representations afford.

Notes

1 However, Lesley Brill (1991) characterises Hitchcock's films as essentially romantic but not in a straightforward manner.
2 A sense of the film's current status is that Canadian artist Stan Douglas made the installation 'Subject to a Film', which recreated (although updated) the tense silent robbery sequence from *Marnie* in a loop of film.
3 In a contemporaneous review, Judith Crist of the *New York Herald Tribune* declared uncharitably that *Marnie* was 'pathetically old fashioned and dismally naïve' (quoted in Kapsis, 1992: 123).
4 According to Richard Allen, Hitchcock's films pose the question of whether romantic love 'harbors a murderous [and] self-annihilating desire' (1999: 226).
5 David Raksin discusses Hitchcock's downward career trajectory at this point, in the documentary *Bernard Herrmann: Music from the Movies* (dir. Joshua Waletzky, American Film Institute, 1992).
6 Original screenwriter Evan Hunter was not happy with the rape scene the way Hitch wanted it. Jay Presson Allen later told him that this scene was the main reason for Hitchcock making the film (Allen, 2002: 208; Hunter, 1976: 75–6; Spoto, 1983: 545).
7 However, Moral reports (from Herrmann's soon to be divorced wife Lucy) that Universal had been pushing Herrmann for a hit song for *Marnie* (2005: 137).
8 According to Spoto (1983: 491), Universal were insistent on a hit song for *Torn Curtain*, as they were certain the film was likely to fail. After *Marnie*, Herrmann scored *Joy in the Morning* (1965, with a title song by Sammy Fain). The love theme from *Vertigo* was also rearranged as the popular song 'Madeleine' (Smith, 1991: 222).
9 The song's disc release date in the USA and UK was 29 June 1964, and was accompanied by a strong cross-media promotional campaign (Moral, 2005: 139).
10 To some degree, film music is almost always able to stand alone without its film. Herrmann's *Marnie* has been made available a number of times as a musical recording, including (in recent years): the 1996 disc for the Sony Classical series conducted by Esa-Pekka Salonen and the Los Angeles Philharmonic (B000024MFE); *Bernard Herrmann, Marnie: Original Motion Picture Score*, by Joel McNeely and the Royal Scottish National Orchestra (Varese Sarabande 302-066-094, released 2000); and *Alfred Hitchcock's Marnie. OST* (Tsunami TCI 0601, released 1994), which is a widely available grey-market CD release of the original film score recording.

11 The *Oxford English Dictionary* defines romantic as 'conducive to or characterized by the expression of love', www.oxforddictionaries.com/definition/english/romantic, accessed 6 June 2015.

12 It is worth noting that Herrmann's '2+2' structure is also strikingly similar to the regularities of song form structure, which is perhaps why the main theme of *Marnie* was easily made into a popular song. This also allows for the first four bars of the main theme melody to be used, but the second four to be replaced with something less stormy and more fitting to a popular song croon.

13 Schneller (2010: 60) notes that there are 'two condensed thematic variants, and five motives derived from "Marnie" that range in length from eight to two notes. The relationship of the prototype to its variants and motivic surrogates resembles a Russian doll that contains within it smaller and smaller versions of itself.'

14 This is not a fully 'diminished seventh' chord, but in essence here the chord change is from major to minor on the same root. This is commonplace in popular music, and in the extended chord form here is also common in jazz. This accounts partially for how easily the theme was made into a Nat King Cole song.

15 This large jump in pitch codes extreme emotion but also is a rare and difficult jump for singers to achieve, and thus has an emotive sound.

16 Indeed, the McNeely re-recording of the score excises some of the score, likely due to it sounding too repetitive.

17 See also Bill Wrobel's website 'Film Score Rundowns', which gives a cue-by-cue analysis of the music in films, www.filmscorerundowns.net/.

18 Herrmann certainly reused fragments of his music elsewhere, and this is also the case with his *Marnie* score. For example, there is an isolated statement of the *Marnie* theme in his 'Echoes' for string quartet of 1965.

19 For example, Raksin in *Bernard Herrmann: Music from the Movies* (see note 5).

20 This development is related to 'audio dissolves' in musicals. These are points of transition between different aesthetic regimes, where music 'wells up' and takes over (Altman, 1987: 110).

21 What Hitchcock referred to as 'pure cinema', an almost purely visual approach (Truffaut, 1984: 214–22).

22 The film is in essence not naturalistic.

23 This arguably embodies a form of aesthetic death drive where the film 'reverts' to disintegrated components.

24 This corresponds with the notion of schizophonia, where sound sources become divorced from their attendant sound (Schafer, 1994: 91).

25 An important part of Freud's notion of the death drive is the unconscious desire to revert to an inert state, away from the complexity and activity of life.

26 Behaviourism is the dominant form of scientific endeavour and is dismissive of most other psychologies – particularly psychoanalysis (which has been deemed 'unscientific', even 'quackery', by some behaviourists).

27 See Konrad Lorenz's groundbreaking investigation of New Caledonian Crows and Eurasian Jackdaws (1961).

28 Robin Wood (1989: 151) suggests that Hitchcock did not face up to what he was doing in making *Psycho*.

29 Robin Wood (1989: 20) points to his extraordinary degree of control in his filmmaking.

30 There was some evidence of Universal executives interfering, as Hitchcock did not get the actors he initially wanted for his films around this time, most obviously with *Torn Curtain*.

31 This was recounted by Herrmann via Raksin in *Bernard Herrmann: Music from the Movies* (see note 5). Herrmann certainly had some latitude: 'Hitchcock himself was not a musically sensitive man, but according to Herrmann, he had "the great sensitivity to leave me alone when I am composing"' (Moral, 2005: 136).

32 This is despite Hitchcock's claim that *Psycho* was a comedy.

33 While musical romanticism is not the same as a romantic film, such music has tended to be the dominant musical language of romance in Hollywood films.

34 Murray Pomerance (2004: 152) suggests that, certainly initially, the relationship of Marnie and Mark is 'ownership' within the scope of the workplace rather than romance as such.

35 In a different interpretation, Tom Schneller (2010: 61) points to the 'conventionally triumphant mediant shift that signals "happy ending" and rings rather hollow, considering the melancholy final scene of the film'.

References

Allen, Richard (1999), 'Hitchcock, or the Pleasures of Metaskepticism', in Richard Allen and Sam Ishii-Gonzalès (eds), *Alfred Hitchcock: Centenary Essays*. London: BFI, pp. 221–37.

Allen, Richard (2002), 'An Interview with Jay Presson Allen', in Sidney Gottlieb and Christopher Brookhouse (eds), *Framing Hitchcock: Selected Essays from The Hitchcock Annual*. Detroit: Wayne State University Press, pp. 206–18.

Altman, Rick (1987), *The American Film Musical*. London: BFI.

Brill, Lesley (1991), *The Hitchcock Romance: Love and Irony in Hitchcock's Films*. Princeton, N.J.: Princeton University Press.

Brown, Royal S. (2004), 'Herrmann, Hitchcock, and the Music of the Irrational', *Cinema Journal*, 21:2: 14–49. Reprinted in Robert Kolker (ed.), *Psycho: A Casebook*. New York: Oxford University Press, pp. 102–17.

Burch, Noël (1981), *Theory of Film Practice*. Princeton, N.J.: Princeton University Press.

Donnelly, K.J. (2014), *Occult Aesthetics: Synchronization in Sound Film*. Oxford: Oxford University Press.

Eisenstein, S.M., Vsevolod Pudovkin, and Grigori Alexandrov (1988), 'Statement on Sound' in Richard Taylor (ed. and trans.), *S. M. Eisenstein: Selected Works*, vol. 1, *Writings 1922–1934*. London: BFI, pp. 113–14.

Eisler, Hanns and Theodor Adorno (1994), *Composing for the Films*. London: Athlone.

Hitchcock, Alfred (1995a), 'Film Production', in Sidney Gottlieb (ed.), *Hitchcock on Hitchcock: Selected Writings and Interviews*. London: Faber and Faber, pp. 210–26.

Hitchcock, Alfred (1995b), 'On Style', interview in Cinema magazine, 5:1, August-September 1963. Reprinted in Sidney Gottlieb (ed.), *Hitchcock on Hitchcock: Selected Writings and Interviews*. London: Faber and Faber, pp. 285–302.

Hubai, Gergely (2011), '"Murder Can Be Fun": The Lost Music of *Frenzy*', *Hitchcock Annual* 17: 169–94.

Hunter, Evan (1976), *Me and Hitch*. London: Faber and Faber.

Kapsis, Robert E. (1992), *Hitchcock: The Making of a Reputation*. Chicago: University of Chicago Press.

Kracauer, Siegfried (1998), *Theory of Film: the Redemption of Physical Reality.* Princeton: Princeton University Press.

Lorenz, Konrad (1961), *King Solomon's Ring*, trans. M. Kerr Wilson. London: Methuen.

McElhaney, Joe (1999), 'Touching the Surface: *Marnie*, Melodrama, Modernism', in Richard Allen and Sam Ishii Gonzalès (eds), *Alfred Hitchcock: Centenary Essays.* London: BFI, pp. 87–105.

McElhaney, Joe (2006), *The Death of Classical Cinema: Hitchcock, Lang, Minnelli.* New York: SUNY Press.

McGilligan Patrick (2004), *Alfred Hitchcock: A Life in Darkness and Light.* London: Wiley.

Moral, Tony Lee (2005), *Hitchcock and the Making of Marnie.* Metuchen, NJ: Scarecrow Press.

Pomerance, Murray (2004), *An Eye for Hitchcock.* New Brunswick: Rutgers University Press.

Rosar, William (2003), 'Bernard Herrmann: The Beethoven of Film Music?', *Journal of Film Music* 1:2–3: 121–51.

Schafer, R. Murray (1994), *Our Sonic Environment and the Soundscape: The Tuning of the World.* Rochester: Destiny.

Schneller, Tom (2010), 'Unconscious Anchors: Bernard Herrmann's Music for *Marnie*', *Popular Music History* 5:1: 55–104.

Smith, Steven C. (1991), *A Heart at Fire's Center: the Life and Music of Bernard Herrmann.* Berkeley: University of California Press.

Spoto, Donald (1983), *The Dark Side of Genius: The Life of Alfred Hitchcock.* London: Ballantine.

Sullivan, Jack (2008), *Hitchcock's Music.* New Haven: Yale University Press.

Truffaut, François (1984), *Hitchcock.* London: Panther.

Vroomen, Jeanne and Beatrice de Gelder (2000), 'Sound Enhances Visual Perception: Cross-Modal Effects of Auditory Organization on Vision', *Journal of Experimental Psychology: Human Perception and Performance* 26:5: 1583–90.

Wood, Robin (1989), *Hitchcock's Films Revisited*, New York: Columbia University Press.

Wrobel, William (2003), 'Self Borrowing in the Music of Bernard Herrmann', *Journal of Film Music* 1:2–3: 249–71.

Žižek, Slavoj (1992), 'Alfred Hitchcock, or the Form and its Historical Mediation', in Žižek (ed.), *Everything You Always Wanted to Know About Lacan But Were Afraid to Ask Hitchcock*, London: Verso, pp. 1–12.

3

The murder of Gromek: theme and variations

Tomas Williams

Many of Alfred Hitchcock's most memorable cinematic moments are insepa-
rable for audiences from the music which accompanied them. Be it the
piercing violins and the piercing of Marion Crane in *Psycho* (1960), or instances
in which musical motifs played an integral part of a film's narrative, such as the
tune whistled in *The 39 Steps* (1935), or the Albert Hall sequences in both versions of *The Man Who Knew Too Much* (1934 and 1956), music was of utmost
importance to Hitchcock, and has been remembered as such by audiences. One
Hitchcock film that has been less fondly remembered by audiences, along with
its music, is *Torn Curtain* (1966). However, it is a crucial film in the musical line-
age of Alfred Hitchcock's career, being the film that would cause the end of the
director's successful collaborative relationship with his best-known composer,
Bernard Herrmann, and as a result is a film which reveals certain key attitudes
in Hitchcock's filmmaking practices (and equally in Herrmann's approach to the
film score).

The end of the Hitchcock–Herrmann relationship came about as a result of
two different approaches to the score for *Torn Curtain*. One particular disparity
related to Hitchcock's intent for a crucial scene in the film, the set-piece murder
of the film's villain, Gromek (Wolfgang Kieling), to be shown without accompanying music. This chapter sets out to analyse this scene in some detail, comparing
Hitchcock's final scoreless version of the film with two other versions of the scene,
featuring unused scores composed by Herrmann and John Addison (who replaced
Herrmann on *Torn Curtain*, but whose music for the murder of Gromek was also
discarded).

Despite a public consciousness that connects Hitchcock's cinematic imagery
to the musical scores accompanying his films, Hitchcock's career has also been
punctuated by a continuing interest in the effect created by an absence of non-
diegetic score. *The Lady Vanishes* (1938) and *Lifeboat* (1944) both feature a non-
diegetic score only at the opening and close of the film, and David Schroeder
(2012: 72) has highlighted how a break in the score is used to crucial effect in
Blackmail (1929). As Stephen Rebello (1998: 136–8) has noted, Hitchcock envis-
aged equally dramatic experiments by minimising the use of a musical score for
Psycho, in which the sparseness of music would reflect the sparseness of dialogue

in the film, granting particular attention to dramatic sound effects. This wish would become fully realised in *The Birds* (which uses the sounds of the birds to form its soundtrack); however, for *Psycho* Herrmann ignored Hitchcock's ideas, and in particular his instruction not to score the shower sequence, with famous results. The case of *Psycho* stood as a precedent for Herrmann, but his success would not be repeated with *Torn Curtain*.

Torn Curtain was the culmination of Herrmann and Hitchcock's successful ten-year period of collaboration, and was a film which Hitchcock was particularly anxious about, following the frosty reception to his previous film, *Marnie* (1964). Adding to his anxieties were complications with the script during pre-production and key casting decisions the director was not wholly committed to. The script that had caused Hitchcock so much concern follows an American scientist, Professor Michael Armstrong (Paul Newman), who on a conference trip to Copenhagen begins to act suspiciously in the eyes of his fiancée Sarah (Julie Andrews). Sarah follows Michael to Berlin and begins to suspect him of acting as a Soviet spy. It soon transpires that Michael is in fact spying for the American government, but his plans are thwarted when Gromek, an East German officer who has been monitoring Michael, becomes suspicious and attempts to report him. This leads Michael to murder Gromek in a quiet farmhouse, with the assistance of the 'farmer's wife' (as she is credited; Carolyn Conwell), which begins a race against time for Armstrong to discover the information he needs and flee the Eastern bloc before the absence of Gromek arouses suspicions and Michael's true intentions are discovered.

The ageing Hitchcock saw *Torn Curtain*, with its contemporary political setting and fresh young stars, as his opportunity to remain relevant to the young audiences dominating the film market, following the disappointing reception of *Marnie*. Hitchcock instructed Herrmann to compose his music accordingly, to discard his dependence upon orchestral scores and to compose something with a more modern sound, along with a pop song for the title music to aid in the marketing of the film. Jack Sullivan quotes the following telegram from Hitchcock to Herrmann regarding his desires for the *Torn Curtain* score:

> We do not have the freedom that we would like to have because we are catering to an audience and that is why you get your money and I get mine. This audience is very different to the one to which we used to cater. It is young, vigorous, and demanding. It is this fact that has been recognized by almost all the European film makers where they have sought to introduce a beat and a rhythm that is more in tune with the requirements of the aforesaid audience. I have made up my mind that this approach to the music is extremely essential. (Sullivan, 2006: 278)

Further to these instructions, Hitchcock – as he had done with *Psycho* – issued an explicit demand that the key dramatic sequence of the film, the murder of Gromek, remain unscored.

Trusting his own instinct and approach to film scoring, which had proven so successful on *Psycho*, Herrmann chose to ignore the director's instructions on the tone and style of the music, and instead composed an orchestral score which adhered to similar conventions as Herrmann's previous compositions for Hitchcock. As with *Psycho*, Herrmann also chose to defy Hitchcock and scored the murder of Gromek with a highly suspenseful music cue, intending to appropriately lend his powers to what Robin Wood describes as 'the most disturbing murder in the whole of Hitchcock' (2002: 202).

Hitchcock reacted furiously when he heard how Herrmann had chosen to score the film and, feeling betrayed by his friend, he fired Herrmann and brought about the end of one of the most successful artistic collaborations of his career. Hitchcock now found himself in post-production on *Torn Curtain* without a score. The British composer John Addison was hastily brought in to replace Herrmann, having recently enjoyed Oscar success with his music for *Tom Jones* (dir. Tony Richardson, 1963), and he produced a score to accompany the final film which is curiously no more modern-sounding than Herrmann's effort. Even more remarkably, Addison chose to follow Herrmann's lead and also composed a cue for the murder of Gromek. Despite this, Hitchcock maintained his early intention and released the film without music over the murder scene.[1]

As a result of these various complications and attempts to score the scene is that three different aural interpretations now exist for the murder of Gromek: Hitchcock's music-free version which appears in the final film, which for the purposes of this analysis I take as the 'Theme', and Herrmann and Addison's unused compositions, which I take as the 'Variations'. Drawing direct comparison between these three ways of viewing Gromek's death allows for an analysis between the appropriateness of Herrmann and Addison's music for Hitchcock's filmmaking, and the ultimate effect created by the final scoreless version of the scene.

In his book on the filmic soundtrack, *Audio-Vision*, Michel Chion describes the 'audiovisual combination', noting 'that one perception influences the other and transforms it. We never see the same thing when we also hear; we don't hear the same thing when we see as well' (1994: xxvi). Therefore each different aural interpretation of the murder of Gromek must create a different meaning when combined with the visual. Such comparison offers the opportunity to illuminate Hitchcock's approach to filmmaking and the film score through a juxtaposition with differing method taken by someone he had worked so closely with before. In this respect, and without wishing to denigrate Addison's artistic interpretation, his variation of the scene offers a form of 'control group', a third interpretation of the scene which is not influenced by past successes and failures, and the politics of a raucous working relationship with Hitchcock.

Theme

Hitchcock discussed his approach to Gromek's murder sequence as part of his famous interview with François Truffaut, and explained that 'In doing that long killing scene, my first thought again was to avoid the cliché ... And I thought it was time to show that it was very difficult, very painful, and it takes a very long time to kill a man' (Truffaut, 1985: 311). Hitchcock's intention was to use techniques of realism to emphasise the brutality of murder, which Truffaut praised Hitchcock for in the same interview. By avoiding the use of a musical score, Hitchcock gives further prominence to the sound effects of the scene with the intention of enhancing the violent nature of the murder.

To explain the scene and its soundscape in more detail, the action begins with the clicking of Gromek's faulty lighter, before a bowl smashes over his head, thus marking the beginning of the violence. We then hear Gromek's footsteps as he paces across the wooden floor towards the farmer's wife, followed by the rustle of clothes as Michael grapples the protesting Gromek, and the policeman's gun falls from his grasp. The absence of music draws attention to Gromek's dialogue and the silence he is met with. Gromek's brief quips ('You've had your fun', 'Now we stop these games') highlight his need to be silenced, and accordingly Michael's hand fixes itself around Gromek's throat, strangling him and stifling his voice, preventing his cries from being heard by the taxi driver waiting outside. Michael holds the policeman steady as the farmer's wife approaches, brandishing a knife which she stabs close to Gromek's neck, reinforcing this attempt to silence him at all costs. As we hear the knife snap, leaving its tip fixed into Gromek's body, his dialogue stops. This is no longer 'fun' and 'games', and instead all we hear is his grunting and his strained breath as he struggles against Michael. Utilising the tools at her disposal, the farmer's wife picks up a shovel and strikes Gromek's shins, a sound which, through the repetition of her action, develops a sense of rhythm. Once Gromek's body has collapsed to the floor, we hear the farmer's wife turn on the gas taps of the oven, and the escaping fumes become an ominous background noise to the sound of Gromek's body being slowly dragged along the floor to his death. Finally, with his head forced into the oven by Michael and the farmer's wife, we hear Gromek's last groans as he struggles for life, while Hitchcock's prolonged shot catches every flutter of Gromek's hands until life finally leaves his body.

The rhythms and nuances of the diegetic soundtrack demonstrate how Hitchcock in fact becomes a form of composer for the sequence, orchestrating the diegetic sounds created by the violent actions of the scene in the manner of *musique concrète*. For, after all, the careful attention Hitchcock took to 'score' the elements of the soundtrack during pre-production is well-known (as in the case of *Psycho*), and although his music notes were less thorough for *Torn Curtain* he was very clear with Herrmann where he did not want music. Laurent Bouzereau has identified how Hitchcock used sound effects similarly elsewhere in the film, when Paul Newman is being followed and attempts to lose his pursuer, explaining, 'Hitchcock in that scene creates a score using only the sound of footsteps. The pacing of the sound alone is what drives the action and suspense' (2010: 151). Hitchcock enjoyed characterising himself in the role of a composer, constructing a film 'just like a composer makes those little black dots to make music' (Sullivan 2006: xv). In the case of *Torn Curtain*, Hitchcock even chose to use the musical term *misterioso* when explaining his approach to the beginning of the film to François Truffaut (1985: 309), demonstrating his musical approach to filmmaking, even during sequences without music.

This may also explain why Herrmann chose to ignore Hitchcock's wishes and provide a score for the scene, for, despite acting as a sound consultant on *The Birds*, Herrmann later made clear his distaste for *musique concrète*. During postproduction work with Herrmann on *Farenheit 451* in 1966, following the breakup from Hitchcock, François Truffaut recorded in his journal that 'From the very start of our discussion we rejected electronic effects or "musique concrète" and, in general, all the commonplace and futuristic clichés into which television, be it in the USA or in Europe, falls head first' (1967: 14). While Hitchcock does not employ electronic sound effects in *Torn Curtain*, it is perhaps the director's interest in sound effects above the musical score that led Herrmann to this opinion.

Using the sound effects of the scene to create a more brutal, realistic murder also has a strong effect upon the spectator's interpretation of the film as a whole. At this point in the narrative the audience has only just discovered the true reasons why Michael has come to East Berlin. We have come to understand that he is a double agent, yet we do not know (in a typical Hitchcock MacGuffin) exactly what information he has come to obtain. This means that we cannot fully understand the motivation for the murder of Gromek, a fact which, combined with the brutality of his murder, distances the audience from identification with Professor Armstrong.

In contrast, the spectator is allowed to view Gromek rather sympathetically throughout the film, largely due to Hitchcock's obvious affection for the character, described by Stephen Gottlieb as a 'Hitchcock self-portrait' (1967: 59). This affection has been sensed by a number of Hitchcock commentators. Michael Walker finds Professor Armstrong guilty of murder, rather than self-defence (2010: 33), and finds sympathy in the feminised gesture of Gromek's fluttering hands during the final moments of his life (2005: 224). Peter Conrad (2001: 158) describes how the Professor and the farmer's wife 'collaborate to kill', and William Rothman (2011: 357) characterises Gromek as 'oddly likeable'. Furthermore, Robin Wood (2002: 199), who in comparing the narrative of *Torn Curtain* to the mythological descent of a hero into the underworld (suggested by the performance of *Francesa da Rimini* in the later stages of the film), finds Gromek to be a 'lost soul', rather than comparing him to a more sinister figure of Roman mythology, such as the god Orcus, the punisher of broken oaths, perhaps a more suitable comparison considering Michael's deceit.

Conversely, David Schroeder comments of Gromek:

> Compared to *Psycho*, in which we see the brutal murder of a woman we have come to identify with and whose love life and moral dilemma we care about, with the minor character Gromek in *Torn Curtain* we have an East German security man whose work will not endear us to him, who seems a bit of a bumbler (he can't make his cigarette lighter work), and makes a series of bad jokes about American expressions. (Schroeder, 2012: 224)

Schroeder uses a comparison with Marion Crane to highlight how little the audience has invested in the fate of Gromek; however, Schroeder has overlooked a key difference between these two characters, which is important to our understanding of this film and the critical role the soundtrack plays. Crucially, the murder of Marion Crane is undertaken by an unknowable assailant, shrouded in mystery, whereas in *Torn Curtain* the violent murder of Gromek is undertaken by the protagonist of the film. The character quirks of Gromek which Schroeder has identified defy stereotypes of a character of his vocation, and it is this unusual juxtaposition that does in fact endear the spectator to his character. Hitchcock offers the spectator enough information to perceive Gromek with sympathy and, in turn, to view Michael unfavourably, who in comparison goes about his shady deeds without full disclosure before the audience. We learn an astonishing amount of information about Gromek and his past during his short screen time – more than we ever discover about Michael.

Of particular interest is Gromek's emulation of American cultural tropes, distancing himself from the Eastern bloc enemy he supposedly represents. We learn of his background in New York and his fondness for the country, and he displays personal character quirks such as repeatedly chewing gum. We also learn of his love for American gangster films, particularly those starring Edward G. Robinson, and of his fondness for 'Pete's Pizza Parlor' of New York City. With this in mind, the threat Gromek offers appears rather innocuous. He seems a rather harmless figure, acting out his understanding of a gangster figure as opposed to offering a true threat, rather like the taxi driver waiting outside who emulates Peter Lorre.[2] This sense of imitating a role is further reinforced by Gromek's gesture of forming his hand into the shape of a gun and 'firing' this towards the farmer's wife; a threat, but one based in child's play. After all, in those films of Robinson's to which Gromek alludes, such as *Little Caesar* (dir. Mervyn LeRoy, 1931), Robinson takes on the role of antihero, who, despite the redemptive elements of his character, must always meet his fate for the crimes he has committed. Gromek's infatuation with Americana even stretches as far as his name, which is a possible reference to the baseball pitcher Steve Gromek, who played in the Major League between 1941 and 1957 for the Cleveland Indians and the Detroit Tigers.

Even the recurring act of Gromek's inability to use his lighter marks him as ineffectual, in a phallic motif which runs throughout his short tenure in the film and renders the phallic symbol impotent and without use (much like Gromek failing to use his gun). Schroeder (2012: 224) argued that Gromek's failure to use a lighter marked him as 'a bumbler', but did not identify that this fact also functions to belie the violence that is acted out upon him. Gromek's dialogue during the scene, with his references to 'fun' and 'games', also positions him as a rather innocent childlike figure, unable to differentiate between play and the true threat of Michael's violent actions. Hitchcock's shot choices similarly show the character sympathetically. When he is stabbed by the farmer's wife the action is shown from Gromek's point of view, and later his last gasps of air are shown in a 40-second-long shot (Figure 11.1), in which his head is forced into a gas oven, with Michael's

Figure 11.1 *Torn Curtain* (1966, Dir: Alfred Hitchcock). Hitchcock shows Gromek's final moments of life in an unrelenting shot lasting 40 seconds (Universal Pictures).

hands clamped firmly around his neck. Now helpless, Gromek's hands are seen to twitch until he finally comes to rest.

The reasons for Hitchcock's favourable characterisation of Gromek can be linked directly to the director's decision to avoid music during the killing scene, as both factors function to emphasise the true brutality of the act of murder. Here we have a villain who the audience like, and a hero who the audience have been given little reason to care for. This allows the spectator to understand the murder as not only physiologically vicious but also ideologically inhuman, which is supported by the filmic techniques that Hitchcock employed, such as extended shot lengths and lack of score, so that our sympathies for Gromek make his ruthless death an even more excruciating sight to behold.

Hitchcock's success in this regard is perhaps at the detriment to the film as a whole. By being so wholly focused upon the realism of murder, Hitchcock creates a character in Michael Armstrong with whom it is very challenging for the audience to ever sympathise. This perhaps explains why the set-piece murder is so often lauded by critics but the film as a whole is not. This was clearly a concern for Hitchcock, evident from a scene which was shot for the film but did not make the final cut. The scene occurs later in the film and shows Michael meeting Gromek's brother, played by the same actor, Wolfgang Kieling. The brother, not knowing of Gromek's demise, asks Michael to take his brother's favourite sausages to him, which he cuts with a knife reminiscent of the one used in the murder of his brother. Ultimately, despite the macabre humour of this scene, Hitchcock felt that it would be taking our sympathies with Gromek too far, preventing the spectator from ever being able to identify with the film's supposed hero (Truffaut, 1985: 313).

Figure 11.2 Herrmann's initial 'Killing' motif (Themes and Variations).

Figure 11.3 Herrmann's use of triplets and the rising pitch, matching the scene's tension (Themes and Variations).

Variations

A far cry from Hitchcock's soundtrack, Herrmann's cue for the murder of Gromek, 'The Killing', called for a brass section comprising an astonishing sixteen horns, nine trombones and two tubas, as well as twelve flutes, eight cellos, eight basses and two sets of timpani (Smith, 1991: 271). In contrast, John Addison, for his cue 'The Murder of Gromek', employed a more typical arrangement of thirteen flutes, three oboes, four clarinets, three bassoons, six horns, three trumpets, three trombones, one harp, one piano, eighteen violins, six violas, six cellos, three basses, bass guitars and percussion. Herrmann's orchestration saw him reject the violins and violas which had been so crucial to his previous scores, instead leading with the rich sound of the dominant horns, resulting in what Brown (1982: 44) describes as a 'more "iron curtain" sound'.

'The Killing' commences as soon as the bowl smashes over Gromek's head (Addison's cue will not begin for some time). Herrmann's music here is strongly thematic. It begins with a dramatic five-note theme, first introduced by the horns, then adopted by the cellos, basses, flutes and trombones (Figure 11.2). This is repeated in variations until the farmer's wife picks up the knife, at which point the music becomes more tense and anxious, an impression created through the use of triplets. A six-note sequence, again introduced by the horns, steadily rises in pitch to reflect the increasing tension of the scene (Figure 11.3). This is, however somewhat derivative of some of Herrmann's earlier work for Hitchcock, such as the theme from *Vertigo* (1958), seen in Figure 11.4 (Brown, 1982: 30).

When offering Herrmann the score to *Torn Curtain*, Hitchcock had expressed concern over tendencies he had identified in the composer to imitate his own work, citing similarities between Herrmann's music for *Marnie* and his subsequent score for Alex Segal's *Joy in the Morning* (1965) (Smith, 1991: 268). Smith has also identified Herrmann's use of the minor third in 'The Killing', which he describes as 'a popular device for danger or fear' (1991: 272). Therefore, despite wanting

Figure 11.4 Herrmann's earlier use of this style of motif in *Vertigo* (Famous Chappell Ltd).

Figure 11.5 *Torn Curtain* (1966, Dir: Alfred Hitchcock). Both composers
choose to emphasise the explosion of violence on screen as the farmer's wife
(Carolyn Conwell) stabs Gromek (Universal Pictures).

something different and new and modern, Hitchcock was presented with a score
which conforms to popular devices, and which, while more brooding and menacing than Herrmann's previous scores for the director, is nonetheless in parts reminiscent of his earlier works.

As the farmer's wife seizes the knife, it is at this point in the scene that Addison's
cue begins. By commencing his musical cue much later than Herrmann's, Addison
acknowledges Hitchcock's original intention for the scene and allows the director's
desire to emphasise the brutal sound effects to register, at least in part, with the
audience. Interestingly, Addison's score for the sequence indicates that he originally began his cue from the same moment as Herrmann; however, he altered
this decision, marking on the top of his score 'start at bar 16', to coincide with the
moment when the farmer's wife picks up the knife. This allows the introduction
of the score to suggest a shift in tone from a violent scuffle to a brutal murder.
Addison's cue begins with the bass guitars giving a driving sense of rhythm to the
scene, mimicking the action onscreen as the farmer's wife stalks slowly towards

Figure 11.6 Herrmann's 'silenced' semibreve (Themes and Variations).

Gromek, while a sense of disquiet is created through the low powerful murmuring of the other bass instruments. This theme is broken by a sudden cry from the orchestra, matching the explosion of violence onscreen as the farmer's wife stabs Gromek (Figure 11.5).

In Herrmann's interpretation, as the farmer's wife stabs Gromek, a high-pitched ringing noise chimes out, created by a tremolo of notes on the piccolo flutes, before a low-pitched rhythmic drumming begins on the timpani. The sequence builds in momentum, and the original theme returns with a driving force, with its semiquaver motif developed to match the power of the rhythmic timpani. However, the developing rhythm, and with it the notion of suspense, is constantly interrupted (silenced, like Gromek) by the pure force of the semibreve played by the trombones, tubas, cellos and basses, creating the impenetrable 'iron curtain sound' that Brown has described (1982: 44) (Figure 11.6).

Such contrast is central to the success of Herrmann's cue. The semibreve denies the building rhythm and suspense of the music, and instead imbues the sequence with the portentous sense of Michael's morally unjustified actions. The music, instead of asking a question of suspense, 'what will happen?', seems to be asking a question of morality, 'what are they doing?', and this is perhaps what Steven C. Smith identifies as 'an emotional gray' in the score (1991: 272). Therefore, despite adopting a markedly different approach to Hitchcock, Herrmann's interpretation of the score also functions to emphasise the brutality of Gromek's murder. Herrmann's score, by interrupting the developing suspense cues, functions to subvert the 'traditional' Hitchcock–Herrmann score, in much the same manner that Hitchcock, through complex questions of audience identification, subverts his own long tradition of murder. With Gromek subdued, Herrmann's cue reaches its conclusion as the farmer's wife turns on the gas taps, allowing the almost silent and deadly hiss of gas to take over on the soundtrack as Gromek is slowly dragged towards his death.

In contrast to these observations, Schroeder (2012: 224–5) finds 'The Killing' to be a failure, and argues that the reason for this is a fundamental misreading of Hitchcock's intentions for the scene on the part of Herrmann. Schroeder identifies a comedic slapstick quality to the sequence, which he argues that Herrmann's score only functions to undermine. If this were Hitchcock's intention for the scene, then

Figure 11.7 Addison's score, imitative of the action on screen (Shamley Music Corp.).

Figure 11.8 Addison's score mirrors Gromek's fall (Shamley Music Corp.).

it seems unlikely that the director would have been so intent on only employing a diegetic soundtrack. A comedic cue to juxtapose the violence onscreen would surely have underlined this intention to greater effect.

Addison's score continues by mimicking and emphasising the action on screen. As the farmer's wife hits Gromek with the shovel, there is a rest in the frantic music to emphasise the painful sound effect. Addison even marked the score 'Bang' during this rest, indicating how his score was to interact with the diegetic soundtrack. The result is counterintuitive, however, diminishing the result of the sound effect by crowding it in the shrill cry of Addison's flutes (Figure 11.7).

Jack Sullivan, suggesting Chion's concept of 'empathetic music' (1994: 8), sums up the general attitude towards Addison's score by saying, '[r]ather than invoking mystery and tension, it imitates and italicises, telling us what we should feel rather than making us feel it' (2006: 286). One such example occurs as Michael grapples with Gromek until he eventually falls to the floor. In the musical quote taken from the brass, we see, in the first bar, a typical punchy action motif as Michael wrestles with Gromek (joined in the score by a frantically rising violin phrase), which then gives way to a descending sequence of triplets, straightforwardly mirroring Gromek's fall (Figure 11.8).

Furthermore, whereas Herrmann's score ended as Gromek is dragged towards the oven, giving full force to the slowly unfolding horror of Michael's actions, in Addison's cue it is at this point that his original motif resumes. This motif had previously accompanied the farmer's wife approaching Gromek with the knife, and its return adds an undue sense of structure to the scene, which further undermines the haphazard nature Hitchcock had tried to capture about this impromptu murder.

Comparisons between Addison's and Herrmann's music for the film have, unsurprisingly, invariably found in favour of Herrmann, and I hope to have added my own understanding as to why this might be the case. Royal S. Brown (1982: 44) dismisses Addison's effort as 'fluff', and for Jack Sullivan (2006: 285) it is 'the dullest score for any Hitchcock film, and the least Hitchcockian'. Whereas Herrmann had succeeded in matching the ideology of the scene and reinforcing the complexity of audience identification, Addison's score serves merely to mimic the action taking place onscreen. By doing so, Addison adds a frantic pace and rhythm to the scene, undermining the lengths that Hitchcock had gone to in order to show how it takes 'a very long time to kill a man' (Truffaut, 1985: 311).

The final curtain

Despite the comparisons I have offered between Herrmann's and Addison's approaches to scoring the scene, for the murder of Gromek the director's own scoreless version is the most successful, creating an excruciatingly drawn-out traumatic sequence to which Herrmann's and Addison's music cannot help but add undue pace and drama. A comparison between the murder of Gromek and Hitchcock's contrasting approach to murder in *Psycho* demonstrates the suitability of Hitchcock's soundtrack choice in *Torn Curtain*, and why the director was willing to accept Herrmann's score to the murder of Marion Crane, but not to the murder of Gromek.

The shower scene in *Psycho* corresponds entirely to the type of murder sequence that Hitchcock was conscious to avoid in the murder of Gromek: 'In every picture somebody gets killed and it goes very quickly. They are stabbed or shot, and the killer never even stops to look and see whether the victim is really dead or not' (Truffaut, 1985: 311). Unlike *Torn Curtain*, the murder in *Psycho* is extremely brief, and Mother departs before Marion Crane takes her last gasps of life and collapses out of the bathtub. Establishing average shot lengths for the two scenes, taking as start and end points the first moment of violence to the last moment of violence, reveals the difference in approach to the two murders. In *Psycho*, the violence perpetrated by Mother lasts only 18 seconds, with 30 rapid shots producing an average shot length of 0.6 seconds. In comparison, the murder of Gromek lasts for three minutes and thirty seconds, spanning 95 shots, producing an average shot length of 2.2 seconds. This fact highlights the suitability of Herrmann's score to the shower scene, compared to Gromek's demise. In *Psycho* the rapidity of camera cuts reflects the rapid cuts of Mother's knife and, similarly, the non-diegetic score functions to mirror the diegesis, whereby the editing and the staccato violins enhance the stabbing of Marion Crane to the point whereby the audience perceives the knife piercing Marion's body, despite this never being shown onscreen.

The shower scene without music was a failure because, as Royal S. Brown argues,

> the existential distance and the emotional gap between a movie audience and what is transpiring on the screen are so great that even the sight of a knife repeatedly entering the body of a nude woman, and even the sounds of her screams and gasps, did not create sufficient involvement in the scene. (Brown, 1982: 15)

For Brown, Hitchcock was in need of music that would 'fully communicate the sequence's irrationality' (1982: 15). However, for *Torn Curtain*, it was realism, or the 'rationality' of the sequence, which Hitchcock sought to emphasise.

Soundtrack choices for both sequences are therefore justified by the diegesis of the scenes. The music of *Psycho* reinforces the dramatic effect created by the rapid editing in representing the violence bestowed upon Marion Crane, and in *Torn Curtain* careful use of the diegetic soundtrack and an absence of music enhance the action of the scene and the key directorial choices, such as pace of editing, and match the motivations of the characters to murder Gromek in silence. Hitchcock has explained how his directorial decisions with regard to the soundscape of the sequence were justified by the action which unfolds onscreen. He notes: 'The public is aware that this must be a silent killing because of the presence of the taxi driver on the farm. Firing a shot is out of the question' (Truffaut, 1985: 311). The silence of the non-diegetic score therefore underlines the necessity of the characters to silently murder Gromek, without drawing attention to their actions. This brings to mind the anecdote surrounding *Lifeboat*, in which Hitchcock insisted upon there being no score to the film, asking, 'Where would the orchestra come from?'

This conclusion in favour of Hitchcock's version of the scene is not just due to the diegetic justification of the aural soundscape, but also the overbearing dominance that the murder of Gromek, and its *silence*, hold over the film as a whole. As part of a *Cahiers du cinéma* dossier of 1967 entitled 'Defence of *Torn Curtain*', a response to the widespread negative criticism received by Hitchcock's fiftieth film, Jean-Louis Comolli argued:

> *Torn Curtain* places itself entirely under the seal of silence. All kinds of silence – questions left without responses (the scientifico-police interrogations); advances or retreats in covert words (Newman's lies and pretenses [sic] to Julie Andrews); dialogues in half-words (the scientific discussions); silences of hearing (the chatter of Gromek [sic], which occurs outside Newman's hearing); and even the frank and beautiful silences of the two explanations. (Comolli, 1967: 52)

In this sense the silencing of Gromek, and in turn the silencing of the non-diegetic soundtrack, becomes a necessity, the black hole at the centre of a film punctuated by moments of silence, the dramatic epicentre of silence which all events prior build towards, and from which all events that succeed are irrevocably changed – from the silent dining hall at the commencement of the film, to the very last moments, in which a photographer gestures to Michael and Sarah through a window wishing to take a photograph of them, but the pair silently dismiss him, entirely through body language.

The sad endnote is, of course, that it was the experience of *Torn Curtain* that fractured the relationship between Herrmann and Hitchcock so severely that the pair never collaborated again. In hindsight this seems even more regrettable considering that Addison's score, which ultimately ended up on the finished film (without his cue 'The Murder of Gromek'), is no more modern or youth-oriented than Herrmann's effort. The small consolation is that Herrmann's score for *Torn Curtain* lived on beyond its rejection by Hitchcock, with Herrmann's close friend Elmer Bernstein rescuing the score by recording it as part of his Film Music Collection in 1977. And Bernstein's connection to the score did not end there. Charged with composing the music to Martin Scorsese's remake of *Cape Fear* in 1991, Bernstein felt that Herrmann's score to the original 1962 film was still the most appropriate music to tell the story. Bernstein recycled the music and, for instances in which there was no appropriate cue from the original score, he turned to Herrmann's unused music to *Torn Curtain*. So, twenty-five years after it was originally composed, and many years after the composer's death, audiences were finally able to hear Herrmann's music to *Torn Curtain* where it was originally intended: in the cinema.

As a final note, perhaps it is not so far-fetched to find, with hindsight, a reference in Gromek's forename to Hitchcock's once favourite composer; Bernard Herrmann had been represented on Hitchcock's screen once before, in a reverential cameo in *The Man Who Knew Too Much* (1956), but he ended his final Hitchcock collaboration brutally and intently dispatched by the director in the form of Hermann Gromek. 'The Killing' was one of the final cues written by Herrmann for Hitchcock. He was fired before he could complete the full score for *Torn Curtain*, allowing Hermann Gromek's death to play out in deadly silence, and denying Bernard Herrmann his final requiem to a Hitchcock murder.

Notes

1 Anecdotal evidence from Hitchcock's production assistant Peggy Robertson suggests that Hitchcock may never even have heard Herrmann's score to the murder sequence, indicating that it was the style of the score that Hitchcock was irked by, rather than necessarily a disagreement surrounding this particular scene (Schroeder, 2012: 222).
2 The actor Eugene Weingand, believing himself to look like Lorre, changed his name to Peter Lorre Jr in an attempt to capitalise upon this resemblance.

References

Bouzereau, Laurent (2010), *Hitchcock, Piece by Piece*. New York: Abrams.

Brown, Royal S. (1982), 'Herrmann, Hitchcock, and the Music of the Irrational', *Cinema Journal* 21:2: 14–49.

Chion, Michel (1994), *Audio-Vision: Sound on screen*, trans. C. Gorbman. New York: Columbia University Press.

Comolli, Jean-Louis (1967), 'The Curtain Lifted, Fallen Again', *Cahiers du Cinéma in English*, May: 52–5.

Conrad, Peter (2001), *The Hitchcock Murders*. London: Faber and Faber.

Gottlieb, Stephen (1967), 'Actors and Directors', *Cahiers du Cinéma in English*, May: 59–60.

Rebello, Stephen (1998), *Alfred Hitchcock and the Making of 'Psycho'*. London: Marion Boyars.

Rothman, William (2011), 'The Universal Hitchcock', in Thomas Leitch and Leland Poague (eds), *A Companion to Alfred Hitchcock*. Chichester: Wiley-Blackwell, pp. 347–64.

Schroeder, David (2012), *Hitchcock's Ear: Music and the Director's Art*. London: Continuum.

Smith, Steven C. (1991), *A Heart At Fire's Center: The Life and Music of Bernard Herrmann*. Los Angeles: University of California Press.

Sullivan, Jack (2006), *Hitchcock's Music*. New Haven: Yale University Press.

Truffaut, François (1967), 'The Journal of *Fahrenheit 451*: Part Three', *Cahiers du Cinéma in English*, May: 8–19.

Truffaut, François (1985), *Hitchcock*. London: Simon & Schuster.

Walker, Michael (2005), *Hitchcock's Motifs*. Amsterdam: Amsterdam University Press.

Walker, Michael (2010), 'A Perfect Place to Die? The Theater in Hitchcock Revisited', *Hitchcock Annual* 16: 23–54.

Wood, Robin (2002), *Hitchcock's Films Revisited*. New York: Columbia University Press.

12

Mending the *Torn Curtain*: a rejected score's place in a discography

Gergely Hubai

A lot has been said about Bernard Herrmann's *Torn Curtain* (1966), ranging from Steven Smith's biography of the composer (1991: 267–74) to Jack Sullivan's *Hitchcock's Music* (2006: 276–89), or my book, *Torn Music*, which gives a chronological overview of rejected scores from all over history (Hubai, 2012: 62–7). Instead of dwelling on the details of that fateful day when Herrmann and Hitchcock called it quits, this chapter examines the musical afterlife of the score and how it became an influential work – of course, not nearly as historically important as the scores for *Citizen Kane* (1941) or *Psycho* (1960), but it's certainly very influential considering it was never used in the film for which it was intended. In order to explain its relative significance, I'd like to draw attention to *Torn Curtain's* importance in Herrmann's discography and how its early re-recording (instigated by Elmer Bernstein) contributed to its continuing influence over the decades.

By looking at what is and what was commercially available from Herrmann's oeuvre, it becomes apparent that the unusually great attention paid to *Torn Curtain* can be attributed to the fact that this unused work was one of the very first Herrmann scores to be released in its entirety on a separate soundtrack recording. This concept is harder to understand nowadays, because almost everything Herrmann wrote for film is available for purchase on soundtracks. The composer's substantial body of work at 20th Century Fox was thoroughly preserved by Varese Sarabande in 2011 with complete releases of seventeen different titles (2011: Varese Sarabande CD Club VCL 1211 1128), while other speciality labels rescued some of the smaller scores – such as Film Score Monthly's release of less discussed works like *On Dangerous Ground* (2003: FSMCD vol. 6, no. 18) or *The Wrong Man* (2006: FSMCD vol. 9, no. 7). By my count of his discography, about 80 per cent of Herrmann's feature film scores have been released in some form or another – and that doesn't even account for his radio and television scores, which still have many titles waiting to be discovered. In order to see the significance of *Torn Curtain*, we must first consider a historical rundown of Herrmann's discography.

The basics of soundtrack release

The Herrmann discography soundtracks can be divided into two separate categories.

- The CD releases of original film tracks which were used in the films – some cues may have been cut in post-production, but that's inconsequential in this discussion. These original tracks are not only important from a historical perspective (after all, these were the ones used in the films), but also because they usually represent an authentic vision of the composer's intention. Herrmann was one of the few composers who tried to conduct all his scores – and he was adamantly critical of the few scores where he was forbidden to conduct his own work (see an explanation about why he had to skip *Vertigo* (1958) and *The 7th Voyage of Sinbad* (1958) in a later section).
- The so-called re-recordings that feature selected highlights or even complete scores in some cases. These re-recordings are done only for soundtrack albums and never appeared in the films themselves. This category can be divided into two further subcategories:
  - Herrmann himself preferred to re-record selected highlights of his own works as he did with his own re-recordings in the Phase 4 series of Decca. With the exception of his complete re-recording of *Psycho* (see later in the chapter), Herrmann never tried to record all the cues from the films and had no interest in doing a full-on reconstruction of how the score sounded in the film. Instead, he optimised the music for the listening experience on the album.
  - Modern re-recordings are also called reconstructions, because they aim to recreate the whole score as written by Herrmann. By using the original manuscript sketches, these reconstructions take meticulous care in catching performance nuances, the right tempo or even re-recording material that was cut from the films. One of the earliest reconstructions of Herrmann's work was Tony Bremner, whom we can thank for a complete *Citizen Kane* (1991: Preamble PRCD 1788) and *The Magnificent Ambersons* (1990: Preamble PRCD 1783) re-recordings, but the busiest teams in this regard were Joel McNeely, who conducted several albums for Varese Sarabande like *The Trouble with Harry* (1998: Varese Sarabande VSD 5971), *Vertigo* (1996: Varese Sarabande VSD 5600) and *Torn Curtain* (1998: Varese Sarabande VSD 5817), whereas John Morgan/William T. Stromberg also recorded a handful of albums featuring Herrmann scores such as *Mysterious Island* (2007: Tribute Film Classics TFC1001) or *Fahrenheit 451* (2007: Tribute Film Classics TFC1002).

These expensive reconstructions are usually done for two reasons. The first one is performance issues with the original tracks. As explained later, the original film tracks of *Vertigo* (1996: Varese Sarabande VSD 5759) were compromised due to a strike, hence Varese Sarabande financed a new re-recording of *Vertigo* – the one conducted by Joel McNeely (1995: Varese Sarabande VSD 5600), and this version was supposed to be closer to Herrmann's original intentions. The other reason re-recordings are done is to fill in the blanks of Herrmann's discography if the original tracks are definitely lost, as in the case of Herrmann's Americana efforts *The Kentuckian/Williamsburg: The Story of a Patriot* and war movies like *The Naked and the Dead/The Battle of Neretva* (2011: Tribute Film Classics TFC1007). Surprise discoveries can always happen, though – Herrmann's *The Egyptian* (co-composed with Alfred Newman) was considered lost and given a lush new re-recording by William T. Stromberg (1999: Marco Polo 8.225078), but the film tracks were discovered a few years later and got released (2001: Film Score Monthly FSMCD vol. 4, no. 5).

In terms of selling points, Herrmann's scores remain bestselling items, as we can observe from the countless reissues of already existing properties. A lot of scores Herrmann did for 20th Century Fox were released two or three times: *The Day the Earth Stood Still* (1951) had three different releases as a complete score (1993: Arista/TCF Film Scores 07822-11010-2; 2011: Varese Sarabande CD Club VCL 1211 1128; 2014: Kritzerland KR 20029-3) and was even given a complete re-recording by Varese Sarabande in 2003 (Varese Sarabande VSD 6314).

The Egyptian (1954) also had no fewer than four different releases (2001: Film Score Monthly FSMCD vol. 4, no. 5; 2011:Varese Sarabande CD Club VCL 0711 1123; 2011: Varese Sarabande CD Club VCL 1211 1128; 2015: La-La Land Records LLLCD 1346) and a re-recording conducted by William Stromberg (1999: Marco Polo 8.225078). In short, whatever is available from Herrmann in its original format usually had at least two different recordings and there are frequently complete re-recordings available as well – *Psycho* for instance has two complete re-recordings (1975: Unicorn RHS 336; 1997: Varese Sarabande VSD 5765) and an almost complete reconstruction (1998: Virgin Records America, Inc. 72438 47657 2 9). Even with so many re-recordings present, it's still interesting to ponder why some seminal works, such as the original recordings of *Psycho* and *Cape Fear* (1962), are still blocked by studio red tape even though we know the original recordings exist.

The historical perspective

While almost everything Herrmann did for film is now available in its original form or re-recordings, things were much bleaker thirty-five years ago. Back when the composer passed away on 25 December 1975 (on the eve of finishing the recording of *Taxi Driver* (1976)), very little of his professional output was available on soundtrack recordings. Part of the reason was that Herrmann himself wasn't keen on putting out the original recordings on soundtracks. He firmly believed that what he recorded for the films should stay there and what becomes a classic through its association with a particularly popular film may not translate well on to a concert or an LP recording. In one of the few surviving audio interviews with Herrmann, authors Leslie T. Zador and Gregory Rose conducted a discussion that reveals much more about the character of the composer than anything about his work (1998: 209–54). In this interview, Herrmann argues that one of arguably most the important scores (*North by Northwest* (1959)) is only represented with three minutes of music on the recent compilation *Music from the Great Hitchcock Movie Thrillers* because that score simply doesn't have more material good enough for an LP. Rose obviously disagreed with the mentality of a fan, having recorded the music off television to a cassette (Zador and Rose, 1998: 245).

The same interview reveals another facet of Herrmann's character, namely that he didn't take that good care of his own work. Composers like Max Steiner, Miklós Rózsa or Henry Mancini actively preserved their own works and kept well-catalogued archives of whatever they could grab from the studios – a good thing, too, since sometimes these personal archives offer the last known copies of certain scores. Steiner, Rózsa and Mancini are mentioned in particular because the copies of their personal tapes were used by producer Tony Thomas to release some of the first soundtracks aimed specifically at collectors through Citadel Records (though many of these were semi-legal, as they had no permission from the studios, only the composers). Herrmann, on the other hand, kept only the written scores with no interest in the film recordings. In the Zador and Rose interview, the two authors ask Herrmann about copying some of his personal tapes, but the composer makes it very clear he doesn't have anything in his possession (1998: 228).

By keeping the written scores to himself, Herrmann did in fact prefer to re-record his own scores for album presentation. His compilation albums released through Decca in their Phase 4 series usually featured highlight suites organised around certain themes such as Alfred Hitchcock on *Great Hitchcock Movie Thrillers* (1968: London Phase 4 SP-44126) or science fiction on *The Fantasy Film World Of Bernard Herrmann* (1974: Decca Phase 4 PFS 4309). Harking back to the composer's day at Columbia, where he could conduct concerts on a regular basis, Herrmann took it upon himself to popularise the film works of well-known composers as well with *Bernard Herrmann Conducts Great British Film Music* (1976: Decca Records SPC 21149). In all these instances, Herrmann created suites even though he barely had to rework his own material – in *The Fantasy Film World*, for instance, the separate cues are indicated within the recordings, while *The Great Hitchcock Movie Thrillers* contains suites where there are no separate lists for the cue titles (with the exception of *Vertigo*).

For collectors of film music, there's another reason why Herrmann's own re-recordings couldn't replace the real things: the tempo. The composer usually conducted at a much slower pace than what appears in his films (Zador and Rose, 1998: 222). The most notorious example of this change is *Psycho*, where the original score runs for about forty-six minutes. Herrmann himself re-recorded the complete score for the Unicorn label (1975: Unicorn RHS 336), the only example of the composer revisiting a prior work with this amount of detail. There's one problem, however – considering that both the original tracks and Herrmann's new recording contain all the same cues in the same order, the LP version runs for fifty-eight minutes – meaning that Herrmann's average tempo on the new album is 20 per cent slower, on average. The record simply misses what made the original score a fan favourite – its frantic pace.

There is another reason why most of Herrmann's original tracks were not released on soundtracks, though – cost-prohibitive reuse fees. The composer recorded most of his scores in Los Angeles, where every soundtrack recording located with the so-called union, the AFM (American Federation of Musicians), is subject to a special treatment. The most important issue in terms of soundtrack releasing is the so-called reuse fees – in short, this means that if the studio wants to release an album featuring musicians under this ruling they must pay the union once more. Scores with more musicians are more expensive than scores that feature fewer musicians, but there are other factors as well. The terms and payments varied from decade to decade, but the current situation allows for reduced prices for very old scores under a so-called historical scale – this essentially means that the age of the score also figures in the calculation of reuse fees.

The true effect of this ruling can be seen in how Herrmann's career was affected by the AFM strike, a film political event that considerably shaped the Hollywood sound. The strike lasted between 20 February and 20 July 1958, during which time frame no original score could be recorded in Hollywood (Wierzbicki, 2009: 184–6). While the big studios were ready to negotiate contracts and find a solution to the problem, they couldn't postpone the premieres of their announced releases just because the music couldn't be recorded. The first few scores to be affected were recorded in nearby Mexico, whose only positive effect was the proximity to Los Angeles, as the quality of the musicians was sorely lacking. The next few films were transported to London, which was unfortunately struck with a solidarity strike a few weeks into the problems. Therefore, the studios moved their operations further to the continent; they most frequently used the Graunke Symphony Orchestra of Munich.

The strike had an ardent effect on two Herrmann scores: *Vertigo* and *The 7th Voyage of Sinbad*. The recording sessions for both films coincided with the time frame of the strike, so therefore they were recorded in other countries. The recording sessions for *Vertigo* originally began in London, but after a solidarity strike started, the remaining cues were recorded in Vienna – there is a noticeable difference in the quality of the cues recorded in the British and Austrian capitals (Smith, 1991: 222). Since London was out on strike by the time of *The 7th Voyage of Sinbad*, the recordings were carried out by the aforementioned Graunke Symphony Orchestra of Munich. This ensemble hosted a number of troubled Hollywood productions and recorded both original scores as well as stock cues to be used in a variety of films during the 1958 strike (Smith, 1991: 225).

While the scores were done in time for the premieres, this didn't mean Herrmann was pleased with the results. Due to other union and co-production restrictions the scores that were recorded in London and Munich had to be conducted by local conductors – *Vertigo* was handled by Muir Mathieson, while the conductor for *The 7th Voyage of Sinbad* was not credited either in the film or anywhere else in the production. Herrmann, always the perfectionist, naturally thought that his scores would have sounded better if he were allowed to conduct Los Angeles musicians (though later in his career he did use more London talent). As fate would have it, these two works were also the first two Herrmann scores to have proper releases of original soundtrack recordings made for the films – after all, the music was not done in Los Angeles, so therefore the reuse fees did not apply to them.

The majority of the London tracks (but none of the Vienna tracks) from *Vertigo* were issued by Mercury Records, who compiled thirty-five minutes of the score (1958: Mercury Records MG-20384), while *The 7th Voyage of Sinbad* was released by Columbia's record label Colpix (1959: Colpix CP 504). To illustrate the scarcity of available Herrmann recordings, both scores were reissued (by Mercury and United Artists respectively) to coincide with the composer's passing (1977: Mercury Records SRI 75117; 1976: United Artists UAS 29763). While some of Herrmann's last scores were also released, all of them had their own problems: Polydor's LP of *Twisted Nerve* was merely the B-side to the more marketable Les Reed score *Les Bicyclettes De Belsize* (1969: Polydor 583.728), while United Artists' French release of *The Bride Wore Black* was merely an EP, containing a fraction of the music (1967: United Artists 36.122 UAE). Finally, the album for Herrmann's ultimate score (*Taxi Driver*) was more like a jazz concept album using his themes interspersed with Robert de Niro's dialogue – basically nothing from the film cues made it to the soundtrack album (1976: Arista Records AB/AL-4079). From the latter scores, only *Obsession* (recorded in London) had a sort of proper release, with thirty-eight minutes of music (1976: London/Decca SPC 21160). At the time of Herrmann's death, his discography of original score recordings was effectively all that's listed in this paragraph.

The historical significance of *Torn Curtain* in the discography

This short rundown of Herrmann's discography shows one of the key issues of studying the composers work – while many of his scores were celebrated within the films, hardly anything was available to be heard on its own. Even the biggest scores could go unreleased (the original tracks of *Psycho* are still officially unreleased as of now), while the short suites selected by Herrmann or other conductors like Charles Gerhardt were hardly representative of the entire work (see the *North by Northwest* example on *Music from the Great Hitchcock Movie Thrillers*). Even when Herrmann himself felt that a score of his deserved a more comprehensive archival treatment; the results were far from becoming a satisfactory representation of what appears in the film (see the example of his *Psycho* re-recording). Fans, filmmakers and researchers alike had access to a limited number of scores, but this gradually changed in no small part due to the first release of *Torn Curtain* – the first ever complete reconstruction of a Herrmann score and a rejected score.

This premiere recording of *Torn Curtain* was initiated by composer Elmer Bernstein as part of his *Film Music Collection* series. The whole enterprise can be dated back to 1972, when Bernstein published an article in *High Fidelity* magazine entitled 'What Ever Happened to Great Movie Music?'. In the article he listed all the important names he felt represented great Hollywood traditions: people such as Max Steiner, Erich Korngold, Alfred Newman, Hugo Friedhofer, Miklós Rózsa, and so on (Bernstein, 1972: 55). Feeling that the works of these composers were unfairly neglected, Bernstein launched his own enterprise entitled the *Film Music Collection*, in which he reconstructed great classical scores and re-recorded them in London. Each LP was accompanied by an issue of the *Filmmusic Notebook* [sic], a quarterly publication that contained interviews, discographies and biographies usually relating to the score of that given issue. The journal wasn't widely available, hence its treasure trove of information was a valuable resource in the pre-internet days (now the whole series can be bought in one handy volume issued by the *Film Music Society* (Bernstein, 2004)).

Bernstein's whole enterprise with the Royal Philharmonic Orchestra was launched in 1974, with Max Steiner's scores for *A Summer Place* and *Helen of Troy*. The first issue was followed by twelve further issues, all but one of which were re-recordings by Bernstein – the only exception was the eleventh issue, which featured the original film tracks from Jerry Fielding's score for *Scorpio* (1973) (Bernstein, 2004: 427). Bernstein recorded Herrmann material score, first for the 1975 summer issue, where he conducted selected highlights from *The Ghost and Mrs Muir* (1947). That issue also featured important articles that contained note-worthy information unavailable anywhere else, including a biographical sketch of Herrmann by John Caps and an obituary for *Vertigo* conductor Muir Mathieson. Previous issues also contained a two-part analysis of *Psycho* by Fred Steiner, though that particular score wasn't reconstructed for the series – after all, Herrmann's own re-recording was still fresh.

For the second issue of 1977, Bernstein unearthed Herrmann's *Torn Curtain* and created the first ever more-or-less-complete recording of the score – even Herrmann's original recording at Universal was unfinished, as the sessions were famously cancelled after only a few cues had been recorded. Bernstein's recon-struction contained twenty-one different cues, or about two-thirds of the entire score. The album sequence was mostly chronological, though a few liberties have been taken in order to accommodate the side A/side B change of the record: the highlight cue 'The Killing' was placed out of sequence to close side A. Bernstein also addressed another concern relating to the score, namely that it seems unfin-ished – the last surviving cue entitled 'The Bus' comes about two-thirds of the way into the movie and nothing else seems to have been written – even the final print of the film has no original music after this point. In order to lend a better closure to the album, Bernstein simply put a reprise of the Prelude at the end of the record.

When it was finally issued, *Torn Curtain* became the first new Herrmann recording to come out after the composer's death. The commercial release (which for some reason Bernstein repeatedly references as *The Torn Curtain*) was also hindered by a very unusual coincidence: the death of Elvis Presley. As explained in the next volume of the collection, the pressing of *Torn Curtain* albums were delayed because record pressing plants were overbooked with producing Elvis compilations and other forms of musical memorabilia; hence Bernstein's album was temporarily 'swept aside' in favour of these recordings (Bernstein, 2004: 428). Curiously enough the issue that actually features the score (vol. 3, no. 2) has no articles pertaining to the score (as was the usual case), with the exception of the front cover that features some sheet music in Herrmann's handwriting. This next issue, however (vol. 3, no. 2), featured a lengthy interview with John Addison, who shared some details about writing the replacement score for *Torn Curtain* (Bernstein, 2004: 444–58).

Thanks to Bernstein's reconstruction and recording of the music, *Torn Curtain* wasn't an abstract historical oddity – it became a real part of Herrmann's discography at a time when other, admittedly more important, scores were still unavailable. To signify the importance of this recording, here's an example of how a single record can influence other scores even if the music didn't appear in its film. In an interview given to author Michael Schelle for his book *The Score*, Christopher Young explained how one of his earliest works, entitled 'Torment', was inspired by Herrmann's unused work. While referencing Herrmann pieces was nothing groundbreaking on Young's part (his music for *Highpoint* (1982) is effectively a remake of *North by Northwest*), even he credits the existence of the Bernstein recording for incorporating the terrifying bass flutes into his repertoire:

> Elmer Bernstein recorded Herrmann's *Torn Curtain* and released it through his Film Music Collection series. The sound of it completely fascinated me. So, I decided that I was going to use the same kind of orchestra. But, of course, we had a shoestring budget. And at the recording session, I discovered that the person playing the bass flute had just rented the instrument, and had never really played it before. I discovered that if you're going to write for a group of flutes, by God, they better all be in tune, especially once you get into alto and bass flutes. What a problem! I think it was a noble idea that kind of misfired. I can't listen to *Torment* [1986] without focusing on all the intonation problems. (Schelle, 1999: 388)

Of course, Young wasn't the only one to reuse parts of *Torn Curtain*. Herrmann himself made use of unused ideas in *The Battle of Neretva* (1969); the opening of 'The Turning Point' is a slightly slower version of what the composer envisioned for the death of Gromek in 'The Killing'. The other main raider of the lost score was Bernstein himself, who made tongue-in-cheek references to *Torn Curtain*'s 'The Killing' in several cues of his music for *Airplane!* (1980) – these nods can be heard in the cues like 'Flash' and 'Panel'. Bernstein also used portions of the music in the 1991 Martin Scorsese remake of *Cape Fear*; though the score was mostly an adaptation of Herrmann's work from the original version of the film, certain musical blank spots were covered with material from the rejected score: the cue entitled 'The Fight' combines material from the 'The Fall' and 'The Killing', while the first forty seconds of 'Destruction' equals the first forty seconds of 'The Killing'.

Conclusion

Elmer Bernstein's comparatively early release of *Torn Curtain* made the unused music available not only to other composers, but also to researchers, academicians and fans of film music. The significance of his recording is especially striking when we compare the discussion surrounding Herrmann's *Torn Curtain* with that of Alex North's rejected score for Stanley Kubrick's *2001: A Space Odyssey* (1968). Both rejections marked a bitter departure between a beloved

Hollywood composer and a legendary director, plus they occurred at around the same time (1966 and 1968). *Torn Curtain*, however, was issued by 1976 and instantly became a part of the Herrmann canon. Compare this with the premiere re-recording of North's score – conducted by Jerry Goldsmith – which was only released in 1993, so the real discussion around that score could only begin some twenty-five years after the film's release (1993: Varese Sarabande VSD 5400).

Thanks to Bernstein's efforts, Herrmann's *Torn Curtain* became available just a short decade after its composition and could grow in stature for a much longer period of time than any other rejected score. Even more importantly, it was released before dozens of better-known Herrmann scores – a fan, a collector or a researcher couldn't buy a copy of *Citizen Kane* or *North by Northwest*, but *Torn Curtain* was readily available, especially after Bernstein's own limited print run was given a wider reissue in 1978 by Warner Bros. Records, who licensed a number of Bernstein *Filmmusic Notebook* re-recordings for their own series. Although there was a more complete reconstruction since this release (Joel McNeely's 1998 recording for Varese Sarabande is more complete, as it misses only two short cues), it was the Bernstein recording that paved the way for the academic discussion that's been carried on since that day.

References

Bernstein, Elmer (1972), 'What Ever Happened to Great Movie Music'?, *High Fidelity*, July: 55–8.

Bernstein, Elmer (2004), *Elmer Bernstein's Film Music Notebook*. Sherman Oaks: Film Music Society.

Hubai, Gergely (2012), *Torn Music: Rejected Film Scores – A Selected History*. Los Angeles: Silman-James Press.

Schelle, Michael (1999), *The Score: Interviews with Film Composers*. Los Angeles: Silman-James Press.

Smith, Steven C. (1991), *A Heart at Fire's Center: The Life and Music of Bernard Herrmann*. Berkeley: University of California Press.

Sullivan, Jack (2006), *Hitchcock's Music*. New Haven: Yale University Press.

Wierzbicki, James (2009), *Film Music: A History*. New York: Routledge.

Zador, Leslie & Rose, Gregory (1998), 'A Conversation with Bernard Herrmann', in Clifford McCarty (ed.), *Film Music I*. Los Angeles: Film Music Society, pp. 209–54.

13

The Herrmann–Hitchcock murder
mysteries: post-mortem[1]

William H. Rosar

In 1965, with the publication of the fourteenth edition of the *Encyclopedia Britannica*, Alfred Hitchcock expressed what might be called the "majority opinion" within the movie business on the role of film scoring, writing in his entry on 'Film Production' of music 'serving to add a dimension of mood and atmosphere to the film' and evidently endorsing the idea that the 'presence of music … is perfectly in accordance with the aim of the motion picture, namely to unfold an action or to tell a story, and thereby stir the emotions' (1995: 222). It is clear from an interview Stephen Watts carried out with him at the time of *Waltzes from Vienna* (1934) that the director was already fully cognisant of the value of film scoring from its long previous use in the silent era, though at the time he was still working out his own ideas about how it might most effectively be used in dialogue scenes, as were many other movie studio personnel in those days (Hitchcock, 1933–34; see also Steiner, 1989: 81–107).

Three decades later, one of the most successful and celebrated associations between a film director and composer ended in 1966 with *Torn Curtain*, a fact that has been lamented ever since by devotees of both Alfred Hitchcock and Bernard Herrmann, all the more since the film itself proved unsuccessful at the box office. But the handwriting was already on the wall well before then, and the seeds of Hitchcock's discontent really originated not so much out of conflict with Herrmann, but with the studio system and its established procedures for film scoring.

In his memoir *Music for the Movies*, Louis Levy recorded quite flattering impressions of having worked with Hitchcock as music director on his English films of the 1930s, so much so that one would think it a musician's dream to work with such a director:

> Hitchcock … has the greatest patience for the musician and the highest apprecia-
> tion of music in the production of the film. In his practical way he has time and
> time again worked out with me a job the music had to do in the particular film
> on which we were engaged. It was obvious that he knew nothing of the notes, and
> tempo, orchestration, or anything of the technicalities. But he has a way of express-
> ing himself so clearly that I always left our musical conferences with a tune written
> clearly in my mind, almost as though Hitchcock himself had written it. [He] has
> always insisted that music should take its proper place in the production of the film,
> just like the selection of the stars, the design of the sets, costumes and so on. With

Hitchcock the musical score is conceived in conjunction with its story, and not as an afterthought. (Levy, 1948: 147)

Yet in commenting on the working relationship he shared with Hitchcock for twelve years, Herrmann remarked, 'Hitchcock is very sensitive: he leaves me alone! Fortunately, because if Hitchcock were left by himself, he would play [Albert Ketèlbey's] "In a Monastery Garden" behind all his pictures!'[2] Herrmann's comment would seem to have been corroborated by Hitchcock himself: 'As far as I'm concerned, he does as he likes!' (Markle, 1964). That was his laconic reply to CBC television journalist Fletcher Markle, who had asked him during the making of *Marnie* (1964) how the two of them went about examining the contribution of music to a film, then only two years prior to *Torn Curtain*. For a self-styled auteur to admit that his composer enjoyed such liberty and, at that, to publicly do so on camera with a smirk as he did in answering Markle, is perplexing, and taken together with Herrmann's remark should cast doubt on the extent of his control over scoring – at least with Herrmann. What is more, in the same interview Hitchcock went further in making this admission: 'I've always found with musicians that you're in their hands anyway. What can you do?' By way of explanation he recalled: So very often I've been asked – not necessarily by Mr. Herrmann, but other musicians [e.g., Dimitri Tiomkin] – they say, "Come down, I want to know what you think of this," and you go down, and you say, "I don't care for it," and they say, "Well, we can't change it, it's all scored." So the next time you take good care to say, "Well, can you play me some, let me hear some of it before you go to the expense of an orchestra and all." "Oh no, you can't – you can't play it on a piano, it's not possible," so that there is no way to find out. So you are in the hands of a musician!"

Though intended to illustrate frustrating experiences he had had with composers, these examples as much reveal Hitchcock's frustration with the very *process* of film scoring itself. This is even more obvious when he repeated the same examples in a subsequent interview, in which he prefaced his remarks with another revealing admission: 'I'll tell you the big problem with music … In a way you have no control for music' (Adriano, 1972). This would seem to contradict views he had expressed some thirty years earlier at the time he directed *Waltzes from Vienna*, when he had also expressed disappointment with the dramatic use of music in the early talkies up to that point:

[T]he coming of sound opened up a great new opportunity. The accompanying *music came at last entirely under the control of the people who made the picture.* That was surely an advance on having a separate score played by cinema orchestras. The tremendous advantage of a film being musically accompanied had been demonstrated by 'silents' such as *Ben Hur* and *Way Down East*. Yet when it became possible to blend film and music together in an artistic entity the opportunity was overlooked, or at least left underdeveloped. (Hitchcock, 1933–34: 81; my emphasis)

We can only guess what it was that had disappointed Hitchcock, but the 'cinema orchestras' to which he referred actually became the studio orchestras that, in some of the very first talkies, recorded scores compiled from the same repertoire of published 'photoplay' music used to accompany silent films, conducted by music directors who had been hired by the studios from movie theatres. The only difference was that the music was now recorded and synchronised to the film, and mixed with dialogue and sound effects. The music directors and studio orchestras could scarcely be thought of as 'the people who made the picture', because they were performing in virtually the same capacity they had in the silent era, and one which for all intents and purposes was performed only *after* a film had been made. This was certainly true of Hitchcock's first sound film, *Blackmail* (1929). Unfortunately for posterity Hitchcock did not explain how he saw music in those first few years of sound as having come 'entirely under the control of the people who made the picture', only then thirty years later to deny having that control himself as a director who had more control than the average studio director of his day.

In any case, it was not just that Hitchcock lacked control over Herrmann, or over composers, but rather that he lacked control over the scoring process itself. He had difficulty getting his composers to audition their musical material for him, quite understandably expecting that he should be able to hear it, much as he would expect studio art directors or costume designers to show him drawings for sets or costumes for his inspection or approval before finalising them. But it is not clear from the anecdotes he related that he had pressed his composers to demonstrate their material, even if inadequately on piano, so that at least he would get some idea of what they had in mind. Yet, to listen to Hitchcock, one would think that composers were just by nature fickle and difficult, even conspiring to thwart his desire to hear what they had written. Obviously any composer seeking approval from a director by previewing his finished score during a scoring session would be disappointed by such a reaction as Hitchcock's (not to mention the reaction of the average producer, ever watchful of cost), and also share his frustration by the limitations and inadequacy of demonstrating orchestral music on piano.

In 1964, then, when *Marnie* was made, the well-established procedure was that film scores were customarily composed to edited, timed, film footage during post-production. Decisions about music placement then (as now) were, as a rule, made during the course of the 'spotting' session or 'music breakdown'. Joseph Gershenson, music supervisor at Universal for many years prior to *Marnie*, wrote a manual on film scoring which most helpfully identifies common factors influencing and determining music placement choices made during the 'music breakdown' process:

> There are no set rules or formulas for the placement of music in a film. Individual taste and one's dramatic sensitivity are the factors that will determine this … The music breakdown procedure is therefore of utmost importance in the preparation to a score and much thought and consideration should be given to the placement of the music. Sitting in with the composer at the music breakdown sessions are usually the producer, director, music editor and an editorial secretary who takes the notes when final decisions as to the music placements are made.[3]

It seems reasonable to suppose that this was common knowledge within the Hollywood studios at the time, much of it already having been the subject of the textbook *Underscore* written several years earlier by Universal film composer

Frank Skinner (1960). It could even be said that many Hitchcock films followed the typical pattern of music placement or 'spotting' described by Gershenson, and even some of the departures from it that he notes as also being effective, which will prove particularly relevant to the Herrmann–Hitchcock 'case'. For example, deciding that a scene would intentionally *not* be scored would usually be determined during spotting, if less commonly than deciding which scenes would be scored.

It is tempting to imagine that Hitchcock would have formulated his own ideas as to music placement, and even something of its character, before consulting his composers. For example, *To Catch a Thief* (1955) was scored by Herrmann's immediate predecessor and close colleague from CBS Radio in New York, Lyn Murray, the composer who actually introduced Herrmann to Hitchcock. A week after a lunch meeting with Hitchcock to discuss the film, Murray screened it at Paramount alone and recorded all of the dialogue in the film using his own tape recorder. Murray noted in his journal at the time, 'It is a wonderful picture, one of Hitchcock's best, and is full of marvelous chances for music. I am elated.' The following week Hitchcock and Murray screened it together, after which the director presented him with 'three pages of single space notes about sound and music', and Murray commented that Hitchcock

> knows exactly what he wants each of these elements to accomplish. For example, in a scene on the beach at Cannes with [Cary] Grant the wind is whipping the umbrellas and the canvas on the cabanas. He said there would be absolutely no sound in this scene – just music. (Murray, 1987: 148–9)

It might be assumed that Murray gave Hitchcock feedback after having screened the film himself, listening to the dialogue as he probably did, and that there was discussion about music when the two of them screened the film together. Yet it would appear that Hitchcock had prepared his music and sound notes before his third meeting with Murray, if he handed them to him immediately after the screening. This does tend to suggest that Hitchcock's method of procedure may have been to first formulate his own ideas about music, and present them to the composer, if then, for questions and discussion.

Like other creative directors of his day, Hitchcock sought to circumvent the limitations imposed by scoring only commenced in post-production, and eventually would involve a composer as soon as the script for a film was written, sometimes even during preliminary story discussions. When interviewed for *Marnie*, Herrmann confirmed that to be the case: 'I'm brought in at the very beginning of the idea of a film, and by the time it has gone through all its stages of being written and rewritten and the final process of photographing it, I'm so much part of the whole thing that we've all begun to think one way' (Markle, 1964).

The scoring of the murder scenes in *Psycho* proves illuminating as to the modus operandi Hitchcock and Herrmann employed in their work together. What emerges from the recorded testimony of both director and composer was that there was at times a battle of wills that would ultimately lead to the dissolution of their work together. Theirs was a dialectical method of procedure, one that might be characterised as 'point/counterpoint', representing two fundamentally different attitudes toward film scoring, in which Hitchcock ultimately held rank as director but often deferred to Herrmann, sometimes giving in to him when there were differences. Though Herrmann would later recall that 'it was a collaboration which I no longer have for many reasons – none of them personal', Hitchcock evidently thought otherwise, saying that 'he is a very good composer, but a very difficult man' (Adriano, 1972; Gilling, 1971–72: 38). The scoring of the *Psycho* murders also offers an exercise in *genetic criticism* (*critique génétique*), showing how, in this case, an artistic collaboration does not necessarily proceed towards a predetermined end – much though Hitchcock may have wished otherwise, production designer par excellence that he was, both by virtue of his early career experience as a film art director in England, and perhaps even by temperament.[4]

Herrmann had evidently been on *Psycho* from the start, often visiting the set during shooting, and it stands to reason that he and Hitchcock would have had opportunities to discuss possibilities for scoring. Presumably he became familiar with the story from the script and from talking with the director. Entitled 'Mr Hitchcock's Suggestions for Placement of Music', preliminary spotting notes for the entire film dated 8 January 1960 referred not solely to edited footage as one would expect of spotting session notes, but evidently to story continuity based on the script, storyboarding, as well as to scenes shot/edited to that date in rough cut, because principal photography had not yet been completed. After the shower murder was shot in mid-December 1959,[5] Herrmann recalled Hitchcock saying to him at the time, '[D]o what you like, but only one thing I ask you: please write nothing for the murder in the shower', since '[t]hat must be without music' (Herrmann, 1980: 132).

Even if initially Hitchcock had seemed to give Herrmann free rein with the sole proviso of having no music during the shower murder, he evidently had second thoughts, given his preliminary spotting, which at the very least bracketed where in the film he wanted music, if saying nothing of its character. In his 'Suggestions', which were prepared only days before principal photography was completed, no music is indicated for the shower sequence. For Arbogast's murder, he specified 'continue music until Mother emerges with the raised knife and shut music off when Arbogast's face is slashed'.[6] Hitchcock's instruction to 'shut music off' is as significant as his decision to have music in a scene, with a history going back at least into the 1940s. After Miklós Rózsa had been signed to score *Spellbound* in 1945, Hollywood columnist Hedda Hopper explained that 'shutting the music off' was integral to Hitchcock's method of film scoring:

> Hitch has his own theory about music. He puts music in pictures so he can stop it. He gets a celebrated composer to write music for him just so he can stop it. But just why, sir, do you get all that expensive music just to stop it? 'You've seen people in danger?' asks Hitch. 'People at some high point of tension? … So … in a psychological mystery, there are appropriate intervals at which I want the music dramatically stopped – with a hush! Well, if we didn't have the music in the picture in the first place we couldn't stop it. Which is to say that we put the music there so we can stop it.' (Hopper, 1945: 3)[7]

In his scrupulously researched study of the genesis of the *Spellbound* score, Nathan Platte found that in at least three instances Hitchcock had specified in his music notes for *Spellbound* that the score be 'stopped' (Platte, 2011: 431). Twenty years later, after *Marnie* was released, Hitchcock was still advocating the same principle, only more succinctly, while addressing the Cambridge Film Society in May 1966 after a screening: 'Sometimes it's best to have music so you can cut it off when you want to, dropping it at the dramatic climax' (quoted in Joyce, 1979: 26). It is clear from the spotting notes for Arbogast's murder that he wanted the music composed that way, not that he planned to shut it off while it was still playing. To his way of thinking, the absence of music in the shower murder could be seen as an instance of the music having already been stopped, in this case, with the cue 'The Bathroom' when Marion flushes the note down the toilet before getting into the shower.

Arbogast's murder was shot on 5 January 1960, only three days prior to Hitchcock's 'Suggestions' for that scene, on 8 January.[8] Herrmann dates composition of the score on his manuscript as starting on 12 January 1960, only four days afterwards, which coincides with the date of the first of four instalments of new spotting session notes for the film broken down by reel into separate, numbered cues.[9] Customarily a composer in those days would have composed working from *timing breakdowns* ('cue sheets') prepared by the music editor of the spotted film segments ('cues'), in which the action is described in detail and the dialogue given and timed to fractions of minutes and seconds. Unfortunately, timing breakdowns for *Psycho* have not been found, so that information is not available for comparison with Herrmann's manuscript score for the cues, though the timings can be related to the film as it was released.

In addition to the surviving autograph score, an Ozalid copy (an alternative photographic process that prints on to translucent media) of it was evidently made at the time. Presumably Herrmann conducted the recording sessions from the autograph, and the copy was made for reference by the personnel in the recording booth on the scoring stage, chiefly the music editor and music recordist. A comparison of the autograph and Ozalid yields some useful clues. It would appear that the Ozalid was made after Herrmann had finished composing, and after he had annotated timings that cued the music to the film, but before the bars were numbered, before the cues were numbered and before final reel and part numbers were assigned to them. For example, the scene of Arbogast going to the Bates house is scored with a cue entitled 'The Stairs'. The autograph is marked 8/4 (Reel 8, Part 4) in ink, but the Ozalid is marked 11/2 (Reel 11, Part 2) in pencil, suggesting either that the film had been shortened considerably or that the preliminary rough-cut reels were shorter. Close inspection of the autograph for the cue reveals that the reel/part number in ink had just been written over the penciled one. The cue number (29) on the autograph is to the left of the cue title, whereas it is to the right of it on the Ozalid. The bar numbers, in ink, correspond exactly between the autograph and Ozalid, except that they have been added to each of the scores individually, as can be discerned from slight differences in writing of the numerals and the position of them below the systems. Herrmann evidently annotated timings on the score in red ballpoint pen prior to the Ozalid being made, as they appear on both scores (monochrome on the Ozalid).

Five timings appear on 'The Stairs': the first and second as Arbogast inspects the open safe in the Bates Motel office and then exits; the third corresponding with the cut to the POV (point of view) exterior shot of the Bates house; the fourth to the cut to the interior of the house as Arbogast enters; and the last, the slow zoom shot pulling back as he walks up the stairs. Significantly the section of the cue starting with the last timing consists solely of a high chord played by divided violins that was evidently intended to last for the remainder of the cue, given the tempo (adagio). It is punctuated three times by a crotchet in the basses, the final bar marked with a fermata. Yet on the verso of the first page of the autograph, the cue has a different and shorter conclusion that has been crossed out in red ball-point pen (presumably by the composer). No fifth timing is indicated on it, but when compared with the film the cue would appear to end exactly as Hitchcock specified in his 'Suggestions', with the music being 'shut off' as Arbogast's face is slashed by 'Mother' (Norman).

Herrmann was in the habit of composing a three- or four-line sketch of each cue in pencil (as most of his Hollywood colleagues did), but customarily discarded them once he completed his orchestration in full score (in ink). Because this version of the cue was orchestrated, and is ostensibly complete, it seems reasonable to assume that it was not preliminary, but intended for the film as written. It differs from the longer, extended version in that, rather than a sustained high chord, an initial tremolo chord (bar 23) in the strings is heard again and sustained till the end instead. The revised ending on a second separate page contains the fifth timing and is four bars longer. That being the case, the final chord in the extended version would presumably have been heard under Arbogast's murder.

There is reason to believe that Herrmann was not working from the aforementioned spotting session notes in composing 'The Stairs', at least initially, and may have composed the first version before receiving them for that reel of the film, perhaps working from another set of preliminary timings. Furthermore, the spotting notes for that scene are dated 2 February 1960, which, by then, was two weeks after Herrmann had commenced composition. The spotting session notes for Reel 11 specify three cues, two of them for that scene:

Cue 11/2
Start music Int. of office of motel after Arbogast shouts 'Bates'. Continue as he looks around parlor – walks out of office – carry through Arbogast entering house and end music when he slowly starts up stairs toward mother's bedroom.

Cue 11/3
Start music when figure appears with raised knife. Continue through Arbogast's death. End music on Dissolve to hardware store.

In the film, however, the sustained chord in high violins is 'shut off', though not by a caesura in the music, but by the famous shower murder music, as Norman suddenly appears in the doorway, and a full two seconds *before* slashing Arbogast. The version of the shower murder music is entitled 'The Knife' (Reel 11, Part 3). The last five bars of the chord in 'The Stairs' are omitted and replaced by 'The Knife'. This suggests that *both* endings of 'The Stairs' were composed prior to the spotting session notes of 2 February, because Herrmann evidently had scored the whole scene with one cue (Reel 11, Part 2) rather than two, as would correspond to the spotting notes, which indicate two cues for the scene.

As Herrmann recounted, Hitchcock originally wanted no music during the 'murder scenes' (plural), yet when Hitchcock became nervous about the film, and initially granted Herrmann free rein, it was with the sole stipulation that there be no music for the shower murder (singular). Yet his written suggestions seem to indicate that he wanted no music for either murder, and the first ending of 'The Stairs' seems to comply with that wish. Why then did Herrmann extend the ending to accompany Arbogast's murder, and why was the latter replaced by the shower murder music? Moreover, do the spotting notes reflect a screening of the film at which both Herrmann and Hitchcock were present or reflect only revised 'suggestions' on Hitchcock's part, perhaps in response to discussion with Herrmann elsewhere, even over the phone? There is still no music indicated for the shower murder in the spotting session notes for Reel 8 containing it (dated 27 January).

Whatever the case may have been, it is evident that the scoring of Arbogast's murder *evolved* and that a whole new approach finally emerged. Whether that may have consisted of more than Herrmann prevailing upon Hitchcock that Norman's sudden appearance with the knife in the doorway called for particularly dramatic music at that point can only be a matter for speculation. In light of Herrmann's account, there is no reason to believe that he had auditioned the music most closely associated with the shower murder for Hitchcock prior to the dubbing session.

It then becomes a chicken-and-egg question of which came first in terms of musicodramatic conception: the shower murder cue ('The Murder') or the one for Arbogast's murder ('The Knife')? It does seem possible that Herrmann wrote 'The Knife' first, given the chronology of spotting notes, and that he then simply extended the music for 'The Murder', adding an introduction and longer ending than those in 'The Knife'. Alternatively, 'The Knife' could be an abbreviated version of 'The Murder'. Either way, if Hitchcock agreed to have music under the Arbogast murder, it was just the licence Herrmann needed to write *a little murder music*. If he realised that he could use virtually the same music for both scenes, as he ultimately did, there was not much to lose, as Hitchcock might only drop the shower music version. At the same time Herrmann had adroitly circumvented the sort of awkward scene Tiomkin experienced with Hitchcock on the scoring stage. Instead, by taking the liberty of recording the music in spite of Hitchcock's request that there be no music for the shower murder, he diplomatically presented it to him as an alternative, leaving the decision to Hitchcock, rather than complaining that it had already been recorded, that it was too late to change it, as evidently Tiomkin had done on previous films he scored for Hitchcock.

Presumably, then, Herrmann gambled that a picture is worth a thousand words and, by demonstrating his shower murder cue with picture during music dubbing, would dramatically provide the necessary impetus to convince Hitchcock of his contention that the scene called for music. This jibes with Hitchcock's own qualification in the *Marnie* interview that it was 'not necessarily … Mr Herrmann, but other musicians' who would only ask him to come and listen to cues when they were being recorded during a scoring session. Herrmann's gamble paid off because when Arbogast's murder on the staircase played with that same music in the dubbing Hitchcock had already approved it and, better still, liked it.

It could be further argued that, prior to writing 'The Knife', Herrmann had no conception of 'murder music' as such, because, even though the murder of Arbogast was eventually scored with a sustained chord, it was the same chord that accompanied him climbing the stairs before being attacked by Norman – it was not even particularly suspenseful, and certainly very different in character from 'The Knife'. Perhaps Herrmann had found a compromise to Hitchcock's suggestion to 'shut off' the music, because the chord would not really in any way mirror the horrific action on the screen, but was just an ethereal background or atmosphere against which it played out.

Obviously thinking about scoring evolved with Hitchcock, whether independently or in discussion with his composer – probably both – and evidently even during music dubbing, since he exerted his prerogative of artistic control on at least one cue in *Psycho*. Here again, he related how he did this in the context of complaining about musicians, which he was still doing in an interview with Swiss composer-conductor Adriano (1972) after making *Frenzy* (1972):

> We had, in *Psycho*, every time a murder nearly took place, *screaming* violins. Let me tell you how composers work: When we got to the end of the picture, the man rushes in with a knife – Tony Perkins. No screaming violins! I said, 'What happened? We had screaming violins in the first two murders and in the last one nothing.' 'Oh, well,' [Herrmann] said, 'We did the last one first, the other two came later.' I said, 'You're crazy! Re-do the end one and make them all the same!' That's musicians for you!

It seems reasonable to suppose that here Hitchcock refers to the same music dubbing session(s) during which Herrmann introduced him for the first time to the music he had written and recorded for the shower murder and for Arbogast's murder. Again, initially Hitchcock had wanted no music during the scene in his initial 'Suggestions'. Yet the spotting notes indicate there was to be music for it:

> Cue 14/4
> Music starts after Lila's reaction and second scream at finding the body. Continue as Sam enters, through Sam and Norman's struggle. End Music on Fade to Police Station.

The complete recording of Herrmann's score conducted by Joel McNeely in 1997 includes a cue entitled 'Discovery', which, according to the sleevenotes, was intended for that scene. This is of significance, because the complete recording

Herrmann himself conducted of the score in 1975 corresponds with the music as heard in the film, which reprises the 'screaming violins', as Hitchcock called them. Herrmann's manuscript for 'Discovery' reveals that 25 of its 40 bars have been crossed out, leaving only the last 15, and that below the cue title he has noted 'Use cue 30', which is 'The Knife'. On the margin of the first page of the Ozalid copy of 'Discovery' in another hand is the annotation 'S.T. 94-01-M-R11/4-3', which tends to suggest that, rather than re-recording 'The Knife' for use in this scene, the music track was just duplicated for it, presumably because the decision was made during dubbing after the music scoring sessions had already been concluded.

The agitato character of 'Discovery' is completely different from the simple, repetitive glissando 'screaming' ostinato of 'The Murder' and 'The Knife'. Going by Hitchcock's recollection, it may be that Herrmann had decided to score the 'Discovery' scene initially, prior to writing 'The Murder' and 'The Knife', if he had not been thinking yet in terms of 'murder music', mindful of Hitchcock's wishes. If, indeed, he scored the 'Discovery' scene first (that is, composed it first), he was in a sense complying with the spirit if not the letter of Hitchcock's wish that there be no music during the murders, simply because no murder is committed in that scene, even though one is attempted – ergo, no need for 'murder' music, and in spite of the fact that Hitchcock did not initially *suggest* there be music in that scene. Even the title of the cue itself reflects a different dramatic purpose than the titles of the other two: along with two of the protagonists, Sam and Lila, the audience is *discovering* the embalmed corpse of Norman's mother and at the same time the identity of the murderer in 'Discovery', whereas in the 'The Murder' and 'The Knife' it is the horrific *act* of murder itself that is being captured in the music. From Hitchcock's perspective, though, hearing 'The Murder' and 'The Knife' in film continuity sequence evidently set up an expectation of hearing the same music again when Norman attacked, and thus his perplexity upon not hearing it and spontaneous directive during dubbing to Herrmann that the murder music be substituted for the part of 'Discovery' that shows Norman wielding the knife. It works because the audience cannot know that a third murder will not be committed at that point. This was much to Hitchcock's credit as the cinematic 'master of suspense', creating a false expectation by reinforcing with the music the audience's initial apprehension that has already been associated with murder, even if it meant abandoning his original conception of having no music during the murders.

Of course, the expectation generated by the murder music which prompted Hitchcock to insist that it be substituted for part of 'Discovery' might not have come about had it been different music – obviously since the discovery music is very different. But evidently Herrmann did not think of the three sequences as being the same musicodramatically. He had a different conception of the third scene as opposed to the other two; otherwise, he would have made the murder music the same as the 'Discovery' music. Presumably, too, Hitchcock would not have made his suggestion insisting that the third be the same had he not heard the first two. Such is the nature of cinematic collaboration between director and composer, highlighting that there was a dialectical process between Hitchcock and

Herrmann, and certainly not one of pure auteurism, at least in musical terms. This is attested to by the fact that Herrmann revised his re-recording of the score for commercial release, as he did to conform with the music as it is heard in the film, not as he had originally written it, and omitted the first part of 'Discovery' for the recording.

In chronicling the artistic and commercial issues that resulted in Hitchcock rejecting the score Herrmann wrote for *Torn Curtain*, their ninth and final film working together, Herrmann biographer Steven C. Smith related that Norman Lloyd recalled Hitchcock telling Herrmann there was to be 'no Richard Strauss' in the score. Smith demurred that this only reflected Hitchcock's 'limited understanding of Herrmann's music, which usually was as thematically and orchestrally understated as Strauss' could be excessive' (1991: 271). Arguably that could be countered with innumerable examples of Wagnerian or Straussian *Sturm und Drang* in Herrmann's output of dramatic music, which, on the face of it, would tend to invalidate Smith's generalisation. But it is curious why, of all Herrmann's musical forebears and influences, Hitchcock would single out Strauss as the one to eschew rather than, for example, the Wagner of *Vertigo*, which was certainly very obvious with its imitation of *Tristan*, something evidently explicitly favoured by Hitchcock himself. Did Hitchcock name Strauss as exemplifying the so-called 'late Romantic' style, which has been used to characterise the so-called 'Golden Age' of Hollywood film music? Or was there perhaps something more specific he had in mind, directly related to their previous work together?

It is a truism that film composers draw upon their own musical traditions much as filmmakers draw upon their cinematic or theatrical ones. In this case, there is one motive in all of opera that might well have suggested itself spontaneously to Herrmann while scoring *Psycho*, and that is the 'axe-stroke' in *Elektra* by Richard Strauss, relevant especially because, unlike the motive of Wotan's spear in Wagner's *Ring* cycle, the deadly blade is wielded by two angry women – by Clytemnestra, who slayed her husband Agamemnon with it; and then by Elektra, the grief-stricken daughter, seeking to avenge his death by slaying her mother in turn (though Clytemnestra is finally slain by the sword of Orestes). When Elektra is first seen on stage digging in the ground for the axe that she has buried in order to hide and preserve it, her maidservant says that she is 'poisonous like a wild cat' (see Del Mar, 1969: ch. 8[b]). What might readily argue for the 'axe-stroke' motive being Herrmann's model is the conjunction of certain details:

- the Strauss motive is well-known by the name 'axe-stroke' in the opera literature and the title of the cue that arguably may have been the first murder music Herrmann wrote for *Psycho* is 'The Knife'
- Whereas Strauss has the violins leaping down alternately in minor tenths and minor sevenths, Herrmann has the strings leaping up in octaves, resembling the imitation bird chirps of "Petit Poucet" ("Little Tom Thumb") in Ravel's *Ma mère l'Oye* (*Mother Goose*), and the 'axe-stroke' is first introduced by fast upward runs spanning minor sixths that resemble glissandi

- the constant downward motion of the Strauss motive is consistent with Herrmann's, even though Herrmann prolongs the downward descent differently: Strauss has all the parts jumping down in different minor chords, whereas Herrmann starts by repeating a single line leaping up and then doubling it below with other pitches, descending through the whole string orchestra in the same rhythm, gradually forming a single dissonant chord
- the Strauss motive rhythm is syncopated from the start, whereas Herrmann's repeats a single time value, followed by a syncopated rhythm similar to Strauss's at the end of 'The Knife' in the lower register.

Though the tempo of the musical 'strokes' is different (Herrmann's being faster than Strauss's), and the main similarity between the two is the leaping violins, I would argue that we may see in the correspondence between the two motives a process Herrmann commonly used with his models: in subjecting choice bits that he borrowed to his technique of *microvariation*, as I have called it elsewhere, he pares them down to essentials, simplifying and streamlining them, and is therefore able to repeat the borrowed idea, slightly varied, ad-lib (see Rosar, 2003).[10] With 'The Murder' and 'The Knife', Herrmann wrote two whole cues from a bar or two borrowed from *Elektra*, if dramatically changing the character of the 'axe-motive' in the process, with the *bravura* result being one of pure *terror*, thanks to his brilliant flair for orchestral effects. As Lyn Murray once said of Herrmann's genius for colouristically transforming even simple musical ideas, 'Benny could make a shower curtain look like a tapestry.'

If this was the 'Richard Strauss' Hitchcock had in mind, it was not what he wanted for *Torn Curtain*. In his biography, *Hitch: The Life and Times of Alfred Hitchcock*, John Russell Taylor explained the situation facing the director at the time: 'Universal signified to Hitch that they did not want Bernard Herrmann to write the score – they would like something less "old-fashioned," more saleable in the form of a soundtrack album. Hitch stood up for Herrmann, and went out on a limb for him' (Taylor, 1978: 277). This was in spite of the fact that Herrmann had scored *Cape Fear* (1962) for Universal only a few years earlier, as well as seventeen episodes of the *Alfred Hitchcock Hour* (1962–65) for Universal TV, the last of which ('Death Scene', 8 March 1965) was telecast only several months prior to production on *Torn Curtain*.

Of the rapport that had existed between the two men collaborating on previous films, Herrmann said to Royal S. Brown in an interview: 'But he wasn't then working for Universal. He became a different man. They made him very rich, and they recalled it to him' (1994: 290). Instrumental in changing Hitchcock's fortunes was Lew Wasserman, his former agent with MCA Artists, who had conceived the idea of Hitchcock's TV show, which made its debut on 2 October 1955, just one day prior to the premiere of *The Trouble with Harry*, the first film Herrmann scored for him (see Christensen, 2012; Phillips, 2010; Taylor, 1978). Wasserman was an uncredited producer on *Psycho* and responsible for it being shot on the Universal Studios lot, which had by then been acquired by Revue Studios, MCA's television subsidiary. In 1962, MCA finally bought Universal Pictures and Hitchcock was signed to a contract, yet when Wasserman had asked Herrmann to score a film he declined the offer. David Raksin recalled, 'Benny had turned down a job from Wasserman, who got angry and said, "All right, Benny, when you get hungry you'll come to see me." Herrmann said, "Lew, when I get hungry I go to Chasen's"', the famous Hollywood restaurant (Smith, 1991: 267). This evidently had no bearing on Herrmann scoring the episodes he did of the *Alfred Hitchcock Hour* for Universal, so it would seem that the desire to use someone other than Herrmann was motivated purely by commercial reasons, since Herrmann scores were not 'hot' in terms of soundtrack sales at the time.

By then Herrmann was living part of the year in London, and in a lengthy cable to him Hitchcock set forth *requirements* for the score, not just *suggestions* this time, as he had made with *Psycho*, and well before production was completed (Smith, 1991: 269). Mostly these just repeated old complaints, likely ones discussed and debated with Herrmann in the context of previous films. At the top of the list was 'the need to break away from the old fashioned cued-in type of music that we have been using for so long'. The pronoun 'we' rather than 'you' implied an acknowledgement on his part that he had gone along with this until then. Already, after *Marnie*, Hitchcock had confessed to the Cambridge Film Society in May 1966 that he was 'a little bothered by *cued music* where the *music* is making the same statement as you have on the screen', and that 'Bringing in *music* on cue is like dialogue which merely confirms what you can see' (Hitchcock, quoted in Joyce, 1979: 26). This was in marked contrast to the concept of 'counterpoint' that Hitchcock espoused, evidently influenced by V. I. Pudovkin, who used the term in an analogy with the art of counterpoint in which two or more independent musical ideas or lines are artfully juxtaposed. More generally, Pudovkin conceived the art of film in quasi-musical terms, as later did Hitchcock, following his lead.

Hitchcock's understanding of Herrmann's art must be called into question, if he truly believed there was nothing more to his *métier* than musically duplicating what was seen or heard onscreen. Yet in his cable he quite frankly states that he was 'extremely disappointed' by the score for *Joy in the Morning*, which was made the same year as *Marnie*, because he found it 'conforming to the old pattern'. Worse still, he felt it was 'extremely reminiscent of the *Marnie* music', noting that 'the theme was almost the same'. This implies that Hitchcock must have already been dissatisfied with the *Marnie* score as exhibiting the 'old pattern', if *Joy in the Morning* was so similar to it in his estimation. Then, possibly for the first time, Hitchcock showed an express interest in the musical *style* of a score, moreover, that it be *in style*. Given Herrmann's quip that 'if Hitchcock were left by himself, he would play "In a Monastery Garden" behind all his pictures', in his experience Hitchcock was not particularly discriminating when it came to the style of music he wanted as scoring in his films, this in spite of the fact that the director was a devotee of classical music and had a large record collection.

Evidently no longer content with a hit song coming out of a film of his – such as 'Que Sera, Sera' had with *The Man Who Knew Too Much*, being sung by Doris Day onscreen – he tried to dictate to Herrmann the musical style of what Herrrmann was to write for the film:

> Unfortunately for we artists, we do not have the freedom that we would like to have, because we are catering to an audience and that is why you get your money and I get mine. This audience is very different from the one to which we used to cater; it is young, vigorous and demanding. It is this fact that has been recognized by almost all of the European film makers where they have sought to introduce a beat and a rhythm that is more in tune with the requirements of the aforesaid audience. This is why I am asking you to approach this problem with a receptive and if possible enthu-siastic mind. If you cannot do this then I am the loser. I have made up my mind that this approach to the music is extremely essential. (Smith, 1991: 268–9)

One can only guess which European filmmakers Hitchcock was alluding to in hav-ing introduced this 'beat and rhythm', apparently assuming that Herrmann would somehow know. Perhaps he was attempting to be diplomatic with his composer by not being more explicit than he was when, as it would appear in hindsight, he was sowing the seeds of disaster by providing such a vaguely worded directive. With his reference to the 'young' audience and a 'beat and a rhythm', the obvious infer-ence to be drawn was that he wanted a 'pop' score, a score written in the style of popular music. But why didn't he just say so and supply Herrmann examples for comparison?

These scarcely seem like the words of an auteur with a personal artistic vision, and one with complete artistic control over his film.[11] Rather, he sounds like a commercial studio hack pandering to his public, which further undermines the conception of Hitchcock qua auteur, at least as relates to scoring. The mandate he gave Herrmann is so meagre that to suggest he was exerting *any* artistic control with it would be generous, and only serves to highlight Herrmann's contribution, and the extent of his own artistic personality that is injected into these films and naively attributed to Hitchcock by auteur theorists.

Accomplished a composer though he was, it is not clear that Herrmann had the knowledge to write music in a popular vein had he tried. Ordinarily a Hollywood composer in those days would have asked an arranger to make pop arrange-ments of his thematic material as the need arose, except in the case of composers with experience writing in that idiom, notably his Hollywood colleagues Henry Mancini, Nelson Riddle, Elmer Bernstein, Earle Hagen and Pete Rugolo, for exam-ple. On top of that, Hitchcock wanted the score 'sketched in' even before principal photography had been completed on the film (Smith, 1991: 269).

Hitchcock's twofold emphasis should perhaps be interpreted that, as in previ-ous films, he had his own ideas about spotting, but with this film he wanted to keep to them, and thus curtail the amount of music in advance, rather than negotiate. As we saw with *Psycho*, the amount of scoring increased as the film was edited and spotted, and it is hard to imagine that this was not due to Herrmann's influ-ence. What becomes apparent is that Hitchcock was averting a battle of wills, and perhaps most telling of all in this regard is that in the draft of Hitchcock's cable to Herrmann, he concluded with the words, 'Will you please cooperate and do not bully me', but omitted that from the actual cable sent. Though Smith noted this omission from the cable, he does not consider the implications of it; clearly it suggests that, had there been differences between the two men, Herrmann may have tended to prevail with Hitchcock not on the merits of his ideas or arguments, but by browbeating.

Evidently determined to rise the occasion, Herrmann accepted the assignment – if, perhaps, somewhat reluctantly, or at the very least with decidedly mixed feelings – in light of his long and successful association with the director. He replied to Hitchcock, 'Delighted to compose vigorous beat score for *Torn Curtain*. Always pleased [to] have your views regarding music for your film. Please send script indicating where you desire music. Can then begin composing here', saying nothing about the style being in a popular idiom (Smith, 1991: 269). Somehow Hitchcock sensed that Herrmann might not be agreeing to his terms and had his assistant Paul Donnelly follow up with: 'Hitch asked me to stress ... that you should not refer to his "views" toward the score, but rather his requirements for vigorous rhythm and a change from what he calls the "old pattern".' Herrmann wrote to Peggy Robertson requesting that Hitchcock specify where in the film he wanted music (spotting) as well as 'his ideas about the kind of music for each cue'. Since the film was not yet in production, he also asked that the script be sent to him, which he received in the last week of November 1965.

Herrmann came to Los Angeles at the end of December to complete the score, though did not receive spotting notes from Hitchcock until the middle of February, though his manuscript is dated January–March 1966, which suggests that he began writing in advance of receiving them. As to the character of the music he wanted, Hitchcock specified that in only one instance, stating that the main title should be an 'an exciting, arresting and rhythmic piece of music whose function would be to immediately rivet the audience's attention' (Smith, 1991: 271).

As Smith put it, 'Herrmann complied, on his terms: his prelude was exciting, rhythmic, and riveting. But it was not jazz or pop music' (1991: 271). Instead, the 'beat' and 'rhythm' were akin to the rhythmic gyrations of Stravinsky's *Le Sacre du printemps* and motor rhythms of Prokofiev from which Herrmann had drawn inspiration before and would again afterwards. It was as if Herrmann sought to achieve the qualities that Hitchcock indicated he wanted without the stylistic trappings of popular music – or, if anything, was mocking them with his furious *oompahs* of band music clichés, there being no strings in the *Torn Curtain* instrumentation. In his own words, Hitchcock would later recall, 'I went down, heard the first segment. I said, "Finished. No other way. Finished. Good-bye. Here is your money. Sorry."' This evidently happened in spite of Hitchcock seeming to have taken 'good care' beforehand, as he would say, to involve Herrmann early on, communicating what he wanted as to the general tone of the score, not wanting much scoring, sending him the script and hearing on piano his ideas prior to the recording. Yet somehow even those measures were not sufficient to ensure the results he desired.

Smith interviewed four of the musicians who played on the session, and also David Raksin, who was with Herrmann later that day. Contrary to Taylor's (1978) account, what Hitchcock heard was not the music performed while Herrmann was conducting it for the recording, but playbacks of what had already been recorded. Some present at the recording session remembered other words having been said in those tense moments. Specifically, horn player Alan Robinson recalled in the documentary *Music for the Movies: Bernard Herrmann* (Joshua Waletzky, 1992), 'Hitchcock walked in and he said after hearing the main title, "What is this? What kind of music is this? This is not what I want!"'. Herrmann then tried to play the cue he had written for the murder scene, even though Hitchcock had the idea of having no scoring under it, so this evidently only incensed him more.[12] Presumably Herrmann planned to do as he had done with *Psycho* and present it to Hitchcock merely as an alternative. The cue, entitled 'The Killing', actually does not cover the whole murder scene, but only the first part of the struggle between Gromek and Armstrong, and ends after Gromek is stabbed and led towards the kitchen stove, where he is then asphyxiated by gas. It recalls Arbogast's murder in that the music is 'shut off' before the actual murder takes place, which could be interpreted to mean that Herrmann was conceding to Hitchcock's wish. It may be that he did not have a chance to explain, given Hitchcock's completely negative reaction to what he heard. Presumably the orchestra musicians were still present on the scoring stage as this was taking place, because a session break was called. They did not resume recording the remaining cues, because Hitchcock cancelled the rest of the session. According to Robert Mayer, who was music editor on the film, Hitchcock accused Herrmann of breaking their agreement as to the style of music the film should have and fired him on the spot. As Hitchcock was leaving, Herrmann shouted, 'What do you know about film music?' and then punctuated his parting shot with a four-letter epithet or two for good measure. Peggy Robertson had the impression that Herrmann was just not listening to what Hitchcock wanted, and said there had been meetings between the two in which it was discussed that, because Herrmann was not up to writing a pop song, he would instead score the film in a light style (Edward Nassour, personal communication).[13]

The events of that fateful day in film music history did not end with the session, though. Herrmann had apparently invited some of the musicians to join him at his home in North Hollywood that evening. As Alan Robinson remembered, '[W]e were just sittin' there, havin' a cocktail, talking it over in his bedroom, because that's where his music room was. He said, "Go to the other line, I want you to hear this, because Alfred Hitchcock is on the line," and he did get a chewing out! They had a yelling conversation between them, yes, both of them, they both had it on, and still never resolved it!' (*Music for the Movies: Bernard Herrmann*, 1992). Something of that exchange would seem to have been conveyed by Herrmann in his interview with Royal S. Brown almost ten years later:

> He just wanted pop stuff, and I said, 'No, I'm not interested.' I told him, 'Hitch, what's the use of my doing more with you? Your pictures, your mathematics, three zeros. My mathematics, quite different.' So it meant forget about it; I said, 'I had a career before you, and I will afterwards. Thank you.' [H]e said he was entitled to

a great pop tune. I said, 'Look, Hitch, you can't out jump your own shadow and you don't make pop pictures. What do you want with me? I don't write pop music.' (Brown, 1976: 65)

Herrmann told Brown that Hitchcock heard 'only the overture', but that 'he wanted the pop tune. It's a shame – it was a good score. I used sixteen horns and eight flutes, among other things' (1976: 65).

Talking again of the matter with Ted Gilling, he expressed much the same view and zeroed in on the problem that faced both Hitchcock and him on *Torn Curtain*:

> It's hard to talk about Hitchcock. It was a collaboration which I no longer have for many different reasons – none of them personal. The people who produce his films feel that he should use a kind of pop music and I don't agree with that, so I prefer not to bother. I think Hitchcock's films depend enormously on music to build his nutcracker of suspense, and to impose on him a kind of pop culture is to deprive him of one of the greatest weapons in his arsenal. However, it's not for me to say. (Gilling, 1971–2: 38)

The following year, in talking about the main title music for *Psycho*, Herrmann said, 'In film studios and among filmmakers, there is a convention that the main titles have to have cymbal crashes and be accompanied by a pop song – no matter what! The real function of a main title, of course, should be to set the pulse of what is going to follow' (1980: 132). He could just as well have been alluding to the situation he encountered on *Torn Curtain*.

Given Hitchcock's ungrateful reaction to the composer's efforts to help the film and Herrmann's riposte, it seems likely the two men would never work again and their professional association had come to an end: Herrmann was not about to endure that kind of professional humiliation again, nor was he willing to subordinate himself to such capricious whims in the name of artistic control, even if the director was Alfred Hitchcock, and a long time close associate at that. There is no indication that Hitchcock ever expressed publicly or privately any remorse over his split with Herrmann. This may partly be explained by something he learned during a sojourn in Hollywood visiting the movie studios in the 1930s:

> A thing … which I confess surprised me … is the way in which stars, directors, writers and others are taken off a picture if they do not seem suitable. In England it is still something of a set-back to one's reputation if such action is taken. In Hollywood it not only does no harm to the withdrawn expert's reputation, but is commonly done if the first experiment does not work out well. (Levy, 1948: 148)

Other than the personal anguish it caused Herrmann, there is no indication that being taken off *Torn Curtain* damaged his professional reputation, considering that his next film was Truffaut's *Fahrenheit 451* – which, ironically, though British-made, was distributed by Universal! If anything, Herrmann's career began to prosper, sought after as he was by young directors who admired him.

In Herrmann's defence, and lacking definite evidence to the contrary, Hitchcock did not *say* he wanted popular music, so Herrmann did not write it, or provide it arranged by another musician, as he might have under the circumstances. He interpreted Hitchcock's mandate literally, to the letter: Herrmann may well have *surmised* Hitchcock wanted a pop score, but in fact that is not what Hitchcock actually wrote him as a *requirement*. Evidently the director thought he had communicated more to his composer than he actually had. Rather, Hitchcock's expectation seems only to have come out in the angry exchange on the phone that took place between the two men following the recording session. Though initially Herrmann blamed Universal for influencing Hitchcock in this regard, later on he was of the opinion that it was due to Hitchcock himself. This came out when Brown asked Herrmann who was responsible: 'Was the Hitchcock break basically the doing of producers who decided they wanted a pop composer?' Herrmann replied, "No, it's Hitchcock" ' (Brown, 1976: 65).

Of course, what Herrmann never said was that he might not even have been capable of writing pop music had he wanted to, which might very well have also been the case. Indeed, it was primarily a colossal failure in communication between two men who had worked closely and successfully together for twelve years, given the box office results alone, at least until *Marnie*. Even years after *Torn Curtain*, and the end of their professional association, Hitchcock was still complaining about the problem of judging music only at recording sessions, so it was a pet peeve for which he held the composers responsible, rather than the established system of motion picture production.

What recourse did Hitchcock have to exert his wishes for scoring? Starting with *Torn Curtain* he left his decision until the scoring session, and simply threw out the score, rather than allowing any provision for revision, had time and budget permitted. There was always the option of the 'remake', the rewriting of a cue or cues, to better conform to his desire, something for which David O. Selznick, for example, was notorious, as Nathan Platte has documented in his extensive research on the music in Selznick films, including *Spellbound*. But Hitchcock seemed not to exert his executive privilege of artistic control in that manner, given the examples shown here from *Psycho* and *Torn Curtain*, which tended to be either proscriptive or by veto. *Psycho* has provided one instance in which he explicitly asked that music be substituted (the 'screaming violins' for part of 'The Discovery'), and with *Torn Curtain* he found Herrmann's musical ideas at audition 'too heavy'.

Hitchcock claimed that artistic control was something that had been contractually granted to him in his studio contracts at least since *North by Northwest* (1959). It may be that he did not have much budgetary control over post-production costs that would include requesting rewrites of cues and re-recordings if music displeased him. But these working conditions were not the fault of composers, and if Hitchcock had wanted the luxury of music revision after scheduled recording sessions, he could have sought to stipulate the provision in his contracts. In their day, however, usually that prerogative was reserved for producers or music department heads.

Though Herrmann came to Hitchcock's defence on *Torn Curtain*, it is clear that Hitchcock invoked then current musical fashion in movies and the pressure he got from Wasserman and the 'front office' at Universal as subterfuge to dictate style to Herrmann, though to do so would have been his prerogative on the previous films they had done together. The way he presented his 'requirements' to Herrmann in the cable seems far from an artistic decision of his own for which he was taking responsibility, though. That he offered to pay Herrmann's fee out of his own pocket in discarding the *Torn Curtain* score after discharging him was evidently only a symbolic gesture, because it was paid by the studio and the budget was sufficient to permit a new score to be written and recorded, not by Herrmann, but by another composer deemed capable of writing what the studio and the director had wanted – English composer, John Addison.

Perhaps most telling is that, years later, when asked if he would use Herrmann again, Hitchcock replied condescendingly, 'Yes, if he does what he is told', as if he had been insubordinate. Hitchcock's retort stands in marked contrast to his line at the time of *Marnie*, when he said of Herrmann, 'As far as I am concerned, he does as he pleases.' It is rumoured that Hitchcock invited Herrmann to score his final film, *Family Plot* (1976), but that he declined because he was working on other films at the time.

The lamentable outcome on *Torn Curtain* exemplified an artistic dilemma that Hitchcock evidently never fully resolved to his own satisfaction. As Herrmann would say after the fact during the scoring of *The Bride Wore Black* (1968) for Truffaut:

> Hitchcock is an extraordinarily well-organized man in making of his films. The actual shooting process to him is already boring because he has made the film in his head. For example he will never give an actor direction how to walk in and out of a room. He will accept the fact that the man had to walk into the room, and if that actor walks that way, and it's done with conviction, he's quite happy with it. And so to work with him with music also is a great deal that way. He will say, 'I have left reel three for you.' (*Music for the Movies: Bernard Herrmann*, 1972)

Even though Hitchcock would publicly praise Herrmann that '33% of the effect of *Psycho* was due to the music' (Smith, 1991: 241), Herrmann knew that the director begrudged him for it, simply because his music had saved the day. Hitchcock had to concede that Herrmann's musicodramatic instinct was right regarding the shower murder, but reluctantly, because it meant he had been wrong in thinking that the film alone without music would have the shocking effect he had envisioned: 'Improper suggestion, my boy, improper', he had to admit. Music had not been part of his own filmic conception of the brutal murder, which he had wanted to succeed to the point of insisting that Herrmann not even write music for the scene.

As Herrmann realised,

> [Hitchcock] only finishes a picture 60%. I have to finish it for him … I think he resented the importance of the role my music played in his films. I always tell the story: A composer writes a score for a picture, and he gives it life. Like a fellow goes to a doctor, says, 'I'm dying,' and the doctor cures him. Then the doctor says, 'Aren't

you pleased? I cured you.' And the fellow says, 'Yeah, that's right, but you didn't make me rich, did you?' (Brown, 1976: 65)

On another occasion Herrmann argued for the *necessity* of music in films:

[F]ilm is one medium that needs other arts, because it's a cooperative, mosaic enterprise, and the use of music has always been necessary even from silent days to the present day. And people always ask me this question 'Why does a film need music?' Well, I'd like to say this – I've never met a producer yet who said to me, 'I've just finished a film and I don't need *you!*' They say, 'You must come and see what you can do to *help* us!' Now, that alone is the crying need of the film, because music is a sort of cement, or veneer, that finalizes the art of making a film. (Herrmann, 1972: 11)

Was Herrmann here perhaps unconsciously thinking of the venerable *play doctor* of the theatre, who is called in to 'doctor' plays by fixing dramaturgical weaknesses or other problems in plays?

In the final analysis, Hitchcock was a production designer trying to plan during pre-production that which was customarily one of the last phases of post-production – scoring a film. When Stephen Watts interviewed Hitchcock at the time *Waltzes from Vienna* was made, and asked him, 'Do you believe, then, that every film should have a complete musical score, before it goes into production?' Hitchcock responded,

I do … [t]hough by 'complete' I do not mean continuous. That would be monotonous. Silence is often very effective and its effect is heightened by the proper handling of the music before and after. There is, somewhere, the correct musical accompaniment for almost any scene – music which will improve the scene. But none at all is better than the wrong music. (Hitchcock, 1933–34: 81)

Because of that, Hitchcock would think of music placement before some scenes had even been filmed, as seen in his preliminary spotting 'suggestions' to Herrmann on *Psycho* and later 'requirements' on *Torn Curtain*. Yet, as a result, he was inevitably faced with an insoluble chicken-and-egg problem in working with his composers, since films are typically scored *in response* to what amounts to a finished work – the film – much as a composer composes a song, a tone poem or opera in response to an existing work or text. In this case, that work is something the composer sees and hears, much as music directors and organists did in the silent era: the films they accompanied were *finished* works. A composer's response to reading a script may not be the same as seeing a scene from it once it has been filmed and edited, so it is not always helpful to read it before seeing (edited) film footage (Heinz Roemheld, personal communication).[14] At most, being involved early in a film at the conceptual stage helps to stir a composer's creative juices and may inspire musical ideas. Given that usually he is writing to edited film, in a fundamental sense his is an *art of accompaniment*.

In 1968, Herrmann wrote a musical tribute entitled 'A Portrait of Hitch' based largely on his first score for Hitchcock – *The Trouble with Harry* – which, in turn, consisted mostly of thematic material he had borrowed from himself for the CBS radio drama programme *Crime Classics* (1953–54). A year after it was written, Herrmann recorded the piece for an album entitled *Music for the Great Movie Thrillers: Music Composed by Bernard Herrmann for Motion Pictures Directed by Alfred Hitchcock*. Given what Hitchcock had to say about the score and theme for *Joy in the Morning* seeming so similar to *Marnie*, we can only wonder what he might have thought had he known the origins of the *Trouble with Harry* score and Herrmann's musical tribute to him.[15] Some have interpreted the *Great Movie Thriller* album as an olive branch Herrmann extended to Hitchcock, especially given the sleevenotes, which paid further tribute to the director's art: 'Most people think of Hitchcock as a master of mystery and suspense. Although this is fundamentally true, he is also a great romantic director. This record displays many of his diversified talents.' That is a strange thing for a composer to say, given that what was presented was his music, not the director's.

Notes

1 I am grateful to Edward Nassour, Stephen Pickard, Robert Swarthe and William Wrobel for information and sources supplied by them and for much beneficial discussion. Also, thanks go to Jenny Romero of the Margaret Herrick Library, Academy of Motion Picture Arts and Sciences, for her capable and generous assistance in supplying primary sources from the Alfred Hitchcock Papers there, and to David Seubert of Special Collections, Davidson Library, University of California, Santa Barbara, for holding information about *Psycho* material in the Bernard Herrmann Papers in the Performing Arts Collection.

2 The 'light classics' of Albert Ketèlbey (1875–1959), this one for orchestra and chorus being the most famous of them, were very popular during the silent era as accompaniment. Three volumes of them containing eighteen numbers are listed in Erdmann, Becce and Brav (1927: 121).

3 Cover note: 'A step by step guide to the techniques and procedures employed in the preparation for and the writing of music for all mediums and films.' Unpublished typescript, *c.* 1965, evidently written after *The Art of Love* (1965) had been scored at Universal by Cy Coleman.

4 'Genetic criticism does not focus on one particular state of the text, but rather in the process by which the text came to be. As explained in *Genetic Criticism*, edited by Ferrer, Deppman and Groder: "the chief concern [of genetic criticism] is not the 'final' text but the reconstruction and analysis of the writing process. Geneticists find endless richness in what they call the 'avant-texte': a critical gathering of a writer's notes, sketches, drafts, manuscripts, typescripts, proofs, and correspondence"' (Macé, n.d.).

5 The *Psycho* Shooting Schedule (Revue Studios), Alfred Hitchcock papers (Folder 611), Margaret Herrick Library. It indicates on p. 12 that the shower murder was to begin shooting on 14 December 1959.

6 Hitchcock papers (Folder 599).

7 I thank Nathan Platte for calling my attention to this article.

8 *Psycho* Shooting Schedule: 26.

9 *Psycho*, autograph score (incomplete), Bernard Herrmann Papers. A microfilm copy of the autograph that also includes Ozalid copies of cues missing from the autograph is in the Music Division of the Library of Congress, Microfilm 87/20,037 <Mus> 33.

10 It might be that Herrmann derived his microvariation technique from the practice of Wagner in varying and transforming the leitmotivs in his musicdramas, given how short most of the leitmotivs are. Herrmann evidently realised that the process of variation of a single musical idea could be extended indefinitely, if systematically.

11 Hitchcock related that, from the time of *North by Northwest*, 'I have complete control. [T]here's a clause in the contract which gives me complete artistic control even though it's their money' (Joyce, 1979: 26). That being so, he must have gone along with what Herrmann did up until *Torn Curtain*.

12 Having evidently requested a timing breakdown for the scene from the music editor, in spite of Hitchcock's intention.

13 Formerly of the editing department at Universal, Nassour had talked to Mayer and Robertson about what happened between Herrmann and Hitchcock on *Torn Curtain*.

14 Hollywood film composer Heinz Roemheld even acquired the nickname 'Doc' because he was so routinely called in by producers to 'save' pictures.

15 According to Smith, Herrmann requested permission from the producer of *Crime Classics*, Elliott Lewis, to reuse music from it, but does not indicate that Hitchcock knew anything of that (Smith, 1991:193).

References

Adriano (1972), 'Alfred Hitchcock on Film Music and Bernard Herrmann', 26 September, www.adrianomusic.com/hitch.html. Accessed 2 July 2014.

Brown, Royal S. (1976), 'An Interview with Bernard Herrmann', *High Fidelity* 26:9: 64–7.

Brown, Royal S. (1994), *Overtones and Undertones: Reading Film Music*. Berkeley and London: University of California Press.

Christensen, Jerome (2012), 'Alfred Hitchcock is Rolling in His Grave', *Salon*, www.salon.com/2012/12/24/alfred_hitchcock_is_rolling_in_his_grave/. Accessed 3 July 2014.

Del Mar, Norman (1969), *Richard Strauss: A Critical Commentary on His Life and Work*, vol. 1. New York: Chilton Book Co.

Erdmann, Hans, Giuseppe Becce and Ludwig Brav (1927), *Allgemeines Handbuch der Film-Musik*, vol. 1. Berlin: Schlesinger'sche Buch und Musikhandlung.

Gilling, Ted (1971–72), 'The Colour of the Music: An Interview with Bernard Herrmann', *Sight and Sound*, 41:1: 36–9.

Herrmann, Bernard (1972), 'Bernard Herrmann: A John Player Lecture', *Pro Musica Sana* 3:1: 10–6.

Herrmann, Bernard (1980), 'Bernard Herrmann, Composer', in Evan William Cameron (ed.), *Sound and the Cinema: The Coming of Sound to American Film*. Pleasantville, NY: Redgrave Publishing, Co., pp. 117–35.

Hitchcock, Alfred (1933–4), 'Alfred Hitchcock on Music in Films', *Cinema Quarterly* 2:2: 80–3. Reprinted in Sidney Gottlieb (ed.), *Hitchcock on Hitchcock: Selected Writings and Interviews*. London: Faber and Faber, pp. 241–5.

Hitchcock, Alfred (1995), 'Film Production', in Sidney Gottlieb (ed.), *Hitchcock on Hitchcock: Selected Writings and Interviews*. London: Faber and Faber, pp. 210–26.

Hopper, Hedda (1945), '"Hitch" Reveals Secret of Making His Pictures', *Los Angeles Times*, 11 March, pp. B1, 3.

Joyce, Paul (1979), 'Hitchcock and the Dying Art: His Recorded Comments', *Film* 79: 25–8.

Levy, Louis (1948), *Music for the Movies*. London: Sampson Low, Marston & Co.

Macé, Caroline (n.d.), *Textual Scholarship*, www.textualscholarship.org/gencrit/index.html. Accessed 3 July 2014.

Markle, Fletcher (1964), 'A Talk with Hitchcock', Part 1, Canadian Broadcasting Corp. Author's transcription.

Murray, Lyn (1987), *Musician: A Hollywood Journal of Wives, Women, Writers, Lawyers, Directors, Producers and Music*. Secaucus: Lyle Stuart Inc.

Phillips, Adam (2010), 'Alfred Hitchcock Presents "Alfred Hitchcock Presents" ', Hitchcock Report, http://thehitchcockreport.wordpress.com/tag/lew-wasserman/. Accessed 3 July 2014.

Platte, Nathan (2011), 'Music for *Spellbound*: A Contested Collaboration', *Journal of Musicology* 28:4: 418–63.

Rosar, William (2003), 'Bernard Herrmann: The Beethoven of Film Music?', *Journal of Film Music* 1:2–3: 121–51.

Skinner, Frank (1960), *Underscore*. New York: Criterion Music Corp.

Smith, Steven C. (1991), *A Heart at Fire's Center: The Life and Music of Bernard Herrmann*. Berkeley: University of California Press.

Steiner, Fred (1989), 'What Were Musicians Saying About Movie Music During the First Decade of Sound? A Symposium of Selected Writings', in Clifford McCarty (ed.), *Film Music 1*. New York: Garland Publishing, pp. 81–107.

Taylor, John Russell (1978), *Hitch: The Life and Times of Alfred Hitchcock*. New York: Pantheon Books.

University of California Santa Barbara (UCSB), Bernard Herrmann Papers, Special Collections, Davidson Library, University of California Santa Barbara.

14

How could you possibly be a Hitchcocko-Herrmannian?: Digitally re-narrativising collaborative authorship

Steven Rawle

The title of this chapter refers quite explicitly to André Bazin's 1955 *Cahiers du cinéma* editorial addressing the criticisms of their issue on Hitchcock, the matter of 'a certain amount of fuss' (1996: 32). Bazin addresses some of the reproaches *Cahiers* experienced about the issue, from those including Lindsay Anderson at *Sight and Sound*, as well as the disputes between him and the 'young Turks' (1996: 33) at the magazine. The critiques, he states, were 'fertile':

> Where criticism is concerned I do not really believe in objective truths or, to put it more precisely, I would rather be forced to consolidate my own judgements in order to deal with opposing ones than have my principles supported by weak arguments. If I remain skeptical about Hitchcock's work, at least I do so for the best reasons. (1996: 33)

Bazin remained indifferent to the excesses of *la politique des auteurs*, although he did embrace the figure of the director as author in much of his criticism. In this particular editorial, Bazin's objection is with the refusal of certain kinds of criticism. He offered a summary, to the young critics at the magazine, and their detractors: 'we all have something in common in spite of our disputes; not "love of the cinema" – that goes without saying – but a vigilant refusal under all circumstances to *reduce* the cinema to the sum of what it expresses' (1996: 33; emphasis in original). In adopting a version of Bazin's title, this chapter wants to emphasise a different type of reductionism in popular approaches to film authorship. To be a Hitchcocko-Herrmannian is not so scandalous as the canonisation of popular filmmakers like Hitchcock and Howard Hawks was in the 1950s, when the notion of the film author expressed degrees of cultural capital. But there is a blockage to thinking about how we conceive of collaboration, especially amongst the digital artefacts of recent and current cinephilia and audiophilia.

One of the key developments over the last few decades of cinema has been the growth of home video, later DVD and Blu-ray, and the creation of new types of cinephilia in the home. The film is no longer accessible simply as a stand-alone feature, although as streaming media through platforms such as Netflix, Hulu and Amazon Prime becomes the default method of home viewing such practices will inevitably be rethought. Coming towards the end of the era of physical media in the home, this chapter is an exploration of something that is soon to pass into another form, or potentially to disappear altogether: the special feature. The supplements and special features collected on the DVD, and on the Blu-ray, constituted an altered mode of cinematic appreciation and film education. Although there is definitely a promotional incentive with the special feature and the special edition DVD or Blu-ray, developed in the 1980s by the Criterion Collection on Laserdisc, and adopted en masse by the film industry in the late 1990s, the DVD offered different kinds of positioning of authorship, the processes of film production and constructions of reception, interpretation and address to the viewer. There have been several explorations of the DVD and the director's audio commentary and each explores the ways in which authorship is re-presented, resituated or simply presented by authors' (often the directors') own biographical or dramatic reconstruction of the creation of the film text. The supplements sometimes create a particular view of a film's meaning, as Brookey and Westerfelhaus (2002) have shown with the audio commentary of *Fight Club* (1999), which seeks to recuperate the film from queer or homoerotic readings, but this presentational material (which works in conjunction with, at the same time as, representational material) works to resituate, or to avoid conceptions of collaboration that unseat, the director-as-sole-author, long after academic theory had really consigned the author as a source of meaning to history.

As Nicholas Rombes has noted, 'Roland Barthes's famous prediction about the death of the author has come to pass, but not because the author is nowhere, but rather because she is everywhere' (2005). Film authors are more available than ever, and we need to think about how they are constituted, how this encompasses older traditional romanticisms, as well as how this responds to digital economies, film production and reception. Now, of course, Hitchcock offers us a different approach to this material, since he isn't around to record new material for DVD. Nevertheless, the DVD and Blu-ray releases work very hard to promote an auteurist reading of his work, with multiple retrospective documentaries and 'expert' insight about Hitchcock's working methods and the films' development and production. This has significant consequences for the re-presentation and conception of collaboration. What I want to address here is how Hitchcock is conceived by the DVD and Blu-ray releases, initially Universal's fiftieth anniversary release of *Psycho* (1960). I choose this particular package for several reasons: first, it is the film which has one of the most significant popular recognitions of Herrmann's contribution to the film; second, it is particularly well packed with special features, certainly more than earlier releases; and finally, it presents authorship in a very clear fashion, in technical and production processes, by resituating it within an historical approach to film production; additionally, the Blu-ray package presents an auteurist conception of cinema – the director as the main source of meaning in the text. The home video text can now encompass several things; the film does take prominence, but it can be time-shifted, combined with new soundtracks, an audio commentary, interspersed with documentary materials which create, as

Bertellini and Reich note, 'value-adding paratexts' (2010: 103). As Paul McDonald has shown, though, the viewer can choose not to engage with these paratexts:

> Rather than presuming DVD has any impact on the viewing experience, it is probably more appropriate to judge that the significance of DVD extras resides in how they offer the possibility of interactivity even if the viewer never chooses to access those options. (2007: 66–7)

Nevertheless, this possibility has an effect on the conception of production, 'creating a particular vision of the processes and conditions of media production' (2007: 66). This includes how collaboration is discussed, framed and positioned. While film authorship has always been a reductive practice critically (something Pauline Kael famously lambasted Andrew Sarris for in her infamous essay 'Circles and Squares' (1963)), this 'publicly disclosed deep text', as John Thornton Caldwell refers to the DVD extra, embeds this in a public discourse. The 'deep text' at once functions as a form of industrial theorising whilst simultaneously intended for public consumption (Caldwell, 2008: 345–50).

Echoing the publicly disclosed nature of Caldwell's 'deep text', Catherine Grant has pointed to 'the potential "deterritorializing" of auteurism' by new media technologies (2000: 101). Offering a critique of Timothy Corrigan's 'deterritorialized' *Cinema without Walls*, Grant argued that 'the increasing commodification of authorship' (108) stimulates, in the new millennium, changes in 'the precise nature and direction of a significant part of the flow of cultural and, especially, economic capital' (105). Although written prior to the widespread popularisation of DVD, Grant's partly speculative meditation on auteurist discourses for 'niche' communities of fan discourse in online forums gives an insight into the ways in which authorship became commodified and mediated via Hollywood blockbuster DVDs. The work done by digital re-releases of classic cinema, however, recuperates the historical spaces of classical Hollywood. I'm thinking here about the documentaries and releases of classic Hollywood films with commentaries by living cast and crew members or with talking-head academics (in some cases including contributors to this book, such as Jack Sullivan, who features in a number of Laurent Bouzereau-produced documentaries, while all of the Network DVD releases of British Hitchcock films include introductions from Charles Barr). Such 'value-adding paratexts' offer a historical perspective on the film, either by revisiting the making of the film or by offering academic or critical readings of the film's text. In the case of the anniversary release of *Psycho*, there is a sustained effort to revisit the making and release of the film, from its conception in Bloch's novel to the 'see it from the beginning' release strategy. While all of this material is already available in print, the situation of that material within the space of the film's text repositions those paratexts that Bertellini and Reich describe. However, whereas Grant talks about the deterritorialisation of auteurism in new communities, the DVD and Blu-ray artefact specifically resituates these discursive processes within the spaces of the disc, the home and the interactive viewing – the film does not have to be watched alone. Some releases even allow the viewer to break the film up with featurettes that place those paratexts within the text itself, supplementing historical information, production trivia, but with a continued placement of the film's author.

In 'Auteur Machines? Auteurism and the DVD' (2008), Grant again addressed these concerns in relation to the very privileged area of DVD audio commentaries that recuperate or recover a film's text via the 'documentary performance of the "drama of the movie's source"' (2008: 112).[1] It is perhaps surprising, given the substantial publishing industry around Hitchcock's films, that only *Psycho* and *Vertigo* (1958) have been released with commentaries.[2] All of the releases do feature some kind of extra material that explores production, release and reception, but the privileged audio commentary has been reserved only for these two Hitchcock films. For Grant, a whole new mode of auteurist reception is created by such artefacts. She notes:

> Contemporary auteurism comprises a complex series of interrelated film production, marketing, and reception practices and discourses which are all underpinned by a shared belief in the specific capability of an individual agent – the director – to marshal and synthesize the multiple, and usually collective, elements of filmmaking for the purposes of individual expression, or to convey in some way a personal or, at least, 'personalized' vision. (2008: 101)

While much of what Grant defined here is common with earlier romanticised notions of auteurism, the location of contemporary readings of authorship within 'production, marketing, and reception practices' highlights the related discourses mobilised by these practices. Many Hitchcock DVDs do give a privileged space for Hitchcock's individual, 'personalised' voice: with *Psycho*, the 2005 release featured archival material (*Masters of Cinema: Alfred Hitchcock*) that allowed us to return to Hitchcock as the originator of the text; while the 2008 Network release of *The Man Who Knew Too Much* (1934) included an archival episode of *Aquarius*, a Thames Television arts programme from 1972 entitled *Alfred the Great*. But, as Grant notes, the

> act of selecting the … commentary turns the 'original' (theatrical) experience of watching the film *as fiction* into one of watching it 're-directed,' or literally re-performed, *as a documentary*, one in which the film's existing visual track is employed as graphic illustration of a teleological story of its own production. (2008: 111)

What's significant here are two things in relation to the digital re-releases of Hitchcock's work – the first is the reperformance of the film as documentary, where the commentary turns the film into an historical document of the production of the film' and the other is the problematic consequence for the musical track. With the audio commentary, the soundtrack of the film is generally turned down, sometimes turned up again for gaps in the commentary. This immediately stresses the secondariness of the aural frame to the visual. This becomes particularly problematic for the anniversary release of *Psycho*, which I will come to in a moment. While the film's visual frame becomes a basis for the documentary source – the images as testimony to the production history being layered on top – the soundtrack becomes replaced, or recombined with other elements to again stress the importance of the visual over the aural. The visual text therefore becomes a documentary performance of the film's imagery in order to present the 'teleological story of its … production'. The performance of that production, for the classical-historical release, is mainly auteurist in nature. While the auteur in this case is not obtainable, as it might be for a more contemporary release, the intentions and activity of the author are situated in the voice of the authoritative 'expert' – usually the author of a book on the film, another film director or composer – to promote the authorial reading of the text as an individual one.

My concern in this chapter is really the effects of this kind of promotion on the reception or construction of auteurist readings of the film text – in relation to classical Hollywood (given the cultural weight given to Hollywood cinema in the study of popular culture), a notion of cultural capital in the reception and knowledge of classic works of cinema. What this also maps on to are distortions in those very things that the work of the DVD paratext works to recuperate: history and the reading of the film text. Paul Sellors' book *Film Authorship: Auteurs and Other Myths* revisits auteur theories as a way of reviving, differently, the notion of authorship in research and reception of cinema. As he ends the book:

> The combination of … growing evidence of film productions and the influence of analytical philosophy on film theory has enabled a shift from a textual to a communicative model of film authorship. This shift allows us to refocus our attention from the coherent picture of a film's reception to the more complicated situation of its production. This I believe is an important development in our understanding of film authorship, not just because it promotes a historically robust understanding of the actual means by which any film comes about, but also because it provides a more accountable analysis of how films are meaningful and culturally significant. Historical research has demonstrated that films are collaborative enterprises and that authors are facts of film production. (2010: 129–30)

Sellors gives a very admirable reclamation of collaboration as a model for thinking about how films are produced and conceived, and, as a historical methodology, his authorial focus on collaboration presents us with a means by which we can revisit authorship and the conception of the work in any given film's production (I refer to production here, rather than thinking about the text as a source for defining and 'reading' authorship). Sellors argues that 'within the production collective is an authorial collective' (2010: 124). Sometimes the production and authorial collectives are the same, but often that production collective is larger than those with authorial bearing on the finished film – we'd include a composer in the authorial collective, but we wouldn't include a grip (as Sellors argues, but a grip may still have bearing on elements of camera movement that contribute to meaning or significance in the finished work, but it may not necessarily be intended). Where I think Sellors' methodology becomes problematic is in making only very short and almost dismissive reference to the ways in which authorship has become, popularly, a very common means of situating the film's production history or the means of reading the text. The DVD makes no such methodological promises about the ways in which authorship is presented or discursively constructed in the audio commentary or in the ways in which the film becomes a documentary performance of the production of the film. I'm more concerned with its discursive dimension, rather than reclaiming it from history – a very different approach to Sellors, who wants to reclaim authorship from textual readings – but I wish to react to how the discourse of authorship, particularly concerning the reframing of collaboration between Hitchcock and Herrmann, and Herrmann's contribution to their work, has been detached from the film text and repositioned in the paratexts of authorship in the DVD supplement.

Re-encountering *Psycho*

The 2010 release of *Psycho* (including box-set repackaging, it was the seventh time the film had been released on disc in the UK), the fiftieth anniversary edition, creates a number of paratexts that reconstruct (rather than re-perform) the documentary performance of the making of the film. What is perhaps most surprising in this collection is the lack of general reference to the work of Herrmann in the production of the film. This is unexpected, due to the prominence of Herrmann's work on the film and the fact that his score is one of the film's most famous aspects. The disc's supplements do recover collaboration in the texts constructed by their participants – one, a documentary entitled *In The Master's Shadow: Hitchcock's Legacy*, does not necessarily figure collaboration, promoting Hitchcock's authorship and influence through interviews with filmmakers such as Martin Scorsese, William Friedkin, Guillermo del Toro and John Carpenter, and biographers and academics David Sterritt and Donald Spoto; Jack Sullivan makes reference to the music of Hitchcock's films, but it isn't in the context of Herrmann's work. A ninety-five-minute documentary, *The Making of Psycho*, revisits the principal living figures of the work, Joseph Stefano, Janet Leigh and Patricia Hitchcock. The documentary, directed by Laurent Bouzereau, presents the drama of the film's production, its problem with censorship, the influence of Ed Gein on Bloch, the adaptation, the first rejected screenplay by Cavanaugh and its release. Surprisingly, however, the reconstruction of the film's production doesn't figure music significantly. A small section on Herrmann is recounted anecdotally by Paul Hirsch, De Palma's editor, who quotes Herrmann's description of the score as 'black and white' and demonstrates the influence of the three-note motif on *Star Wars* (1977). Peggy Robertson recounts how Hitchcock suggested to Herrmann to repeat the staccato strings over the basement scene at the end of the film. However, the focus in the documentary lies largely on how Hitchcock acted as the principal organiser and author of the film. Collaborators like Stefano appear to present their own role in the drama of the film's construction, but there is a general deferral to Hitchcock at the chief source of the film's meaning and intention. Robertson's anecdote goes some way to present an image of Hitchcock's collaboration with Herrmann, but this is only a very small portion of the supplementary material on the DVD, which is liberally intercut with Hitchcock's appearances from *Alfred Hitchcock Presents*, his presence testifying to the documentary's true subject.

The main source by which this drama is reconstructed in traditional auteurist fashion is in Stephen Rebello's audio commentary. Rebello, the author of *Alfred Hitchcock and the Making of Psycho*, presents a commentary that chiefly does two things. First, it presents a reading and identification of key motifs, symbols, character interpretation and meaning in key scenes. This provides the viewer with a template for how to read the film, a source of cultural capital, as Rebello takes the viewer further into the text. Essentially, this is the commentary as 'How-To' guide; Rebello's authority can never be challenged in this respect and the viewer is not invited to debate his viewpoint. Second, the commentary offers a further re-presentation of the making of the film. Again, Hitchcock is the chief protagonist of the drama, as Rebello recounts his role on set directing Janet Leigh in the car sequences, his storyboards (by Saul Bass), his trust for actors and his varying of the size of the mother. Collaborators are mentioned throughout the commentary, creating a historical record focusing almost entirely on Hitchcock's intentions and work on the film. Collaboration seems only to enable Hitchcock's 'personalised' vision, in keeping with traditional romantic views of the auteur. Herrmann crops up in the commentary just three times: once over his credit, as Rebello refers to him as a 'genius'; again as Marion drives to the Bates Motel, as Herrmann's music is timed to the 'slashing' of the windscreen wipers, foreshadowing later events; and then after the shower sequence, where Rebello recounts an anecdote about Herrmann conflicting with Hitchcock's intentions for the sequence to have no music on the scene. Again, we might see this as the traditional focus on the visual over the aural –the commentary plays over a muted soundtrack, the images the 'teleological story' of the film's production. Herrmann is acknowledged as a member of an authorial collective, but that role seems surprisingly small.

There is one more supplement on the disc that does, more than others, attest to the contribution of Herrmann to the film's final construction. A short feature allows the viewer to play the excerpted shower scene with or without music (although they could do this themselves with their remote control). The isolated scene emphasises the role of music. Although this deviates from what I've been speaking about in terms of the re-narrativisation and dramatising of the film's production and authorship in the main documentary and commentary supplements, it does draw attention to the musical text in a way that other supplements do not. Whether this draws the viewer's attention to Herrmann is another matter, as the paratexts that run across and throughout the disc tend to emphasise Hitchcock the author, not Herrmann the collaborator. This is the Hitchcockian, rather than a Hitchcocko-Herrmannian.

Vertigo

The commentary from the *Vertigo* release does more to promote the authorship of Herrmann. It is primarily framed around a conversation between the producer Herbert Coleman and the restoration team of Robert A. Harris and James C. Katz. As might be expected, the commentary is very technical about the restoration process, but also frames Coleman's reminiscence about the production of the film, and in particular working with Hitchcock. The primary source of authorship during the commentary is made clear to be Hitchcock, and the commentary charts a number of his preoccupations and intentions. There are also interventions in the patchwork commentary from Patricia Hitchcock, screenwriter Sam Taylor and Kim Novak. At around the halfway point of the film, though, there is a mini-essay, unrelated to the images over which it plays (the death of Madeleine) by Steven C. Smith, Herrmann's biographer. Now, while Smith doesn't frame the essay around the notion of collaboration – he points to Herrmann's difficulties of working with Hitchcock – he does contextualise Herrmann's authorship of key parts of *Vertigo*. He points to the obsessive, repetitive motifs in the music, the influence of Wagner and Herrmann's disappointment with the finished project, especially the 'sloppy' conducting of the score by Muir Mathieson, necessitated by an American musician strike, via Vienna and London. Smith also places Herrmann's work into biographical context: Juilliard, work with Welles, and the development of his signature style. The essay also highlights Herrmann's later work with Brian De Palma, on *Obsession* (1976), which, Smith notes, Herrmann thought a superior film to *Vertigo*. Smith's commentary segment (just over twelve minutes in length) doesn't place Herrmann in a context of collaboration with Hitchcock, although he does emphasise Herrmann's place within an authorial collective, and stresses the importance of Herrmann's work for Hitchcock's oeuvre. He does so within a biographical narrative for Herrmann, stressing his sole authorship for the music in Hitchcock's work during those eleven years. The commentary becomes an authorised documentary source, as Grant noted the text became, although here not synchronised with the visual text. The *Vertigo* commentary is effectively radio, creating a 'value-adding paratext'. The information fits with conventional notions of film appreciation, the 'value' provided here by this paratext is cultural capital that adds a biographical and textual reading of Herrmann's work, contributing more to a notion of the paratextual Hitchcocko-Herrmannian, certainly, than the *Psycho* edition.

Having acted as paratextual value on the 1998 and later editions of *Vertigo*, the substitution of this commentary with one by William Friedkin in the 2012 re-release is redressed by the addition of new documentary material. This is detached from the documentary performance of the film's creation, but set more in textual focus of narrativising collaboration. A section on the disc looks at several of Hitchcock's key collaborators: Saul Bass, Edith Head, Alma Reville and Herrmann. The Herrmann documentary *Hitchcock's Maestro* takes on some of the burden from the previous audio commentary, especially the contribution of

Steven C. Smith, although the content is drawn from similar sources as other documentary material that accompanies the Universal-released Hitchcock films, with contributions from Jack Sullivan, David Sterritt, Donald Spoto, alongside directors including Scorsese, del Toro and Carpenter. In some ways, it emphasises the repetitive nature of these features, culled from a single set of interviews, but it also testifies to the viewing of these featurettes, not meant to be consumed as a single block but as paratextual supplements to individual films, not as overviews of an entire oeuvre.

The documentary, however, makes more of an attempt to narrativise the collaboration between Hitchcock and Herrmann. While the title implies some sense of ownership of Herrmann by Hitchcock, Sullivan frames the documentary by contending the partnership to be 'the most famous collaboration between director and composer in history'. The fourteen-minute featurette covers the length of their partnership, from *The Trouble with Harry* (1955) to *Torn Curtain* (1966), combining biographical information with analysis of Herrmann's motifs from academic experts and composers, general appreciation from other directors, in the context of an overview of the nature of the collaboration between the two, and the contribution made to Hitchcock's work by Herrmann's music. It also reflects on Herrmann's final work with Scorsese on *Taxi Driver* (1976), and his death immediately after the film's final mixing session. One of the more curious aspects of the feature is that, while it does not dramatise the performance of *Vertigo's* production in the same way as the commentary had done, it characterises the Herrmann–Hitchcock collaboration in particularly generic terms. While it is understandable for the *Psycho* discs' paratextual content to contextualise the film's history, meaning and significance in terms of the horror film, it's perhaps surprising to do so with *Vertigo* (unless the documentary is considered as a spin-off of the *Psycho* interviews). Herrmann's collaboration with Hitchcock is repeatedly positioned in relation to commentary from experts associated with the horror film – by del Toro and Carpenter, whose best-known works are predominantly in the genre, but also by composers including Nathan Barr (*Hostel* (Eli Roth, 2005)) and John Murphy (*28 Days Later* (Danny Boyle, 2002)). While this is partly explained by the proximity to the newer *Psycho* supplements and that the material covers *Psycho* and *The Birds*, the fact that the collaboration is framed partly in its generic terms (including comparison with John Williams' score for *Jaws* (Steven Spielberg, 1975), the rights to which are also owned by Universal) is somewhat unexpected, although it adds an extra dimension to the ways in which Hitchcock's authorship is conceived in these supplements but also to how the legacy of the collaboration between the two has significance historically. However, that Herrmann is positioned equally with other collaborators in this regard, but subservient to the overall Hitchcock brand, promotes an idea of a Hitchcocko-Herrmannian, although it is a part of other authorial, generic and collaborative paratexts that situate how Hitchcock's partnership with Herrmann is presented in these cinephilic materials.

North by Northwest

Alternatively, the 2000 DVD release of *North by Northwest* (1959) features very specific focus on Herrmann's music, with the inclusion of a music-only score, which allows the viewer to remove all dialogue and sound effects to listen only to the music alongside the images. The back cover of the package even refers to the device 'showcasing' Herrmann's score. The music-only soundtrack offers a different kind of paratext to that over the more traditional commentary – it doesn't turn the film into a documentary performance of production of the film, but creates a space in which the music takes prominence over the voice (Michel Chion's argument in the *The Voice in Cinema* (1999) is that the voice takes precedence over all other sounds), albeit artificially, since the score is intended to be a sound alongside others in the film's overall soundscape. In effectively returning the film to silent cinema, it promotes the specific reading of Herrmann's work (albeit not guided by an 'expert') to understand how cues are constructed and placed and how music and image work together. While it allows the viewer a partial authorship of their viewing experience, it sidesteps the issue of collaboration altogether in its 'showcasing' of the score and Herrmann's contribution to the work overall. The 2009 fiftieth anniversary edition of the film on Blu-ray, however, removes the option to watch the film with only the score. Some of the supplements are retained from the earlier edition, such as writer Ernest Lehman's audio commentary and the now (according to the edition's cover) 'vintage' 2000 documentary *Destination Hitchcock: The Making of North by Northwest* (directed by Peter Fitzgerald). Two new documentaries are included about Hitchcock and the making of the film: *The Master's Touch: Hitchcock's Signature Style* (directed by Gary Leva), an analysis of key tropes in Hitchcock's films (the ones where rights reside with Warner Bros.); and *North by Northwest: One for the Ages*, an appreciation of the film by noted filmmakers such as Friedkin and del Toro. Such paratexts reintroduce the role of the expert in offering not a 'teleological story' of the story's production (that is, handled by the older documentary), but the promotion of authorship in Hitchcock's work. The removal of the option to watch with only the score means Herrmann's contribution to the film is relegated to a notable footnote, in both the film's production and Hitchcock's oeuvre overall. In the making-of documentary, Herrmann's contribution is described in the most serious terms, but only as an anecdote about introducing Lehman to Hitchcock – his music isn't discussed at all. Likewise, in the Leva documentary, Herrmann's music receives no specific discussion, although the film does frame Hitchcock's expressionistic use of music with a sequence from *The Wrong Man* (1956) featuring Herrmann's music (reminding us that here only the Warner-owned films can be discussed or evidenced, which reminds us of the commodity value of these paratexts). Mentioned in the same breath as Dimitri Tiomkin, Herrmann is positioned again as a key contributor to Hitchcock's authorship, although music receives just over a minute's discussion to this framing of key Hitchcockian motifs.

If we turn towards another digital medium, the CD, we see a very different framing of the Hitchcock–Herrmann relationship. Sony's 1995 release of the *North by Northwest* score positions the relationship in a different manner – perhaps understandably, because there is no visual frame of reference, unlike an isolated music-only soundtrack on a DVD, and Herrmann is the primary contributor (Hitchcock's name is larger on the front cover than Herrmann's, although this is reversed on the back). Again unlike the DVD, the accompanying paratextual material is detached from the performance of the work (although the viewer/listener can choose to put those texts back together again at their own leisure), but the hierarchy of authorship is largely reversed. Here, Herrmann is promoted as the author of the work. The package features two paratextual documents, two commentaries (one autobiographical on Herrmann, the other a guide to spotting in the film, as the narrative is recounted step-by-step and cue-by-cue). Christopher Husted's (1995) notes on Herrmann comment on his distinctive contribution to the score of *North by Northwest*: 'use of South American rhythms', and the role of the Fandango in response to Cary Grant's 'Astaire-like agility' (1995: 8). Moreover, Husted comments on Herrmann's repetition of his earlier work and the manner in which the film's love theme 'borrowed' from an earlier score for *White Witch Doctor* (Henry Hathaway, 1953) (1995: 9). The CD paratexts promote an alternative reading of the work, and of the partnership, and the ways in which Herrmann brought a distinctive set of creative solutions to the authorship collective in his work with Hitchcock. While the CD produces a very different experience than the combined audiovisual text of the DVD (not to mention often talking to different audiences), there is a similar promotion of authorship and the listener's textual expertise in relation to the work being experienced. This is closer to the recuperation of the authorial collective discussed by Sellors, and subject to the same process of turning fiction to documentary (the burden of labour here is on the reader/listener rather than on the DVD itself and its promise of interactivity), and a more promising Hitchcocko-Herrmannian than that more commonly experienced in the public domain.

Torn Curtain

As might be expected, the final collaboration between Herrmann and Hitchcock provides an important comparison between Herrmann's rejected score and John Addison's music in the final film. Although the paratextual materials provided on the *Torn Curtain* DVDs and Blu-ray are fairly scant – reflecting the film's status as a 'lesser' Hitchcock work (and therefore undeserving of the more lavish spending on editions of key works like *Psycho* and *Vertigo*) – they do reveal a significant focus on Herrmann's contribution to Hitchcock's oeuvre, now in the past tense. Alongside production photographs and the film's original trailer are a fifteen-minute remixed set of Herrmann's recorded but rejected cues for the film in their intended locations. This is included as a single video rather than an alternative track, so that the viewer is not offered the ability to interact with the material, to switch between Herrmann's cues and those featured in the finished film by John Addison. It is effectively a curio, to speculate on what might have been. As a more productive comparison between Herrmann's cues and Addison's, the documentary that accompanies the film, written and directed by Bouzereau (narrated by Trev Broudy rather than featuring the talking-head interviews that are featured on other discs), mixes a close reading of the film with some contextual material on its production and reception, narrated in a voice-of-God style rather than with the expert testimony seen elsewhere. The thirty-two-minute documentary includes a short focus on the firing of Herrmann and the hiring of Addison. It frames this around analysis of the death of Gromek with both the rejected cues by Herrmann and Addison, again lamenting what-might-have-been had Hitchcock not been pressured to include a more contemporary score by Lew Wasserman. It is in the *Hitchcock's Maestro* documentary on the *Vertigo* Blu-ray that the story of the break-up of the partnership is told – with Jack Sullivan's defence of Hitchcock (that Herrmann did not write the score he was engaged to produce) – but that is not so much the focus here as the products of the work that came not to reach the screen.

The elements considered throughout this chapter have demonstrated the ways in which the supplements of the releases of Hitchcock's work by Universal and Warner Bros. have functioned to produce an image of the partnership and collaboration between Hitchcock and Herrmann. In returning to Bazin's refusal to reduce the cinema to something less than its parts, the ways in which collaboration and authorship have been framed digitally by DVD and subsequently Blu-ray (just as they threaten to recede into history like earlier home video formats) have in some respects worked to some degree not to be so reductive. While the traditional romantic workings of authorship remain as a primary focus of such supplements, in the historical documentation of the films' production and as Hitchcock's individual expression, such supplements have promoted collaboration and the work of practitioners other than directors in ways previously impossible on earlier home video formats, often either in stand-alone documentaries or in the printed word.

The CD releases have worked to do something slightly different in framing the work of the composer as a separate artefact, albeit in a shared narrative of production, with more of a focus on parts of an authorship collective. However, those works are situated for a different audience, an audiophile rather than cinephile or more mainstream one, but share ways in which the artefacts transform the role of the viewer or listener, should they wish to participate (since the sleevenotes or supplements can easily be ignored). As Parker and Parker note, the DVD supplements can become 'a particularly useful kind of language game, one that organizes production and experience of film, but which is capable of transformation as interpreters adopt different roles in the game, such as director, writer, cinematographers, critic, or fan' (2005: 131). While the prospect of interactivity can be ignored, the game (if played) can allow collaboration to be seen from a number of different perspectives, as explored above.

The texts created by the supplements of DVD and Blu-ray require reflection and theorising to address how discourses of authorship continue to run very prominently through film cultures. The authoritative (fatherly in most cases) voice of the documentary constructs authorship in the paratexts of the DVD artefact in a way that film texts do not of their own accord. The shift away from authorship as a reading or textual artefact needs to be conceptualised to understand how the DVD/Blu-ray promotes authorial readings of works, especially in the context of film history and the serious appreciation of classical Hollywood. Most of the texts I've cited here invoke concepts of intention and investigation of the production of the film rather than an understanding of the ways in which authorship is textually re-programmed by the digital re-narrativising of cinema history. The failure of the Hitchcocko-Herrmannian to fully emerge from a reading of these home video products is symptomatic of digital auteurism's retention of the film director as sole author (now much more publicly than before), as well as the visual frame of cinema continuing to stand above (literally in the case of the audio commentary) the consideration of the aural or musical frame of the film's text.

Notes

1 Grant is again quoting from Timothy Corrigan's *A Cinema without Walls: Movies and Culture after Vietnam* (1991: 118).
2 The commentary on the *Vertigo* DVD, featuring associate producer Herbert Coleman, Robert A. Harris and James C. Katz, the film's restorers and Steven C. Smith, dating back to the first release in 1998, was replaced on the 2012 Blu-ray with one by director William Friedkin that offers an expert 'reading' instead of historical background. All of the UK and US releases of *Psycho* have included the same commentary by Stephen Rebello, the author of *Alfred Hitchcock and the Making of 'Psycho'*.

References

Bazin, André (1996), 'How Could You Possibly Be a Hitchcocko-Hawksian?', in Jim Hillier and Peter Wollen (eds), *Howard Hawks: American Artist*, trans. J. Moore. London: BFI, pp. 32–4.

Bertellini, Giorgio and Jacqueline Reich (2010), 'DVD Supplements: A Commentary on Commentaries', *Cinema Journal* 49:3: 103–5.

Brookey, Robert Alan and Robert Westerfelhaus (2002), 'Hiding Homoeroticism in Plain View: the *Fight Club* DVD as Digital Closet', *Critical Studies in Media Communication* 19:1: 21–43.

Brookey, Robert Alan and Robert Westerfelhaus (2005), 'The Digital Auteur: Branding Identity on the *Monsters, Inc.* DVD', *Western Journal of Communication* 69:2: 1019–128.

Caldwell, John Thornton (2008), *Production Culture: Industrial Reflexivity and Critical Practice in Film and Television*. Durham, NC: Duke University Press.

Chion, Michel (1999), *The Voice in Cinema*, trans. C. Gorbman. New York: Columbia University Press.

Corrigan, Timothy (1991), *A Cinema without Walls: Movies and Culture after Vietnam*. New Brunswick: Rutgers University Press.

Grant, Catherine (2000), 'www.auteur.com?', *Screen* 41:1: 101–8.

Grant, Catherine (2008), 'Auteur Machines? Auteurism and the DVD', in James Bennett and Tom Brown (eds), *Film and Television after DVD*. New York: Routledge, pp. 101–15.

Husted, Christopher (1995), 'About Bernard Herrmann and His Score to *North by Northwest*' (CD sleevenotes), Sony Music Entertainment.

Kael, Pauline (1963), 'Circles and Squares: Joys and Sarris', *Film Quarterly* 17:1: 62–4.

McDonald, Paul (2007), *Video and DVD Industries*. London: BFI.

Parker, Deborah and Mark Parker (2004), 'Directors and DVD Commentary: The Specifics of Intention', in Thomas E. Wartenberg and Angela Curran (eds), *The Philosophy of Film: Introductory Text and Readings*. Oxford: Blackwell, pp. 123–32.

Rebello, Stephen (1998), *Alfred Hitchcock and the Making of 'Psycho'*. London: Marion Boyars.

Rombes, Nicholas (2005), 'The Rebirth of the Author', CTheory.net. www.ctheory.net/articles.aspx?id=480. Accessed 30 June 2014.

Sellors, C. Paul (2010), *Film Authorship: Auteurs and Other Myths*. London and New York: Wallflower.

Selected bibliography

Adriano (1972), 'Alfred Hitchcock on Film Music and Bernard Herrmann', 26 September, www.adrianomusic.com/hitch.html. Accessed 2 July 2014.

Allen, Richard (1999), 'Hitchcock, or the Pleasures of Metaskepticism', in Richard Allen and Sam Ishii-Gonzalès (eds), *Alfred Hitchcock: Centenary Essays*. London: BFI, pp. 221–37.

Allen, Richard (2002), 'An Interview with Jay Presson Allen', in Sidney Gottlieb and Christopher Brookhouse (eds), *Framing Hitchcock: Selected Essays from the 'Hitchcock Annual'*. Detroit: Wayne State University Press, pp. 3–22.

Allen, Richard (2007), *Hitchcock's Romantic Irony*. New York: Columbia University Press.

Allen, Richard (2013), 'Hitchcock and the Wandering Woman: The Influence of Italian Art Cinema on *The Birds*', *Hitchcock Annual* 18: 149–94.

AllMusic (n.d.), 'Carnegie Hall Concert: December 25, 1938 – Paul Whiteman | Credits', AllMusic, www.allmusic.com/album/carnegie-hall-concert-december-25-1938-mw0000349896/credits. Accessed 8 February 2011.

Altman, Rick (1987), *The American Film Musical*. London: BFI.

Auiler, Dan (1999), *Hitchcock's Secret Notebooks*. London: Bloomsbury.

Balázs, Béla (1952), *Theory of the Film: Character and Growth of a New Art*, trans. Edith Bone. London: Denis Dobson Ltd.

Barr, Charles (2002), *Vertigo*. London: BFI/Palgrave Macmillan.

Bazelon, Irwin (1975), *Knowing the Score: Notes on Film Music*. New York: Van Nostrand Reinhold.

Bazin, André (1996), 'How Could You Possibly Be a Hitchcocko-Hawksian?', in Jim Hillier and Peter Wollen (eds), *Howard Hawks: American Artist*, trans. J. Moore. London: BFI, pp. 32–4.

Bernstein, Elmer (1972), 'What Ever Happened to Great Movie Music?', *High Fidelity*, July: 55–8.

Bernstein, Elmer (2004), *Elmer Bernstein's Film Music Notebook*. Sherman Oaks: Film Music Society.

Bertellini, Giorgio and Jacqueline Reich (2010), 'DVD Supplements: A Commentary on Commentaries', *Cinema Journal* 49:3: 103–5.

Blim, Dan (2013), 'Design in Bernard Herrmann's Prelude to *Vertigo*', *Music and the Moving Image* 6:2: 21–31.

Borden, Iain (2013), *Drive: Journeys Through Film, Cities and Landscapes*. London: Reaktion Books.

Bordwell, David and Kristin Thompson (2013), *Film Art: An Introduction*, 10th ed. New York: McGraw-Hill.

Bouzereau, Laurent (2010), *Hitchcock, Piece by Piece*. New York: Abrams.

Bowser, Eileen (1973), *Biograph Bulletins, 1908–1912*. New York: Octagon Press.

Bresson, Robert (1977), *Notes on Cinematography*. New York: Urizen Books.

Brill, Lesley (1991), *The Hitchcock Romance: Love and Irony in Hitchcock's Films*. Princeton: Princeton University Press.

Brindle, Reginald Smith (1987), *The New Music: The Avant-Garde Since 1945*, 2nd ed. New York: Oxford University Press.

Brookey, Robert Alan and Robert Westerfelhaus (2002), 'Hiding Homoeroticism in Plain View: The *Fight Club* DVD as Digital Closet', *Critical Studies in Media Communication* 19:1: 21–43.

Brookey, Robert Alan and Robert Westerfelhaus (2005), 'The Digital Auteur: Branding Identity on the *Monsters, Inc.* DVD', *Western Journal of Communication* 69:2: 1019–128.

Brophy, Philip (1999), '*The Birds*: The Triumph of Noise Over Music', www.philipbrophy. com/projects/sncnm/Birds.html. First published in Alessio Cavallaro et al. (eds), *Essays in Sound 4*. Sydney: Contemporary Sound Arts. Accessed 25 October 2013.

Brown, Royal S. (1994), *Overtones and Undertones: Reading Film Music*. Berkeley: University of California Press.

Brown, Royal S. (2004), 'Herrmann, Hitchcock, and the Music of the Irrational', *Cinema Journal*, 21:2: 14–49. Reprinted in Robert Kolker (ed.), *Psycho: A Casebook*. New York: Oxford University Press, pp. 102–17.

Bruce, Graham (1985), *Bernard Herrmann: Film Music and Narrative*. Michigan: UMI Research Press.

Burch, Noël (1981), *Theory of Film Practice*. Princeton: Princeton University Press.

Caldwell, John Thornton (2008), *Production Culture: Industrial Reflexivity and Critical Practice in Film and Television*. Durham, NC.: Duke University Press.

Carringer, Robert (1985), *The Making of Citizen Kane*. Berkeley: University of California Press.

Chion, Michel (1994), *Audio-Vision: Sound on Screen*, trans. C. Gorbman. New York: Columbia University Press.

Chion, Michel (1999), *The Voice in Cinema*, trans. C. Gorbman. New York: Columbia University Press.

Chion, Michel (2009), *Film, A Sound Art*, trans. C. Gorbman. New York: Columbia University Press.

Christensen, Jerome (2012), 'Alfred Hitchcock is Rolling in His Grave', *Salon*, www.salon. com/2012/12/24/alfred_hitchcock_is_rolling_in_his_grave/. Accessed 3 July 2014.

Clifton, Kevin (2013a), 'Sound and Semiotics in Hitchcock's Coming Attraction: Locating and Unraveling Meaning in *Rope*'s Movie Trailer', published proceedings for 12th International Congress on Musical Signification, Canterbury, UK.

Clifton, Kevin (2013b), 'Unravelling Music in Hitchcock's *Rope*', *Horror Studies* 4:1: 63–74.

Comolli, Jean-Louis (1967), 'The Curtain Lifted, Fallen Again', *Cahiers du Cinéma in English*: 52–5.

Conrad, Joseph (1910), *The Secret Sharer*. New York: Signet.

Conrad, Peter (2001), *The Hitchcock Murders*. London: Faber and Faber.

Cooper, David (1991), *Bernard Herrmann's 'Vertigo'*. Westport: Greenwood Press.

Cooper, David (2001), *Bernard Herrmann's Vertigo: A Film Score Handbook*. Westport, CT: Greenwood Press.

Cooper, David (2003), 'Film Form and Musical Form in Bernard Herrmann's Score to *Vertigo*', *Journal of Film Music*, 1:2/3: 239–48.

Cooper, David (2005), *Bernard Herrmann's The Ghost and Mrs Muir: A Film Score Guide*. Lanham, MD: Scarecrow Press.

Cope, David (1989), *New Directions in Music*. Dubuque, IA: William C. Brown, 5th ed.

Corrigan, Timothy (1991), *A Cinema without Walls: Movies and Culture after Vietnam*. New Brunswick: Rutgers University Press.

Davies, Hugh (1968), *International Electronic Music Catalogue*. Cambridge, MA: MIT Press.

Davies, Hugh (2002), 'Electronic Instruments: Classifications and Mechanisms', in Hans Joachim Braun (ed.), *Music and Technology in the Twentieth Century*. Baltimore: Johns Hopkins University Press, pp. 43–58.

Del Mar, Norman (1969), *Richard Strauss: A Critical Commentary on His Life and Work*, vol. 1. New York: Chilton Book Co.

DeRosa, Steven (2001), *Writing with Hitchcock: The Collaboration of Alfred Hitchcock and John Michael Hayes*. New York: Faber and Faber.

Donnelly, K. J. (2014), *Occult Aesthetics: Synchronization in Sound Film*. Oxford: Oxford University Press.

Duke, Vernon (1947), 'Gershwin, Schillinger, and Dukelsky: Some Reminiscences', *Musical Quarterly*, 33:1: 102–15.

Durgnat, Raymond (2002), *A Long Hard Look at Psycho*. London: BFI/Palgrave Macmillan.

Edelman, Lee (1999), 'Hitchcock's Future', in Richard Allen and Sam Ishii-Gonzalez (eds), *Alfred Hitchcock Centenary Essays*. London: BFI, pp. 239–62.

Eisenstein, S. M., Vsevolod Pudovkin and Grigori Alexandrov (1988), 'Statement on Sound', in Richard Taylor (ed. and trans.), *S. M. Eisenstein: Selected Works*, vol. 1, *Writings 1922–1934*. London: BFI, pp. 113–14.

Eisler, Hanns and Theodor Adorno (1994), *Composing for the Films*. London: Athlone.

Eliot, T. S. (1933), *The Use of Poetry and the Use of Criticism*. London: Faber and Faber.

Erdmann, Hans, Giuseppe Becce and Ludwig Brav (1927), *Allgemeines Handbuch der Film-Musik*, vol. 1. Berlin: Schlesinger'sche Buch und Musikhandlung.

Fawell, John (2001), *Hitchcock's Rear Window: The Well-Made Film*. Carbondale: Southern Illinois University Press.

Gilling, Ted (1971–72), 'The Colour of the Music: An Interview with Bernard Herrmann', *Sight and Sound*, 41:1: 36–9.

Gorbman, Claudia (1987), *Unheard Melodies: Narrative Film Music*. Bloomington: Indiana University Press.

Gottlieb, Sidney (ed.) (1995), *Hitchcock on Hitchcock*. London: Faber and Faber.

Gottlieb, Sidney (2005–6), 'Hitchcock on Griffith', *Hitchcock Annual* 14: 32–45.

Gottlieb, Stephen (1967), 'Actors and Directors', *Cahiers du Cinéma in English*, May: 59–60.

Grant, Catherine (2000), 'www.auteur.com?', *Screen* 41:1: 101–8.

Grant, Catherine (2008), 'Auteur Machines? Auteurism and the DVD', in James Bennett and Tom Brown (eds), *Film and Television after DVD*. New York: Routledge, pp. 101–15.

Hanlon, Lindley (1985), 'Sound in Bresson's *Mouchette*', in Elisabeth Weis and John Belton (eds), *Film Sound: Theory and Practice*. New York: Columbia University Press, pp. 323–31.

Hansen, Miriam (1991), *Babel and Babylon: Spectatorship in American Silent Film*. Cambridge: Harvard University Press.

Herrmann, Bernard (1932), 'Charles Ives', *Trend: A Quarterly of the Seven Arts* 1:3: 99–101.

Herrmann, Bernard (1957), 'Elgar, A Constant Source of Joy', in H. A. Chambers (ed.), *Edward Elgar Centenary Sketches*. Novello.

Herrmann, Bernard (1974), 'Bernard Herrmann: A John Player Lecture', *Pro Musica Sana* 3:1: 10–6.

Herrmann, Bernard (1980), 'Bernard Herrmann, Composer', in Evan William Cameron (ed.), *Sound and the Cinema: The Coming of Sound to American Film*. Pleasantville, NY: Redgrave Publishing Co., pp. 117–35.

Hitchcock, Alfred (1931), 'A Columbus of the Screen', *Film Weekly*, 21 February. Reprinted in *Hitchcock Annual* 14 (2005): 46–9.

Hitchcock, Alfred (1933–34), 'Alfred Hitchcock on Music in Films', *Cinema Quarterly* 2:2, 80–3. Reprinted in Sidney Gottlieb (ed.), *Hitchcock on Hitchcock: Selected Writings and Interviews*. London: Faber and Faber, pp. 241–5.

Hitchcock, Alfred (1995), 'On Style', interview in Cinema magazine, 5:1, August–September 1963. Reprinted in Sidney Gottlieb (ed.), *Hitchcock on Hitchcock: Selected Writings and Interviews*. London: Faber and Faber, pp. 285–302.

Hitchcock, Alfred (1995), 'Film Production', in Sidney Gottlieb (ed.), *Hitchcock on Hitchcock: Selected Writings and Interviews*. London: Faber and Faber, pp. 210–26.

Hitchcock, Alfred and François Truffaut (1962), 'Alfred Hitchcock and François Truffaut (Aug/1962)', www.hitchcockwiki.com/wiki/Interview:_Alfred_Hitchcock_and_François_Truffaut_(Aug/1962). Accessed 13 October 2013.

Holmes, Thomas B. (1985), *Electronic and Experimental Music*. New York: Charles Scribner's and Sons.

Hopper, Hedda (1945), '"Hitch" Reveals Secret of Making His Pictures', *Los Angeles Times*, 11 March, pp. B1, 3.

Horosko, Marian (1996), 'Balanchine's Guide to a Young Choreographer – Excerpts from Diary of choreographer Gloria Contreras about Conversations with Choreographer George Balanchine', *Dance Magazine*, http://findarticles.com/p/articles/mi_m1083/is_n12_v70/ai_18905905/ Accessed 8 March 2011.

Hubai, Gergely (2011), '"Murder Can Be Fun": The Lost Music of *Frenzy*', *Hitchcock Annual* 17: 169–94.

Hubai, Gergely (2012), *Torn Music: Rejected Film Scores – A Selected History*. Los Angeles: Silman-James Press.

Hunter, Evan (1976), *Me and Hitch*. London: Faber and Faber.

Husted, Christopher (1995), 'About Bernard Herrmann and His Score to *North by Northwest*' (CD sleevenotes), Sony Music Entertainment.

Jaubert, Maurice (1938), 'Music on the Screen', in Charles Davy (ed.), *Footnotes to the Film*. London: Lovat Dickson Ltd, pp. 101–15.

John, Antony (2001), '"The Moment That I Dreaded and Hoped For": Ambivalence and Order in Bernard Herrmann's Score for *Vertigo*', *Musical Quarterly* 85:3: 516–44.

Joyce, Paul (1979), 'Hitchcock and the Dying Art: His Recorded Comments', *Film* 79: 25–8.

Kael, Pauline (1963), 'Circles and Squares: Joys and Sarris', *Film Quarterly* 17:1: 62–4.

Kapsis, Robert E. (1992), *Hitchcock: The Making of a Reputation*. Chicago: University of Chicago Press.

Kinderman, William and Joseph E. Jones (eds) (2009), *Genetic Criticism and the Creative Process: Essays from Music, Literature, and Theater*. Rochester, NY: University of Rochester Press.

Kracauer, Siegfried (1998), *Theory of Film: The Redemption of Physical Reality*. Princeton: Princeton University Press.

Kristeva, Julia (1974). *La Révolution du langage poétique*. Paris: Éditions du Seuil.
Kristeva, Julia (1975), 'Ellipse sur la frayeur et la séduction spéculaire', *Communications* 23: 73–78.
Krohn, Bill (2000), *Hitchcock at Work*. London: Phaidon.
Langer, Suzanne K. (1957), *Philosophy in a New Key: A Study in the Symbolism of Reason, Rite, and Art*. Cambridge, MA: Harvard University Press, 3rd ed.
Larsen, Peter (2005), *Film Music*. London: Reaktion.
Lev, Peter (2003), *The Fifties: Transforming the Screen 1950–1959*. Berkeley: University of California Press, 2003.
Levy, Louis (1948), *Music for the Movies*. London: Sampson Low, Marston & Co.
Lorenz, Konrad (1961), *King Solomon's Ring*, trans. M. Kerr Wilson. London: Methuen.
McCarten, John (1958), '*Vertigo*', *New Yorker* 34: 65.
MacDonald, Malcolm (1967), 'Herrmann: Echoes for String Quartet. Rubbra: String Quartet No. 2 in E flat major, Op. 73', *Gramophone*, 45:533: 213.
McDonald, Paul (2007), *Video and DVD Industries*. London: BFI.
McElhaney, Joe (1999), 'Touching the Surface: *Marnie*, Melodrama, Modernism', in Richard Allen and Sam Ishii Gonzalès (eds), *Alfred Hitchcock: Centenary Essays*. London: BFI, pp. 87–105.
McElhaney, Joe (2006), *The Death of Classical Cinema: Hitchcock, Lang, Minnelli*. New York: SUNY Press.
McGilligan, Patrick (2003), *Alfred Hitchcock: A Life in Darkness and Light*. New York: Regan.
Macé, Caroline (n.d.), Textual Scholarship, www.textualscholarship.org/gencrit/index.html. Accessed 3 July 2014.
Manvell, Roger and John Huntley (1975), *The Technique of Film Music*. London: Focal Press.
Moral, Tony Lee (2002), *Hitchcock and the Making of Marnie*. Manchester: Manchester University Press.
Mulvey, Laura (1975), 'Visual Pleasure and Narrative Cinema', *Screen* 16:3: 6–18.
Mulvey, Laura (1989), *Visual and Other Pleasures*. Bloomington: Indiana University Press.
Murray, Lyn (1987), *Musician: A Hollywood Journal of Wives, Women, Writers, Lawyers, Directors, Producers and Music*. Secaucus: Lyle Stuart Inc.
Nattiez, Jean-Jacques (1993), *Wagner Androgyne*, trans. Stewart Spencer. Princeton: Princeton University Press.
Ong, Walter J. (2002), *Orality and Literacy: The Technologizing of the Word*. New York: Routledge.
Parker, Deborah and Mark Parker (2004), 'Directors and DVD Commentary: The Specifics of Intention', in Thomas E. Wartenberg and Angela Curran (eds), *The Philosophy of Film: Introductory Text and Readings*. Oxford: Blackwell, pp. 123–32.
Petley, Julian (1978), *BFI Distribution Library Catalogue*. London: BFI.
Phillips, Adam (2010), 'Alfred Hitchcock Presents "Alfred Hitchcock Presents"', Hitchcock Report, http://thehitchcockreport.wordpress.com/tag/lew-wasserman/. Accessed 3 July 2014.
Phillips, Craig (2013), 'Alfred Hitchcock Presents San Francisco: The Master and the City by the Bay', in Scott Jordan Harris (ed.), *World Film Locations: San Francisco*. London: Intellect, pp. 48–9.
Platte, Nathan (2011), 'Music for *Spellbound*: A Contested Collaboration', *Journal of Musicology* 28:4: 418–63.
Pomerance, Murray (2000), 'Finding Release: "Storm Clouds" and *The Man Who Knew Too Much*', in James Buhler, Caryl Flinn, and David Neumeyer (eds), *Music and Cinema*, Hanover, NH: University Press of New England, pp. 207–46.

Pomerance, Murray (2004), *An Eye for Hitchcock*. New Brunswick: Rutgers University Press.

Pomerance, Murray (2005), 'Why Hides the Sun in Shame?: Ambrose Chapel and *The Man Who Knew Too Much* (1956)', *The MacGuffin*, www.labyrinth.net.au/~muffin/ambrose_chapel.html. Accessed 29 January 2014.

Pomerance, Murray (2011), 'Some Hitchcockian Shots', in Thomas Leitch and Leland Poague (eds), *A Companion to Alfred Hitchcock*, Malden, MA.: Wiley-Blackwell, pp. 237–52.

Pomerance, Murray (2014), *Marnie*. London: BFI.

Rebello, Stephen (1998), *Alfred Hitchcock and the Making of Psycho*. London: Marion Boyars.

Rohmer, Eric and Claude Chabrol (1979), *Hitchcock: The First Forty-Four Films*, trans. Stanley Hochman. New York: Frederick Ungar Publishing Co.

Rombes, Nicholas (2005), 'The Rebirth of the Author', CTheory.net. www.ctheory.net/articles.aspx?id=480. Accessed 30 June 2014.

Rosar, William (2001), 'The Dies Irae in *Citizen Kane*: Musical Hermeneutics Applied to Film Music', in K. J. Donnelly (ed.), *Film Music: Critical Approaches*. Edinburgh: Edinburgh University Press, pp. 103–16.

Rosar, William (2003), 'Bernard Herrmann: The Beethoven of Film Music?', *Journal of Film Music* 1:2–3: 121–51.

Rosenbaum, Jonathan (1976), '*Family Plot*', *Sight and Sound* 45:3: 188–9.

Ross, Alex (1997), 'Casting the Spells of 'Vertigo', *New York Times*, 6 October, p. H17.

Rotha, Paul (1930), *The Film Till Now: A Survey of the Cinema*. London: Jonathan Cape.

Rothman, William (2011), 'The Universal Hitchcock', in Thomas Leitch and Leland Poague (eds), *A Companion to Alfred Hitchcock*. Chichester: Wiley-Blackwell, pp. 347–64.

Schaeffer, Pierre (1967), *Traité des objets musicaux*. Paris: Seuil, 1967.

Schafer, R. Murray (1994), *Our Sonic Environment and the Soundscape: The Tuning of the World*. Rochester: Destiny.

Schelle, Michael (2002), *The Score: Interviews with Film Composers*. Los Angeles: Silman-James Press.

Schneller, Tom (2010), 'Unconscious Anchors: Bernard Herrmann's Music for *Marnie*', *Popular Music History* 5:1: 55–104.

Schneller, Tom (2012), 'Easy to Cut: Modular Form in the Film Scores of Bernard Herrmann', *Journal of Film Music* 5:1–2: 127–51.

Schroeder, David (2012), *Hitchcock's Ear: Music and the Director's Art*. London: Continuum.

Sellors, C. Paul (2010), *Film Authorship: Auteurs and Other Myths*. London and New York: Wallflower.

Shepherd, John (1991), *Music as Social Text*. Cambridge: Polity Press.

Silk, Sally M. (1994), 'The Orphic Moment and the Problematics of the Signified in Blanchot', *Neophilologus*, 78:4: 537–47.

Simmon, Scott (1993), *The Films of D. W. Griffith*. New York: Cambridge University Press.

Skinner, Frank (1960), *Underscore*. New York: Criterion Music Corp.

Smith, Steven C. (1991), *A Heart at Fire's Center: The Life and Music of Bernard Herrmann*. Berkeley: University of California Press.

Spoto, Donald (1999), *The Dark Side of Genius: The Life of Alfred Hitchcock*. London: Da Capo.

Steiner, Fred (1989), 'What Were Musicians Saying About Movie Music During the First Decade of Sound? A Symposium of Selected Writings', in Clifford McCarty (ed.), *Film Music I*. New York: Garland Publishing, pp. 81–107.

Stevens, Leith (2006), 'Film Scoring: The UCLA Lectures', annotation by Mark Brill (ed.), *Journal of Film Music*, 1:4: 341–88.
Sullivan, Jack (2006), *Hitchcock's Music*. New Haven and London: Yale University Press.
Sullivan, Jack (2011), 'Hitchcock and Music', in Thomas Leitch and Leland Poague (eds), *A Companion to Alfred Hitchcock*. Chichester: John Wiley, pp. 219–36.
Taylor, John Russell (1978), *Hitch: The Life and Times of Alfred Hitchcock*. New York: Pantheon Books.
Truffaut, François (1967), 'The Journal of *Farenheit 451*: Part Three', *Cahiers du Cinéma in English*, May: 8–19.
Truffaut, François (1985), *Hitchcock*, London: Simon & Schuster.
Truffaut, François (1988), *Correspondence, 1945–1984*, ed. Gilles Jacob and Claude de Givray, trans. Gilbert Adair. New York: Cooper Square Press.
Vroomen, Jeanne and Beatrice de Gelder (2000), 'Sound Enhances Visual Perception: Cross-Modal Effects of Auditory Organization on Vision', *Journal of Experimental Psychology: Human Perception and Performance* 26:5: 1583–90.
Walker, Michael (2005), *Hitchcock's Motifs*. Amsterdam: Amsterdam University Press.
Walker, Michael (2010), 'A Perfect Place to Die? The Theater in Hitchcock Revisited', *Hitchcock Annual* 16: 23–54.
Weis, Elisabeth (1982), *The Silent Scream: Alfred Hitchcock's Sound Track*. East Brunswick, NJ and London: Associated University Press.
Weis, Elisabeth and Randy Thom (2007), 'The City That Never Shuts Up', in Murray Pomerance (ed.), *The City That Never Sleeps*. New Brunswick: Rutgers University Press, pp. 214–27.
Wierzbicki, James (2005), *Forbidden Planet*. Metuchen, NJ: Scarecrow Press.
Wierzbicki, James (2008), 'Shrieks, Flutters, Vocal Curtains: Electronic Sound/Electronic Music in Hitchcock's *The Birds*', *Music and the Moving Image* 1:2: 14–15.
Wierzbicki, James (2008), *Film Music: A History*. New York: Routledge.
Wood, Robin (1989), *Hitchcock's Films Revisited*, New York: Columbia University Press.
Wrobel, William (2003), 'Self Borrowing in the Music of Bernard Herrmann', *Journal of Film Music* 1: 2/3: 249–71.
Zador, Leslie and Gregory Rose (1998), 'A Conversation with Bernard Herrmann', in Clifford McCarty (ed.), *Film Music I*. Los Angeles: Film Music Society, pp. 209–54.
Žižek, Slavoj (1992a), *Looking Awry: An Introduction to Lacan through Popular Culture*. Cambridge, MA: MIT Press.
Žižek, Slavoj (1992b), 'Alfred Hitchcock, or the Form and its Historical Mediation', in *Everything You Always Wanted to Know About Lacan But Were Afraid to Ask Hitchcock*, London: Verso, pp. 1–12.

Index